METHUEN'S MANUALS OF MODERN PSYCHOLOGY
GENERAL EDITOR: PROFESSOR C. A. MACE

★

THE PSYCHOLOGY OF PERSONALITY

METHUEN'S MANUALS OF MODERN PSYCHOLOGY

General Editor: Professor C. A. Mace

★

THE STRUCTURE OF HUMAN ABILITIES
Philip E. Vernon

GESTALT PSYCHOLOGY
David Katz

THINKING
G. Humphrey

SOCIAL PSYCHOLOGY
W. J. H. Sprott

THE STRUCTURE OF HUMAN PERSONALITY
H. J. Eysenck

PERSONALITY TESTS AND ASSESSMENTS
Philip E. Vernon

★

THE PSYCHOLOGY
OF PERSONALITY

by

BERNARD NOTCUTT

Professor of Psychology in the University of Natal

METHUEN & CO. LTD. LONDON
36 *Essex Street, Strand, W.C.*2

First published in 1953

CATALOGUE NO. 5419/U
PRNITED IN GREAT BRTIAIN
BY THE ALCUIN PRESS,
WELWYN GARDEN CITY, HERTS.

PREFACE

THE main purpose of this book is that of direction-finding in the field of Personality. It is an attempt to choose, from among the great variety of current psychological concepts and methods, those that have the best promise for the future.

We may mention three purposes that we have not attempted to fulfil: this is not a book about personalities; it does not contain vivid descriptions of particular human beings, or absorbing case histories; nor is it a technical manual of instructions for measuring a galvanic skin reflex, scoring a Rorschach protocol, or factorizing a correlation matrix; nor is it a résumé of research findings. The purpose is more to evaluate than to describe the activities of psychologists.

The less digestible items of information have been segregated into special tables. It is hoped that these will supply useful references, while the main body of the text will be kept free of an excess of learned detail.

September, 1952   B. N.

CONTENTS

CHAPTER I

THE MEANING OF PERSONALITY, AND ITS PLACE IN PSYCHOLOGY

THIS book proposes to give an account of current knowledge about personality; to describe the ideas used by psychologists in this field, the techniques available, the results obtained, and some of their applications. We begin by considering briefly the meaning of the term personality, and go on to explain how this branch of psychology has come to organize itself, and what is its place in the general history of modern thought.

Personality is the pattern of an individual life. If we know someone's personality, we can predict how he will behave in a great variety of circumstances. It should enable us to know what he will notice and what he will miss, what he will seek and what avoid, where he is likely to succeed, and where fail. It is the meaning and coherence of his acts and omissions, some principle that we derive from observing meaningful recurrences in his conduct.

Personality is not a separable part of an individual, like an arm or a liver. It is rather a way of regarding everything that he does. It includes his abilities (his acts regarded from the point of view of their efficiency); his disposition (his acts regarded from the point of view of their motives); his temperament (including such traits as emotionality, persistence, and impulsiveness), and his character (the way in which his motives are integrated, the manner in which he deals with conflicting demands, etc.). Personality is a general term used to include all these aspects. There are many respects in which one can generalize about human beings as a whole, or large groups of them. There are other respects in which we have to study the individual before we can say anything effective about him.

It is these respects that we are particularly concerned with
when we speak of personality. Personality is mainly concerned
with ways in which the individual is particularly himself, and
is marked off from other people in the group to which he
belongs. Getting to know a person means becoming familiar
with the patterns or recurrences that characterize his behaviour
and enable us to anticipate his responses. Everybody has to
get to know something about the persons he associates with:
understanding other people's personalities is as essential a
skill as being able to walk or talk. Children begin to learn the
elementary skills quite early in life. Will mother be angry if
I wet my bed? Will little brother surrender the toy if I ask
for it? Will the other children let me play on the swing if I
yell loudly enough? The successful solution of these problems
depends on knowing other people's personalities. The most
important part of this knowledge is drawn from our own life
experience—our successes and failures in manipulating and
adjusting to other people.

The personal experience from which we draw our lessons
is not experience of human nature in general. It is the experience of a series of culturally defined situations, which have
affected most of our neighbours and contemporaries in a
similar way. Our experience serves as a guide for dealing with
other people, because it resembles the experience of most of
the people we know. Apart from the costly and often painful
lessons of experience, there is a large body of culturally transmitted knowledge about personality. A child does not necessarily have to be burnt in order to dread the fire. The experience of others, passed on through language, literature and
custom, may be sufficient. In European novels and plays there
is a great body of accumulated wisdom about human nature.
There are patterns showing one how to understand and
deal with a great variety of characters; how to recognize
the significance of small acts or omissions, subtle tones
and expressive movements. This body of literature serves
to amplify and enrich the lessons of experience, to extend

our understanding beyond the narrow bounds of direct contact.

The two main sources of our understanding of personality are then shared experience and transmitted knowledge. In recent years a third source has begun to be available—knowledge derived from the scientific study of personality. This is of course not a totally new kind of knowledge. It draws from the general cultural pool. But it does use some distinctive ideas. So far as the psychology of personality is concerned, three aspects of scientific method are particularly important. (i) The scientific psychologist tries to make his hypotheses as exact as possible, and subject to verification. He wants to formulate his ideas in a form in which they can be proved true or false. If he sees less deeply than the poet or the philosopher he tries at any rate to be sure of what he has seen. (ii) He wants objective evidence, which is public and generally available, so that his observations can be repeated by any competent observer. (iii) He is not so much controlled by aesthetic or moral considerations as the ordinary citizen; he discards the usual rules of what is mentionable or unmentionable, and is not deterred by the accusation that his subject matter is prosy, trivial or disgusting. Other characteristic features of scientific method may also often enter into psychological studies—the use of quantitative measurement and instrumentation, the design of controlled experiments, the development of systematic classification, the search for general principles, the listing of references and authorities. Not all of these features will be found in every study, nevertheless they exercise a pervading influence on those who adopt the scientific attitude.

The use of scientific method does not supersede intuitive understanding, just as meteorology has not made it unnecessary for the fisherman to keep his eye on the weather, and the science of genetics has not eliminated the art of the animal breeder. But the scientific study of personality can add something to existing knowledge, can repair its deficiencies in certain respects, and illuminate its blind spots.

To fulfil his purposes, the psychologist has developed certain new methods, which supplement our ordinary ways of knowing about other people with observations that are more amenable to scientific analysis; and a good deal of our book will be concerned with describing and discussing these methods. Many scientific psychologists have been inordinately concerned with questions of method, perhaps because the results obtained by them have often been of so little interest or importance. No subject has suffered more than psychology from the disease that Hayek called scientism. Scientism is to science as the Pharisee is to the man of God. In the psychology of scientism there is everything to impress the onlooker—enormous libraries, and a systematic search of the journals, expensive instruments of exquisite precision and shining brass, complicated formulas, multi-dimensional geometries and differential equations, long strange words of Greek origin, freshly minted, enormous calculating machines and white-coated girls to punch them—all the equipment is there to make the psychologist feel that he is being really scientific—everything, in fact, except ideas and results. Full many a glorious thesis have I seen wending its dignified way to a trivial and predestined inconclusion, armed cap-á-pie with all the trappings of scientism; the decimals correct, the references in order, only the mind lacking. It must not be supposed that when we speak of the application of scientific method to the study of personality, we are setting out to praise that sort of stuff. The psychology of personality has had its share of pedants, though it may be that this topic, by reason of its breadth and ambitious scope, has attracted the pedant less than minuter themes. But there have been other workers in the field, who have been distinguished by an eye for what is of central importance, fertility of hypothesis, a rigid logic in testing their expectations, and a readiness to admit error when confronted with hostile fact; and these are qualities that mark the genuine scientist. As we explore our subject we shall come to see that, while the full rigours of scientific proof are sometimes applicable, the intuitive observer often obtains far more valuable results. The most effective ways of studying personality depend, not on rejecting subjective insights, but on validating them. It is in the study of personality most of all that scientific and subjective psychology come to terms with one another.

The psychology of personality is not a highly integrated body of thought, with a single clearly formulated doctrine. There are, in fact, several conflicting points of view about the subject, and marked disagreements are common enough, as in all psychological matters. Nevertheless, there are some respects in which there is general agreement. One is in the emphasis on continuity, the insistence that the child is father of the man. This continuity may be interpreted in various ways, as the working out of a rigid genetic endowment, or as the generalization of early conditioning, or the fixation of stereotyped responses to traumatic experiences. But the search for continuity is a common theme.

Another point of general agreement is the attitude to the mind-body problem. Psychologists are for the most part agreed that 'mind' and 'body' are some kind of unity, though they are wary of attempts to define it too exactly. The words 'mind' and 'mental' are now commonly avoided, as though they do not want to be committed to a theory of the 'ghost in the machine'. Words like 'organism', 'psychosoma', 'behaviour', 'psychobiology', are popular, because they indicate some notion that is believed to transcend the unwelcome antithesis of mind and body. Without committing themselves to any detailed or well-defined theory of mind-body relations, writers on personality have learnt to talk about some entity which includes both mind and body. A personality is not ordinarily classified as 'mental' or 'physical'. It has both mental and physical attributes, or to put it another way, both social and physical causes operate on personality.

In the field of pathology, inabilities, anxieties and delusions, accidents, crimes, moral lapses and physical illness are considered to belong to a single system of symptoms, which are alternative expressions of the same underlying disorder. Halliday speaks of a patient who suffered from lumbago and acute religious conversion, or rheumatism and go-slow tactics in the coal-mine. Alexander describes the relation between gastritis and unsatisfied cravings for dependency. Menninger describes motor accidents resulting from aggression turned against the self. While many of the examples quoted are difficult to prove in a solid and convincing way to the sceptical outsider, and the mechanisms are only very partially understood, the new view of personality makes possible a synthetic view of human conduct that marks the beginning of a great advance in our understanding.

When Samuel Butler published *Erewhon* in 1872, describing an imaginary society in which our attitudes towards health and crime were interchanged, his fantasy was considered to be wildly paradoxical. To-day one knows that a great deal of what he said is mere common sense. It has long been the fashion to speak of crime among slum-dwellers as resembling a disease or infection for which they cannot be held responsible. And Groddeck and Freud made us familiar with the complementary notion that many allergies, diseases of metabolism, and even infections, may in some subtle way be willed by the sufferer, so that he is, at any rate in part, guilty of his own illness. Available notions of responsibility (whether medico-legal or theological) are clearly inadequate to deal with such situations. Current views of personality require a very different system of ideas from those to which we are accustomed. This 'organismic' point of view would to-day be shared by most workers on personality.

The common reader usually thinks of psychology as the study of personality, the art of working out the subtle patterns of an individual's motives, finding the threads connecting past and future, act and fantasy, the small expressive movement and the attitude symbolized. The psychological writings that have appealed most to the public have been of this kind—Freud, Adler, Havelock Ellis, Karen Horney, Margaret Mead, and others, at a somewhat lower intellectual level, such as Beran Wolfe and Dale Carnegie; not to speak of those dank hinterlands haunted by graphologists, mind-readers, palmists, phrenologists, theosophists, astrologers, teacup-readers and miscellaneous haruspices. (There is believed to be a woman in Johannesburg who can read the bubbles in a milk-shake.) All these writers have been concerned with the person as their unit of study, trying to find ways in which a single act may be expressive of the whole. Academic and scientific psychology has, however, until recently made rather little use of the concept of personality; and even now the study of personality belongs to the adventurous and not wholly respectable frontier regions of psychology, which it is not altogether wise to explore without a safe academic reputation in some entirely reputable field, like colour vision, or the ability of rats to learn their way through a maze. To understand how this separation between popular and scientific psychology came about requires a little history.

Psychology was established as an independent field of study in Germany, in the second half of the nineteenth century. University departments look back to the founding of Wundt's laboratory of experimental psychology at Leipzig University in 1879, as the effective beginning of their discipline. Stumpf in Berlin, Ebbinghaus in Breslau, established the patterns of teaching, and devised many of the experiments that are still standard parts of a laboratory course. Much of their teaching was carried to America by enthusiastic pupils who founded the psychology departments of American universities.

These workers thought of the new psychology as a science of mind. It was to establish laws of mind just as physics and chemistry established laws of matter. The vague notion of such a science of mind had been drifting about Europe for a long time. It was commonly said that the principle of association of ideas, as formulated by Locke, would do for mind what the law of gravitation had done for matter. James Mill had spoken of 'mental chemistry'. But until the work of Fechner and

B

Wundt this natural science of mind had remained an idle dream. For Wundt and his fellow-experimentalists the model of physics and chemistry was decisive. Psychology must measure, it must experiment, and the aim of these activities must be to discover general laws of mind, laws that would hold good for everyone indifferently. A physicist investigating the law of falling bodies does not have to know whether the stone dropped from Galileo's fingers, or was used to sink a net, or to kill two birds. Its mass and shape are his concern, and the rest, as a physicist, he neglects. Similarly the experimental psychologist wanted to study mind in general—sensation, perception of learning as universal processes, not as expressive of individuals.

Personality, if it was noticed at all in his experiments, appeared only as an unwelcome intrusion, an unavoidable fallibility liable to turn up occasionally in even the best experimental subject. So far as introspection was required in experiments, the observer needed to be skilled and practised, just as an experienced bacteriologist can observe far more through a microscope than a beginner can. So experimenters often used themselves or one another as subjects. But it was the subject's business to be as unobtrusive as possible, to serve as a clear mirror for the stimuli he received, without contaminating them by any subjective additions. It was expected that mind would be the same everywhere, just as matter is. Helmholtz had in 1850 established the speed of the nerve impulse; it was found to vary with certain conditions—the type of nerve studied, temperature, and so forth, just as any other physical quality might vary. When Wundt and his collaborators began to make time measurements of mental processes, they expected to establish similar general principles to those of nerve conduction; the true time or sensation would be so-and-so, of discrimination would be something else. More and more accurate instruments were devised for measuring reaction times in thousandths of a second, and hopes were entertained that the timing of mental processes would prove to be as important a clue in psychology, as the timing of physical motion had been in mechanics.

In all experimental work certain variations in results are not accounted for, and this is especially so in work with living organisms; as Leibniz had observed, no two leaves are ever exactly alike; and the scientist who wants to generalize must be content that his principles will be only approximately confirmed by observations; but in much psychological work, and noticeably in these measurements of reaction times, variations were so great that no reliable generalization emerged.

It proved to be impossible to designate any one time as the true reaction time for human beings. A Hipp Chronoscope, designed to measure reaction times in thousandths of a second, was once the pride of the psychological laboratory. It still adorns the cupboards, and may be occasionally demonstrated to first-year students, though few now remember in what way reaction times were originally thought to be important. General experimental psychology achieved notable successes in the analysis of vision and hearing, and minor conquests of the less organized senses. As early as 1840 Weber, experimenting with the discrimination of lifted weights, found that the ratio of weights that could just be discriminated was approximately constant, over a considerable range. Fechner extended this principle to other senses, and proposed to use it as the beginning of a new science of psychophysics. Fundamental quantitative relations were to be established between sensations and the physical stimuli corresponding to them. The Weber-Fechner law seemed to offer a splendid opportunity for bringing mental events into the sphere of natural law. In 1890 the prospects looked wonderful. Great realms of nature were open to conquest and pacification. Nevertheless, the expected triumphs of experimental psychology did not follow. When in 1938 R. S. Woodworth[1] completed his great review of the subject he was also writing its obituary. Another race has been won, and other palms gained. While experimental physiology has continued to make rapid advances, the corresponding kind of experimental psychology has proved successful only in small areas of the subject. The rat psychology of the Behaviourists, and the child study movement, were notable extensions of the psychological landscape, and involved a shift from physical to biological analogies. Both worked within the concepts of general psychology, and in a few instances, such as the study of motor development in babies, notable generalizations were achieved. Yet, considering the enormous amount of study and research that have been devoted to the subject, advances in general psychology have been somewhat disappointing. The ways in which men resemble one another in thought and behaviour have proved to be less impressive than their differences. Many observers, despairing of finding uniformity in human affairs, made their variability the object of study. The founder of differential psychology was Sir Francis Galton, and in both Britain and America these studies. have been energetically pursued. In the enormous production of these workers, we can distinguish three main types of problem that they set themselves to solve—the problem of norms, the relation of one variable to another, and the problem of factors.

The problem of norms. It proved very difficult to find suitable units of measurement for many mental qualities. Eventually the device was adopted of using some representative group of people as the standard, and measuring the performance of an individual by comparison with that of the standard group. Thus Binet measured intelligence in terms of mental age: a person had a mental age of five if his performance on an intelligence test equalled that of the average five-year-old. Stern and Terman, by using the intelligence quotient, sought to devise a measure that would represent a fairly stable and permanent quality of the person measured. Since those days the establishment of norms has been greatly improved by the adoption of better sampling procedures, and by using measures of dispersion or scatter as units of distance from the mean. The application of these techniques has been extended from intelligence to other traits, such as introversion or ascendance. However much statistical sophistication goes into the construction of these norms (and nowadays there is a good deal), they are really continuing the familiar procedure of ordinary language by which, when we call a man ill-tempered, we mean that he is more often or more intensely in a bad temper than most of the people we know; when we say he is greedy, we are comparing his demands for food with those of most people like him. The units in which we are measuring are excellent for many practical purposes, but, like an index of retail prices or a comparison of national incomes in economics, they do not stand up successfully to considerable shifts of environment, or to exceptional cases. The I.Q. is a useful administrative device for classifying large groups in a school or military system; it is less impressive when one is exploring the development of an individual. Norms have not been very much used outside the English-speaking countries. Although Binet invented the concept of mental age, the establishment of norms has found little favour in France, and in Germany the method was specifically rejected. It was in America that the method found most favour; Margaret Mead[2] has suggested that the passion for norms is symptomatic of the competitive pressure, of the need for reassurance about one's status, of the uneasy desire for conformity and acceptance in the group, which are said to be characteristic of contemporary America, and in particular of the second generation of immigrants. The great national paradox of the equality of man is here uncomfortably imaged.

The relation of one variable to another. Differential psychology has provided many opportunities for analysing the operation of causal factors. Every conceivable feature of the environment has been studied in relation to psychometric intelligence—social and economic status, education, position in the family, employment and so on; qualities of age, sex, physical measurements, race, diet and exposure to infections have been similarly studied. Penetrating analyses of the relative influences of heredity and environment on intellectual performance have been made by means of studies of identical and fraternal twins, and of children reared in foster-homes. We shall not treat the topic further here, nor attempt to review it systematically, though we shall often want to quote results from this field. The analysis of the variables affecting psychometric intelligence has been one of the most solidly effective regions of differential psychology. If the method of norms has not been applied in the same detail, and as successfully, with other variables of personality, that is because no other quality beside intelligence has been so effectively measured.

The problem of factors. The third region in which differential psychology has been vigorously pursued has been in trying to arrive at the basic variables of human nature by a statistical analysis of scores on tests. These studies grew out of disputes between faculty psychologists who held that the mind is composed of several distinct faculties, such as attention, memory and imagination, and those who believed in the unity of the mind. The idea of how to tackle the problem came from Spearman who first formulated the conditions that had to be fulfilled if the existence of his general factor of intelligence were to be established.

If a battery of tests is given to a group of subjects, it is possible to calculate coefficients of correlation between each pair of tests, and to prepare a matrix of correlations showing the relation of each test to every other. This matrix is then examined to find out what factors or faculties must be assumed to account for the intercorrelations of the tests. There is no unique way of doing this; many different solutions to the same matrix are possible, and it is hard to say which of several criteria will give one the most valid solution. Spearman was not a great mathematician, and his method of analysis was long ago outmoded, but his astonishing vigour and single-mindedness canalized the work of a whole generation of British psychologists. While the work of this school was directed pri-

marily to the analysis of abilities, some attention was also paid
to other qualities of personality. Among Spearman's pupils
evidence was produced for the existence of the W factor (persistence, will-power, determination), the P factor (perseveration,
mental inertia) and the O factor (fluctuations in efficiency).
Since then a large part of the Roman alphabet has been absorbed
in the naming of newly discovered factors.

Factor analysts have extended the method to a great
number of other traits of personality, mostly by the analysis
of answers to rating scales and questionnaires.   In this
way they have sought to include within differential psychology many concepts that have arisen out of clinical studies.
Factor analysis is a trait psychology.   In applying the method
one assumes that people have fairly stable traits, and that
the boundaries and grouping of these traits will be much
the same for everyone.   The earlier approach was to design
a group of tests to explore the existence of a factor defined
by theoretical discussion.   To-day the practice appears to
be to feed almost any kind of material into the sausage machine,
and hang about at the other end waiting to see what comes out.
In so far as people change their traits, and enlarge or contract
the boundaries of them, factor analysis becomes unsatisfactory
and difficult to apply.   Thus it has been more effective in the
analysis of abilities than of other traits of personality that are
more protean and fluctuating.   Though we can no longer
claim a rigid constancy for the I.Q., intellectual traits on the
whole show a greater stability than moral or temperamental
traits.

There is much disagreement among psychologists about the
value of factor analysis in the study of personality. Those whose
daily work is with people, who are accustomed to deal with
living human beings, make little use of its results, because they
cannot picture a person as a collection of traits. Those whose
business is with tests and scores and systems are often enthusiastic about the possibilities of the method, and consider
that many important results have already been established.

This is something like the divergence that occasionally occurs in medicine between physiologist and physician.

Although a factor analyst may sometimes speak of himself as studying personality, we should prefer to speak of him as studying differential psychology. Two features may be taken to distinguish the psychology of personality—that it deals with total persons, rather than with abstracted traits, and that it takes the temporal dimension seriously; its view of human nature is not confined to snapshots or cross-sections. It is not possible, however, to legislate about the use of such a word as 'personality', and in current usage studies of trait distributions are often spoken of as part of the psychology of personality, particularly when the studies are concerned with dynamic or temperamental traits, rather than with abilities.

The origins of psychology of personality are quite separate from those of general and differential psychology. We must look to the French and German physicians who in the second half of the nineteenth century were beginning to develop ideas about psychopathology. In his autobiography Freud has described how the lectures of the French physicians at the Salpêtrière aroused his interest, and converted him from the narrow and dogmatic materialism then orthodox in Viennese medical circles. Freud was one of a number of sexologists who set out consciously to shock their generation, to destroy the strongholds of Victorian hypocrisy, to set Western man free from the burden of sexual guilt. Krafft-Ebing, Havelock Ellis, van der Velde, Marie Stopes, René Guyon were working towards the same goal; and in certain respects we should class them with Ibsen, Dostoievsky, Proust, James Joyce and D. H. Lawrence, as explorers of the repressed unconscious and enemies of conventional morality.

Freud began as a rather straightforward sexologist; his early papers were demonstrations of the sexual origin of various mental disorders: hysteria is a delayed after-effect of rape, anxiety neurosis is a by-product of birth control, neurasthenia results from excessive masturbation, dreams are disguised sexual wishes, and so on. Freud made a vitally important step forward and when he realized that many of the rapes and juvenile seductions uncovered in the buried memories of his hysterical patients had never really happened, and were merely imagined. A lesser man would have confessed himself mistaken, and returned to the respectable practice of neurology. But Freud turned his necessity to glorious gain, and invented the Oedipus Complex. If people described such distressing experiences when they had not really occurred, that must be because they secretly wanted them to occur; the fictitious stories they told were to be understood as wishfulfilment fantasies. Thus the doctrines of psycho-analysis developed from straightforward sexology into something considerably wider; gradually Freud worked out a general theory of the origin and development of personality. As it developed, psycho-analysis incorporated several other strands of nineteenth-century thought—the Nietzschean will to power was accepted as another element in man's animal nature, co-equal with sexuality. Freud shared Nietzsche's contempt for tenderminded moralists, and many of his characteristic doctrines are formulated in phrases that are specially designed to *épater le bourgeois*.

Evolutionary doctrines of a rather Lamarckian kind were enthusiastically absorbed into psycho-analysis (Freud's blandly comfortable acceptance of the inheritance of acquired characters has always been a stumbling block to his English and American admirers). Late nineteenth-century anthropology also drew extensively on evolutionary theory, treating successive stages of human society as analogous to the sequence of organic forms. By using their common fund of evolutionary ideas, Freud was able to link his work with anthropological theory, and develop his delightful speculations about the primal horde, the origins of morality and the death of Moses.

Psycho-analysis and its derivatives (individual and analytical psychology) have had much more influence in English-speaking countries than other varieties of subjective character description, and we have thus given them most of our attention.   But in the German-speaking countries there have been several other systems of characterology with a wide popularity.   Kretschmer, Jaensch and Klages will be only briefly mentioned in this book, but their work has been highly valued in Europe; and even the vagaries of Szondi have attracted adherents.

Psycho-analysts, making it their mission to shock people, earned a good deal of abuse and hostility.   Organized authority was nearly always against them.   Psycho-analysis was rejected by the greater part of the medical profession, and by nearly all the universities, and condemned by German National Socialism, Soviet Communism and the Roman Catholic Church.   In spite of official opposition it has shown an astonishing power to win adherents, and for many of them it has had the force of a religion or a way of life.   But an unfortunate result of all the abuse to which the psycho-analysts have been subjected has been their tendency to form a sect, to pursue their own meditations in sympathetic company, protected from outside criticism, and reading only one another's works.   At times psycho-analysts appear to have been contented with standards of evidence that would hardly have satisfied anyone more critical than a palmist or a teacup reader.   Early in the development of the subject the method was adopted of explaining away criticism as resistance; and this too useful device has often made psychoanalysts complacent about the scientific short-comings of their procedures.   Freud always claimed that psycho-analysis was a science, but many of his conclusions were reached without benefit of the usual procedures of scientific method.   Indeed, if Freud had been more fussy about his evidence, more insistent on the objectivity of his results, the whole enterprise would have been slowed up in about 1886.   Too much academic research has used impeccable procedures to establish nothing of importance.   When Freud claimed that his method was scientific, he was referring mainly to his determination not to be influenced by wishful thinking; and in this respect he was justified.   But the lack of interest shown by psycho-analysts in other aspects

of scientific method retarded their reconciliation with the rest
of the psychological world.

In German nineteenth-century thought a distinction was
commonly drawn between the methods of *Naturwissenschaft*
(natural science), and those of *Geisteswissenschaft* (moral science).
The distinction was stressed by Dilthey[3], and influenced
many subsequent writers, including Spranger and Stern.
Dilthey held that there are ways of understanding events other
than through the classificatory concepts of natural science.
In America many experimental psychologists have tried to
formulate the fluid concepts of psycho-analysis in terms of
precise observable situations. In particular, resolute attempts
have been made to apply experimental methods to the analysis
and verification of the defence mechanisms. In his studies of
the processes of unconscious thinking, Freud devised terms to
describe characteristic ways in which wishes unacceptable by
the conscious mind were distorted or deflected. He called these
defence mechanisms—projection, reaction-formation, repression, isolation and so on.

It is these interesting but somewhat elusive concepts that
form the starting-point for what is now coming to be called
psychodynamics. Psychodynamics aspires to be an abstract
formulation of the logic of emotions in the same way as
physical dynamics is an abstract formulation of the movements of bodies. (The essay of Sears[4] provides a convenient summary of this work.) Some workers have thought
the purpose of these experiments to be the experimental
demonstration of the existence of the mechanisms. As Masserman[5] pointed out in relation to his own experimental work
with cats, an experiment might prove the validity of a mechanism, but could hardly disprove it. It is possible to think of
experimental psychodynamics as being mainly concerned with
providing quotable examples for use in lectures of processes
that are already known from clinical experience. Saul[6]
remarked that the evidence for the reality of these mechanisms
from the daily work of the analyst is far more convincing than

anything that could be established by analogical experiments. But such demonstrations have other and more important purposes to serve. It is not so much a matter of proving that repression or introjection sometimes occur. Everybody knows that they do, and most of the mechanisms have been familiar for centuries as part of proverbial philosophy. The point is rather to determine the kind of occasions on which they occur, the kind of persons that are most likely to use them, and the results they have—to make them precise enough to approach the status of psychological laws. The verification of psychoanalytic concepts could not occur without a considerable transformation and hardening of the concepts in the process. An example is some of the experimental work on animals with a view to investigating the nature of regression. Experimenters have found it necessary to distinguish two different meanings of the term—a tendency to revert to historically earlier forms of reaction, and a tendency to produce simpler, less organized, or more childish kinds of behaviour, whether or not they had occurred before in that individual. It is only in experimentally controlled situations that it is possible to separate these two kinds of regression, whose phenomena would normally overlap.

We can now define the distinctive features of the psychology of personality. We distinguish general psychology, in which laws are established that hold good for men as a whole, in the analysis of particular kinds of processes; and differential psychology, in which quantitative variations in the distribution of traits are studied, and the psychology of personality, in which the organization of individuals is studied. In general psychology we consider the individual merely as exemplifyng the processes that are being studied; in differential psychology we consider at most a few traits; but in psychology of personality we have to look at our subject as a growing, developing individual, and we have to consider the meaning of events for him, without assuming that they will have the same meaning for others as well. In terms of divergences between various schools of psychology it is an attempt on the one hand, to extend the methods of objective science into regions where conclusions have so far been reached in more subjective ways, and on the other hand a dissatisfaction with the dullness and triviality that has been characteristic of so much objective psychology. Its aims are well expressed in Denham's lines likening the ideals of Augustan poetry to the River Thames:

Though deep, yet smooth; though gentle, yet not dull;
Strong without rage, without o'erflowing full.

From another point of view, the study of personality often emphasizes motives, in contrast with the stress on cognition and action found in general psychology. It is characteristic of this approach that the psychologist should be on the watch for subjective influences, and the expression of private motives, even on tasks, like the description of a picture, that would formerly have been used for the assessment of an ability. We deliberately set up situations in which (in Koffka's phrase) "the external forces of organization are weakened, so that the internal forces of organization will be relatively stronger". It is in the patterning of general motives into sentiments that so much individuation occurs.

The life histories that were studied by psycho-analysts were mainly those of mentally disordered people, and the patterns of development that they recognized first were those leading to various forms of illness. For a long time psycho-analysis, if it was mentioned at all in academic works on psychology, appeared as a branch or theory of psychopathology. The defence mechanisms were thought of as various ways in which people deceived themselves, or became ill. From early days Freud was interested in extending his theories to include phenomena of everyday life, but he regarded this as a more speculative part of his discoveries. The term 'psychology of personality' has come into use as attempts have been made to describe normal and fairly healthy people in terms of their motives and defence systems. The transition is only gradually being made to new concepts that are suitable to normal people. For a long time personality or character has been described mainly in terms of neurosis. To understand a person has meant to know what was wrong with him. We are only gradually building a vocabulary for describing healthy personalities.

As with other subjects, those who work in the field are prone to think of its distinctiveness less in terms of doctrine than of technique. Although, as we shall see in subsequent chapters, a great range of methods is used in the study of personality, certain devices are distinctive and characteristic. These are the use of unstructured social situations, such as improvised psychodrama and the leaderless group test; the use of projective techniques for investigating fantasy; and the validation of subjective insights by matching and specific prediction. The development of these methods has come from those who have stressed the unity of personality, and they are typical of this branch of psychology.

Many writers have drawn careful distinctions between temperament, character and personality. But usage has varied so much that it is impossible to say that this or that is the 'real' meaning of each term. In England the term 'temperament tests' was used to describe measures of various qualities, such as perseveration and oscillation, which were believed to be constitutional, and possibly influenced by endocrine or other physiological factors. In both Britain and America 'character' has been used to describe qualities of integration and personality organization; qualities of determination or weakness, conflict or singleness of purpose, honesty, self-control, self-sacrifice or selfishness—these would often be called qualities of character. In France and Germany, however, the term characterology is used to include everything that we should call psychology of personality. For Europe the meaning of the term was established by the work of Bahnsen[7].

Ours is not a region in which the reader should expect to find an organized body of well-established facts. We are dealing rather with a region of hypothesis, experiment, and obstinate questioning. We are on the boundary of knowledge, and the hills are hidden in mist.

REFERENCES

1. WOODWORTH, R. S. *Experimental Psychology.* London, Methuen, 1938.
2. MEAD, M. *The American Character.* Harmondsworth, Penguin Books, 1944.
3. HODGES, H. *Wilhelm Dilthey: An Introduction.* Survey of objective studies of Soc. Sci. Res. Coun. London, Kegan Paul, 1944.
4. SEARS, R. R. *Psycho-analytic Concepts.* Bull., No. 51, 1943.
5. MASSERMAN, J. H. *Behaviour and Neurosis:* An experimental psycho-analytic approach to psycho-biologic principles. Chicago Univ. Press, 1946.
6. ALEXANDER, F. AND FRENCH, T. *Psycho-analytic Therapy.* New York: Ronald Press, 1946.
7. BAHNSEN, H. *Beiträge zur Charakterologie.* Leipzig, 1867, reprinted 1932.

CHAPTER II

THEORIES OF PERSONALITY

THE variety of current notions about personality is so bewildering that in order to make any sense of the business we shall have to do some rather firm classification. In doing so we shall be doing grave injustices to many of the theories that we are concerned with—selecting for comment one feature of an elaborate and rounded theory, and pigeon-holing it, perhaps in company that the author would heartily disapprove of. Anyhow, it is no use placing unsorted heaps of hundreds of miscellaneous theories before the reader.

We begin by excluding from consideration a number of theories which, in the opinion of nearly everybody who has a respectable scientific reputation, are held to be 'wild', 'cranky', or 'superstitious'. Many of these theories are popular in the intellectual underworld, and it is hard to disprove them finally. It is easy, however, to show that there is no evidence to support them, and also to find historical or personal reasons why people have come to believe them. We exclude on these grounds all varieties of astrological theory (although astrology was generally accepted by educated Europeans for about 1,600 years), and other notions, also of respectable antiquity, such as numerology, palmistry, and telling fortunes by cards. We are still left with an enormous variety of concepts, which may leave the reader with the impression that no two psychologists can agree, that everything in this field is subjective and uncertain, and that no science of personality exists. An impression of variety is of course correct—there are many rival systems of ideas, and at present no way of deciding between them. But in two respects the situation is less chaotic than might appear; terminology is far more variable than concepts, and many theories can be con-

sidered as parallel rather than opposed. Let us consider each
of these points in turn.

Confusions about terminology plague all the sciences,
especially in regions where there are rapid new developments.
Psychology, with its mixture of scientific and unscientific procedures, is worse off than most. Each theorist or investigator
who has a new idea wants to underline its distinctiveness and
his originality by inventing a new term for it. It often happens
that a writer is afraid to use a well-established term, because the
use of it suggests to his readers implications that he does not
intend.

Ever since the great instinct controversy in America in
the second and third decades of the century, most British and
American psychologists have been shy about the term 'instinct',
because they did not want to be committed, in the expectations
of their readers, to accepting all McDougall's views on the
subject; so they used some other term around which they could
develop their own theories. A serious and simple-minded
reader who took all these terms seriously might complain:
'McDougall[1] says that the basic motives in human beings are
instincts, but later he changed his mind and said that they are
propensities. Holt[2] and Murphy[3] say they are *drives*, F. H.
Allport[4] says they are *prepotent reflexes*, Dunlap[30] says
they are *primary desires*, Cattell[5] says they are *ergs*, Murray[6]
says they are *needs*; how am I to know which of these eminent
men is right?' The answer is that all these terms mean roughly
the same, and are introduced to take sides, or avoid taking sides,
in some current controversy. F. H. Allport's term meant: 'I
am talking about the same sort of thing as McDougall meant,
but I think that man's hereditary equipment is less elaborate
than he supposed, and I want to ally myself with the Behaviourists, who (in 1920) seem to me the most progressive and vigorous
group of American psychologists.' Murray's term meant: 'I
am referring to the same facts as these other people, but I don't
want to restrict myself to motives that have a recognizable
organic basis, and I don't want to get myself involved in incon-

c

clusive disputes about heredity and environment.' Thus while each of these terms has some shade of individual meaning, there are many contexts in which they could be used interchangeably without serious error.

It may need very careful analysis for us to discover the underlying identity of different terms. In a society where scholars pride themselves on originality, we are likely to find many instances of a distinction without a difference, while in a society where orthodoxy, tradition and continuity are highly valued, we meet the contrasting kind—real and important shifts of meaning hidden in a conventional vocabulary, as the Christian philosophers added new meanings to the pagan concept of *anima*, while retaining the term. It is noticeable that British psychologists invent new terms rather seldom, compared with American psychologists.

The second point is this—that theories which at first glance appear contradictory may, on more careful examination, turn out to be parallel, and even complementary. Many apparent contradictions are like the conversation in which A says 'I like cheese', and B says 'No, I don't'. What is stated as an absolute opposition may turn out to be no more than a preference for emphasizing one feature or another out of a complex totality, influenced by multiple causes. Take, for instance, the following statements attributed, for the sake of definiteness, to a particular author:

(1)   Climate influences aggressiveness (Huntington)[7].
(2)   Pituitary activity influences aggressiveness (Berman)[8].
(3)   Diet influences aggressiveness (Marett)[9].
(4)   There are inborn tendencies to aggressiveness (Freud)[10]:
(5)   Aggression depends on the amount of frustration to which a child is subjected (Dollard)[11].
(6)   Some cultures teach children to be aggressive, other cultures teach children to inhibit their aggression (Benedict)[12].

If these statements are contrasted with one another as six

'theories of aggression', the impression might easily be given that it was necessary to choose between them, that if one is true, then the others are all necessarily false. In reality, as we have stated them, all these statements could be true at once, and indeed they probably are. For the sake of emphasis and contrast, psychologists stress one aspect of a complex situation and may even claim exclusive validity for their own pet variable; so that A may claim to refute the theories of B and C. Yet, if we remove a few arrogant exaggerations from his statement, there may be little in it to contradict what others have said. For didactic or exhibitionistic purposes, theories may be stated in forms that make them sound more different than they are. Indeed, a discussion that is fair to everybody, and gives adequate weight to every point of view, is likely to be platitudinous and unbearably dull. We are merely underlining what Hegel's Logic long ago made clear, but the principle is easily forgotten.

TABLE 1: THEORIES OF PERSONALITY

A. Systems describing a person in terms of basic traits:
   1. Common traits
   2. Factors.
   3. Types.
      (a) based on psychotic syndromes.
      (b) based on endocrine and other physiological processes.
      (c) based on general bodily form.
      (d) based on values, lifepath.
      (e) based on perceptual processes.

B. Systems describing a person in terms of the external forces acting on them.
   1. Theories based on habit, association, conditioning.
   2. Descriptions of personality in terms of culture and social role.

C. Systems describing interaction of person and environment.
   1. Systems using basic motives (a) passions.
                                   (b) instincts.
                                   (c) vectors.
   2. Systems stressing functional autonomy of motives.
   3. Systems stressing maturational patterns.
   4. Systems stressing defence mechanisms, psychodynamics.

How then shall we sort out this immense rag-bag of systems, theories and notions? Where are the main lines of cleavage, the differences that really matter, and when is it safe to throw a dozen scuffling rivals together in one heap? Our first sorting gives three piles—(a) systems that use basic traits, (b) systems that describe persons in terms of the pressures exerted upon them by the environment, and (c) systems that describe the interaction of persons with the environment.

We begin by trying to get the trait notion clear. If we are asked to give an account of some person, to say what sort of person he is, we are quite likely to do so by ascribing to him various traits. He is avaricious, aggressive, insolent, prim, demure, generous, neurotic, introverted and so on. A trait is any quality of a person, particularly one that is used to describe his life processes, how he thinks, feels or acts. To use a trait-name of a person implies some uniformity in his behaviour. A trait is a quality that turns up reliably and predictably in the person concerned. It is not a momentary state, such as being angry or elated, but a relatively enduring pattern. It is a quality of the person as a whole, not of any particular thing he does, and we suppose the quality to have some sort of continuous existence even when it is not being exhibited. We can call a man intelligent, even when he is asleep or shaving. There is, of course, nothing peculiar or metaphysical about this. We likewise suppose the continuous existence of chairs and tables even when they are not perceived, and the supposition does not often let us down.

Most trait-names describe some deviation from what is ordinary or average, and so imply some social norm. To say that a man is aggressive is to say that he is more often or more violently aggressive than most other men of the same kind. The phrase 'of the same kind' is, of course, crucial. In ordinary speech the normal group against whom an individual is being assessed, is not specified, or even known. This is one reason why most trait-names used in ordinary speech are vague.

It is interesting to try and classify the trait-terms in common use. In Table 2 (page 33) we have tried to do this, though no great importance or validity is claimed for our scheme. Still, **most** of the trait-adjectives in the English language can be pigeon-holed in this way. Allport[13] and Odbert[26], in their mono-graph on trait-names, found 17,953 of them (obsolete terms excluded) in Webster's *New International Dictionary*, edition of 1925. When William James said of German experimental psychology that it could be done only by a nation that could not be bored, he lived too soon to enjoy the work of Odbert. If we are to build a scientific psychology of traits, it must obviously be done with something fewer than all the 17,953 terms that are offered us. And if every psychologist makes his own private selection, how shall science advance?

From these considerations begins the search for basic traits. There are various ways in which this search is carried on—observational and experimental studies of particular traits, a statistical search for factors, and various typological approaches. We shall leave the discussion of these till later, because our first concern is to mark out the main divisions of our field. In general we may say of trait psychologies that they are likely to emphasize what is biologically determined, inborn, relatively invariant with environment, and resistant to change. Characters found in the works of Ben Jonson, Smollett and Dickens are the right sort of people from this point of view. People who grow up, change their minds, experience a conversion, adapt themselves to their wives, get old and tired, are not altogether welcome to the trait psychologist. They are vaguely felt to be cheating. To the factorialist and the typologist the environment is little more than a nuisance obscuring the clean outlines of personality.

In contrast with trait psychologies are the systems (Group B) that stress the influence of external forces acting on people. These systems are of two kinds, those stressing biological determinism, and those stressing sociological determinism. The behaviourist, who describes a person in terms of conditioning, association, habit, treats a person as little more than a place where various influences have an opportunity to operate. In conditioned reflex theory, the arbitrary relation between the sign and what is signified means that under various external pressures a person might develop into almost anything.   By emphasizing environmental influences it is possible to make constitution, original nature, or heredity appear as a vanishing quantity.   During the great instinct controversy in America, techniques of argument were developed by which instincts could be made to appear almost wholly the result of external forces.   Anything which could be influenced from without was considered to have been removed from the sphere of original nature, and handed over to the environment.   If cats could be reared not to kill mice, then mouse-killing ceased to be instinctive.   Every new freak of the conditioning lab was felt to be a fresh triumph for environmentalism.   A personality was considered to be nothing more than the resultant of the various conditioning processes to which he had been subjected.

Side by side with the biological conditioned response theory grew up the sociologists' theories of cultural determinism. Earlier theories of social anthropology stressed the transmission of beliefs and customs; from the time of Malinowski onwards the theory extended to the explanation of central traits of personality in terms of cultural influences.   For a while it was a favourite anthropological game to find (or invent) tribes who were exceptions to any conceivable generalization that could be made about human nature.   Everyone who has associated with anthropologists is familiar with the kind of sentence that begins 'Yes, but among the Bongo-Bongo. . . .'

Arguments about the relative importance of constitution and environment often took on a political colouring.   Typologies were sometimes used in the interests of Nazism and race theory, for the purpose of disparaging people who were not Germans; and extreme environmentalist theories were often developed as a counter weight. Watsonian behaviourism stressed the original equality of man, and much of its appeal lay in its emphatic Americanism, equalizing the farmer's son with the high-hatting aristocrat, and promising the good things of the world to anyone with the right childhood.   At the same time,

Watson's[15] arrogant claim that he could turn a healthy child into any kind of person that he liked, foreshadowed the totalitarian technocrat, whose menacing figure loomed ever larger as the political 'thirties moved on towards the bloody 'forties. What had begun as a salesman's idle boast had become, in Russia and Germany, a dreadful reality.

The attitude of the cultural anthropologist was somewhat different, as his life path is different. Instead of standing around in overalls dominating the lives and manipulating the passions of albino rats, the anthropologist goes to distant places, often under a foreign government, where his business is not to order people about, but to adapt himself to a strange community, and to learn to accept its ways. His original choice of profession was often influenced by a desire to find some alternative to Western civilization, rather than to exploit it. British and American anthropologists used their cultural theories to refute race-theory and anti-Semitism; indeed, they confused people about race to such an extent that some of their readers may have come away with the impression that they could no longer tell the difference between a Swede and a Bushman. But the anthropologists did not use their doctrines of cultural determinism to show the government new ways of dominating people, but rather to create new freedoms by suggesting possible alternatives to existing custom. They agreed with the behaviourists, however, in regarding man as so largely a creature of circumstance that his beliefs, morals and actions could hardly be considered his own, or as having any validity other than a purely pragmatic one.

Our third main group of theories (Group C) consists of those that stress the interaction of the person and the environment. Here the person is described neither as a self-subsistent being who retains an unchanging identity amid the vagaries of circumstance, nor as a mere incident in the play of external forces, but rather as the result of a continuous interaction. In a way it is easy to state this as an ideal, a facile Hegelian synthesis that points towards a goal without showing how to

get there. The justification of it must consist in recording
certain achievements, and certain lines of development, that
show how the solution is attained. Effective theory must be
able to interpret interaction, and suggest methods for predicting
the resultant behaviour. Results will not come merely from
being tiresomely fair to everyone. For the moment, however,
our concern is with theories, and not with the techniques of
applying them.

The first lot of theories in Group C is united by the attempt
to find a list of basic motives in terms of which to describe all
human actions. Among these attempts are the instinct theory
of McDougall[16], as well as comparable theories of drive,
desire and need.

It might appear to the reader that there is no very important difference between a theory of basic traits and a
theory of basic motives; so it is necessary to emphasize that the
difference is very important indeed. A trait is a quality of a
person; a motive is a quality of an act. When we say 'that is an
aggressive act', we are concerned with the motive, intention
and effect of a particular act; when we say 'that is an aggressive
person', we are stating, not merely that this person sometimes
shows aggression, but that he does so more often, or more
violently, than most people. There is an implicit reference to a
social norm, so that the statement cannot help being rather
vague. However careful our verbal definitions may be, trait
terms are almost always vague, if only because of the vagueness
of the norm. But the description of an act in terms of a motive
contains no reference to a norm; it is an absolute statement, not
a relative one.

It is important to stress this distinction, because the
writers who use concepts of basic motives often use the same
terms also for traits, so that the distinction becomes blurred.
H. A. Murray[17], for instance, defines his system of needs
in terms of the goals of particular acts, and in discussing the
differences between his language and that of G. W. Allport[18],
shows that he fully appreciates the importance of the distinction.

But at other times, for instance in his personality questionnaire, he uses his needs also as names for traits. McDougall[19] similarly used his instincts primarily for analysing acts; any act is taken to be the expression of one or more instincts, and since every person is a bearer of all the instincts, one would not think of using the instincts primarily for describing the person; but he did at other times speak of a person's *disposition* as his predominant instinct, thus using the instinct also as a trait. It is important, however, to realize that one can have a system of basic motives without treating them as basic traits. And in fact this is what is done in the later development of Murray's system. In his descriptions, the elements of personality are not unconditional traits, but *themas* or press-need-outcome sequences, i.e. characteristic ways of responding to various defined situations. Similarly McDougall[20] mainly uses his instincts, not as traits, but as components of a *sentiment*.

We may thus regard a trait as the extreme case of a sentiment or *thema* so pervasive that it is unnecessary to specify the kind of situation that evokes it. Aggressiveness would be an unconditional trait in a person who was so aggressive that he was angry nearly all the time, no matter how other people behaved. Such traits are very seldom found, and the sort of thing we get in practice is aggression-when-somebody-tries-to-dominate-you, or aggression-towards-people-who-are-timid-and-submissive, or aggression-towards-anybody-who-reminds-you-of-father, and not just aggression in general. Thus it is quite possible to use a system of *basic motives* for analysing acts, without using a system of *basic traits* for describing persons. We distinguish three kinds of such lists of basic motives—the seventeenth-century kind found in the usual treatise on the passions, the functional kind based on evolutionary theory, and the vector kind based on topology.

There are other theories making no use, or little use, of basic motives. G. W. Allport,[21] in his well-known book *Personality*, put forward an eloquent argument for the functional autonomy of motives, a theory which denies the possibility of deriving all motives from a list of basic motives. The functional autonomy of motives is not in itself, however, a theory of personality, and does not give one a clear method for describing a person. The kind of theory that is likely to develop out of such a doctrine (though Allport does not himself develop it) is some form of psychodynamics. The term describes attempts to give a precise formulation to the sort of processes that Freud described as mechanisms of defence. Others have described the same sort of thing under the names of mechanisms of escape (Fromm)[22] or neurotic trends (Horney)[23] or defence dynamisms (Healy)[24]. Freud used as his foundation a very broad grouping of motives-at first into sexual and self-preservative motives, later regrouped in various ways; his main interest in these motives was in what happened to them afterwards. Freud's broad groups were determined by his desire to sort them out in such a way that the main inner conflicts would occur between groups. Instincts were studied not, as in McDougall, to provide a direct explanation of acts, but to show the sort of occasions that would arouse conflict, and hence defence mechanisms. The main explanations of actions were thus defence mechanisms.

The method of psychoanalysis is largely an explanation by the analyst to the patient of the way these mechanisms can be seen operating in his dreams and associations. Freud never gave a systematic account of them, but invented terms whenever he seemed to need them. Various attempts at a full list have been made, but they are rendered unsatisfactory by the vagueness and flexibility of the terms, and their tendency to overlap. Terms like projection and re-action-formation are clear examples of defence mechanisms, but such terms are often used even when the defensive aspect of the situation is not prominent. In spite of their irritating ambiguity, these concepts are some of the most fertile and valuable that we possess. They are more effective than a concept of basic motives because they describe the organism in continuous interaction with the environment.

To make these ideas hard and exact enough to take an experimental analysis should be one of the main tasks of psychology.

TABLE 2: CLASSIFICATION OF TRAITS

W. McDougall[25] distinguished four main aspects of personality (this account is based on *The Energies of Men*, one of his late works, without attempting to describe developments in his thought).

I Disposition: variation of the native propensities in strength or urgency.

II Temper: variation of the way in which these propensities worked towards their goals. Three aspects of temper were distinguished: (*a*) the degree of perseverance, expressed by the antithesis steadfast-fickle. (*b*) intensity or emotionality, expressed by the antithesis urgent-placid. (*c*) affectability, the degree to which the working of propensities is affected by pleasant or unpleasant feeling, expressed by the antithesis mercurial-even.

III Temperament: McDougall defined temperament as 'the personal qualities that are determined by the chemical influences of the bodily metabolism exerted upon the general working of the brain or nervous system'. Among these qualities he included fatiguability, activity, and extraversion-introversion.

IV Character: the organization of native propensities. Elsewhere he added two other classes: V abilities and VI moods.

Allport and Odbert[26] classify traits into four groups:

I 'Real' traits, designating generalized and personalized determining tendencies-consistent and stable modes of an individual's adjustment to his environment, e.g. aggressive, introverted, sociable.

II Terms descriptive of present activity, temporary states of mind, and mood, e.g. abashed, rejoicing, frantic.

III Judgments of value, including phrases indicating the effect on others of some trait: insignificant, worthy, dazzling.

IV Miscellaneous.

R. B. Cattell[27] divides traits as follows:

I Abilities, or cognitive traits, either as constitutional potentialities, or as achievements or skills.

II Temperamental traits, including what he regards as temperamental in the narrower sense (e.g. excitability, emotionality, speed of response, fatiguability, sensitivity, and a group of traits classified under temper, e.g. perseveration, impulsiveness.

III Dynamic, conative or motivational traits: in their constitutional form these are disposition, needs or ergs; in their environmental mould form, these become sentiments, character, attitude and complexes.

Ludwig Klages[28] used the term 'Character' where we should use 'Personality'. The aspects he distinguished are:

I Talents or abilities, including both intellectual abilities and qualities of will-energy, determination, etc., which McDougall would call 'temper'.

II Driving forces, motives, i.e. McDougall's 'disposition'.
III Temperament: this includes three aspects—emotionality, impulsiveness and 'capacity for expression'.
IV Harmony or disharmony of qualities with one another; this is McDougall's 'character'.
V Consequences of character traits for social life; these are Allport's 'judgments of value'.

H. Eysenck[29] distinguishes four sectors of personality:
I A cognitive sector (intelligence).
II A conative sector (character) this is said to be closely related to 'will' as defined by James, Ach, Michotte, Aveling, etc., to Freud's ego, Webb's 'W' and McDougall's self-regarding sentiment.
III An affective sector (temperament).
IV A somatic sector (constitution). (This corresponds to McDougall's 'temperament'.)

REFERENCES

1 and 16, 19 and 20
  McDougall, W.   *Outline of Psychology.*   London, Methuen, 5th Ed. 1931.

2. Holt, E. B.   *Animal Drive and Learning Process* (in Experimental Social Psychology. Murphy & Newcomb).   London, Harper Bros., 1937.

3. Murphy, G.   *General Psychology.*   London, Harper Bros., 1933.

4. Allport, F. H.   *Social Psychology.*   Boston, Houghton Mifflin, 1924.

5. Cattell, R. B.   *General Psychology.*   Cambridge, Mass. Sci.-Art Publishers, 1941.

6. Murray, H. A.   *Explorations in Personality.*   New York, Oxford Univ. Press, 1938.

7. Huntington, E.   *Mainsprings of Civilization.*   London, Chapman and Hall, 1945.

8. Berman, L.   *The Glands Regulating Personality.*   London, Macmillan, 1922.

9. Marett, H. R. R.   *Psychology and Folklore.*   London, Methuen, 1920.
10. Freud, S.   *Mourning and Melancholia* 1917 (Collected Papers Vol. IV.)   London, Hogarth Press, 1934.

11. Dollard, J. et al.   *Frustration and Aggression.*   London, Kegan Paul, Trench, Trubner & Co., Ltd., 1944.

12. Benedict, R.   *Patterns of Culture.*   Boston, Houghton Mifflin, 1946.

13 and 26
  Allport, G. W. and Odbert, H. S.   *Trait-names: a Psycholexical study.*   Psychol. Monog. No. 211, 1936.

14. JAMES, W.   *Principles of Psychology.*   London, Macmillan, 1890.

15. WATSON, J.   *Psychology from the Standpoint of a Behaviourist.*   Philadelphia, J. B. Lippincott & Co., 1929.

17. MURRAY, H. A.   *Explorations in Personality.*   New York, Oxford Univ. Press, 1938.

18. and 21. ALLPORT, G. W.   *Personality: A Psychological Interpretation.*   London, Constable, 1937.

22. FROMM, E.   *The Fear of Freedom.*   London, Kegan Paul, 1941.

23. HORNEY, K.   *Our Inner Conflicts.*   London, Kegan Paul, 1946.

24. HEALY, W., BRONNER, A. F. AND BOWERS, A. M.   *Structure and Meaning of Psycho-analysis.*   New York, Knopf, 1930.

25. McDOUGALL, W.   *The Energies of Men.*   London, Methuen, 1933.

27. CATTELL, R. B.   *Description and Measurement of Personality.*   Yonkers-on-Hudson, World Book Co., 1946.

28. KLAGES, L.   *The Science of Character.*   London, Allen & Unwin, 1929 (original German edition, 1910).

29. EYSENCK, H. J.   *Dimensions of Personality.*   London, Kegan Paul, 1947.

30. DUNLAP, K.   *Civilized Life.*   London, George Allen & Unwin, 1934.

CHAPTER III

TRAITS

WE have distinguished three large groups of theories about personality—those using some concept of basic traits, those describing a person in terms of environmental pressures, and those describing the interaction of person and environment. This chapter deals with the first of these three groups. We shall discuss first the problems that arise in the assessment and identification of traits, and shall then consider two ways of trying to discover which traits are basic to the personality— theories of types and theories of factors. Here as elsewhere, discussion of techniques will go along with discussion of theories because they are in some measure dependent on one another. It is natural to associate with trait theories the use of rating scales, of quantitative laboratory tests, and of anatomical and physiological measurements. To some extent the identity of theory and technique may be exaggerated by the arrangement of our chapters; but it is not likely that serious injustice will be done.

The description of a personality by trait adjectives must be about as old as language itself. It is a standard method in Homer. It is natural that the psychologist who wanted to found a science of personality should try refining upon this familiar and successful method. Instead of merely calling a person greedy, hopeful, selfish, determined, disagreeable, and so on, according to our whim, we may try to refine the language we use until it is adequate for scientific purposes. The ordinary trait-names have several defects that are not difficult to recognize:

(i) They are vague, and often variously understood by various people. Discussions about 'the real meaning' of some trait-name serve to bring out the great variety of meanings attached to an apparently simple term, and how easy it is for people to misunderstand one another. There is a constant tendency for traits to begin with some fairly clear-cut meaning in a single kind of situation, and then to be used in many other situations until the meaning becomes complex and obscure. Thus courage begins as a quality of men in battle, but may be extended to 'moral courage'. Thus also the parable of the Good Samaritan generalized the concept of 'neighbour'.

(ii) A trait-name usually contains a concealed reference to a social norm. When we say that a person is greedy we mean that he wants food more than most people of his kind; we do not define precisely who these other people are; usually the person we are talking to will have the same kind of reference group in mind, and when this is so then communication is more likely to be successful. It often happens that disagreement about the application of a trait term is really disagreement about the standard group with which comparison is made. One might say 'He is very excitable' and the other reply 'Yes, but he comes from Southern Italy', meaning: if you compare him with Italians then he is not noticeably excitable. Or one might say 'He is rebellious', and the other reply: 'Yes, but he is adolescent', where the standard refers to age-expectations, instead of national stereotypes. It is obvious that in ordinary speech one does not have a very definite group of people in mind who are to act as standard, nor does one decide exactly how far a person has to deviate from the average in order to have a trait. How much ruder than most people does he have to be, in order to be considered a rude man? Such questions have never been determined, and the terms we use in ordinary speech always have this kind of vagueness. Perhaps this is the main and inescapable defect of the rating scale method, that we cannot extract from the results any information more exact than the rater's knowledge.

(iii) A common error arising in the use of ratings is the 'halo' effect. This is the tendency to introduce a concealed value judgment of the total person into what purports to be a rating of a specific trait. Very often we have separate terms for the same trait, according to whether we like the person or not. 'I am determined, you are obstinate, he is a pig-headed fool'.

In *Man and Superman* Don Juan shows how every trait has two names, favourable and unfavourable, according to the speaker's point of view. (Only a fragment of his ingenious tirade will be quoted): . . . 'They are not moral; they are only conventional. They are not virtuous: they are only cowardly. They are not even vicious: they are only "frail". They are not artistic: they are only lascivious. They are not prosperous: they are only rich. They are not loyal, they are only servile; not public-spirited, only patriotic; not courageous, only quarrelsome; not determined only obstinate; not masterful, only domineering; not self-controlled, only obtuse; not self-respecting, only vain; not considerate, only polite; not intelligent, only opinionated; not progressive, only factious; not imaginative, only superstitious; not just, only vindictive. . . . Beauty, purity, respectability, religion, morality, art, patriotism, bravery and the rest are nothing but words that I or anyone else can turn inside out like a glove.'

To measure this 'halo' effect is difficult, because there is no way of determining what the true or correct value would have been; in fact, considering the intrinsic vagueness of such trait-adjectives, there is no real or objective quantity of the trait inherent in the person. One way of showing the magnitude of the effect is to arrange all the traits to be rated in such a way that one end is always 'good' or acceptable, and the other end is always 'bad' or despised. If we then ask a judge to rate several subjects on these traits, we may find that there is a positive correlation between scores on traits that are logically unrelated. The magnitude of this correlation is a measure of the halo effect for that judge, i.e. the tendency to rate them as generally 'good' or 'bad'. Trait terms are constantly shifting their 'halo' meanings. 'Charity', 'gentleman', 'humble', are words that began the nineteenth century as words of praise, and ended it as sneers.

(iv) The question of trait unity also poses difficult problems for the rater. When we use terms like sociable, ill-tempered, cautious, to describe a person, we do not specify what range of situations we are considering. The rater would like his subject to be 'consistent', i.e. to exhibit his trait in a great variety of situations. If he is ill-tempered, then, to be 'consistent' in this way, he should be ill-tempered with his wife, his children, his dog, his boss, his subordinates, the ticket inspector, his golf-clubs, and the weather. The character writers from Theophrastus onwards, have delighted to describe such consistent trait-behaviour.

Here is part of Sir Thomas Overbury's description of a Covetous Man (early seventeenth century).

'This man would love, honour and adore God, if there were an L more in his name: he hath coffined up his soul in his chests before his body; he could wish he were in Midas his taking for hunger, on condition he had his chemical quality. ... His morning prayer is to overlook his bags, whose every parcel begets his adoration. Then to his studies, which are to cozen this tenant, beggar that widow, or undo some orphan. Then his bonds are viewed, the well-known days of payment coined by heart; and if he ever pray, it is, some one may break his day, that the beloved forfeiture may be obtained.... He never spends candle but at Christmas (when he has them for New Year's gifts) in hope that his servants will break glasses for want of light, which they doubly pay for in their wages. His actions are guilty of more crimes than other men's thoughts, and he conceives no sin which he dare not act save only lust, from which he abstains for fear he should be charged with keeping bastards: once a year he feasts, the relics of which meal shall serve him the next quarter. In his talk he rails against the eating of breakfasts, drinking betwixt meals, and swears he is impoverished with paying of tithes. He had rather have the frame of the world fall, than the price of corn.'

In real life, however, we know that such unconditional traits are not common. Most people do not exhibit a trait in

D

the same degree on every conceivable occasion. Overbury himself knew well enough that most men were not 'characters'. 'To square out a character by our English level,' he wrote, 'it is a picture (real or personal) quaintly drawn, in various colours, all of them heightened by one shadowing. It is a quick and soft touch of many strings, all shutting up in one musical close, it is wit's descent on any plain song.'

In Hartshorne and May's[1] famous study of honesty, there were some children who would cheat at school but not at home, there were some who would tell lies but would not steal money, and so on. The experimenters seem to have felt somewhat irritated by the 'inconsistency' displayed by these children, and to have felt that their results invalidated the search for general traits. Perhaps they despaired too quickly; it may be that people do have general traits, even though not everybody has the same ones. To make the point less abstractly: suppose we are considering a trait of aggression, and, fearing the trait is too general, we distinguish six modes of aggression, objects towards which it is directed, or situations in which it appears, for instance, aggression against parents, against rivals, against the weak; aggression when sexually frustrated, when experiencing insecurity about status, when suffering physical pain. Suppose further that we represent the range of possible behaviour by a line, in which the aggressive extreme comes at the left-hand end, and the extreme of non-aggression comes as the right-hand end, and we mark the amount that an individual possesses by a stroke through the line. Then a person A who comes at the aggressive extreme in every relation and situation would show the trait consistently.

A

aggression   non-aggression

B, who is never aggressive, is equally consistent

B

aggression   non-aggression

C, who is about average in all these respects, can also be
rated on the trait. (This kind is theoretically respectable, and often turns up when ratings are done
though one may suspect that the appearance of it is
often due to laziness or defective analysis.)

C

————————/-/-/-/-/-/———————————

aggression   non-aggression

But we sometimes get people like D

D

-/-/-/————————————————/-/-/-/———

aggressive   non-aggressive

For instance, the poet Shelley, who was markedly aggressive
against parents and persons in authority, but in most other
respects was a pacifist; or the authoritarian character described
by Erich Fromm,[2] who is submissive to the strong and cruel
to the weak. To average the ratings, so that their scores both
come somewhere near the middle, would be a ridiculous
proceeding. It would be more sensible to say that such a
person as Shelley does not possess any degree of aggression as
a general trait, that the trait is inapplicable to him. Once we
have recognized the possibility of this, we shall soon find that
it is the rule rather than the exception. It is only rather rarely
that one finds anybody exhibiting the rigid and unconditional
trait consistency that many theoretical constructs represent
as being normal. The point of this discussion is not that
traits are highly specific, not that conduct is usually fragment-
ary, inconsistent, or disconnected; but rather that the grouping

of behaviour patterns varies from one person to another, so that a group of minor traits that are meaningfully associated in one person may not be similarly arranged in the next one. A pattern that seems reasonable or convenient to the investigator may not be meaningful or relevant to all his subjects.

Now let us see how psychologists have attempted to deal with these obstacles. How have they constructed their rating scales to avoid or minimize these difficulties?

First, the vagueness of traits. Instead of merely asking whether or not a particular adjective applies to a person, one may consider the trait as a variation between two extremes, and offer the judge various degrees of the trait as possible ratings. We may take as an example Heidbreder's[3] Minnesota Personal Traits Rating Scales Test Blank, which was constructed to assess two traits—inferiority feeling and introversion—extraversion. The instructions read as follows:

'In rating yourself on a particular trait, disregard every trait but that one. Let your ratings represent your usual behaviour and attitude. The masculine pronoun has been used throughout for convenience.

Rate yourself on each trait. Do not skip any.

If the trait characterizes you *to a marked degree* place a check (X) in the column marked + +.

If the trait characterizes you to a slight degree, place a check in the column marked +.

If the opposite of the trait characterizes you to a slight degree, place a check in the column marked —.

If the opposite of the trait characterizes you to a marked degree, place a check in the column marked — —. If neither the trait nor its opposite characterizes you, place a check in the column marked 0.'

The items for rating then follow; the following are examples:
from the Inferiority Scale

— —   —   0+   ++   22. Is content with his lot.

— —   —   0+   ++   35. Is misunderstood by most
                                          people.

− − − 0+ ++ 40. Is moved to sympathy by the
                         misfortunes of his friends.

Webb[4] employed a pair of antithetical terms, followed by
careful descriptive definitions to make sure that terms were
understood in the same way by everyone.

Sometimes alternatives are given descriptively, instead of
by symbols; as in Rogers' Test of Personal Adjustment.[5]
Item 15.   Do you like to join in rough games, wrestling
matches, football games and things like that?
   (*a*) I like them very much.
   (*b*) I like them a little.
   (*c*) I don't like them.
   (*d*) I hate people pushing and pulling me about.
Freyd's rating scale for teachers[6] made a graphic rating
scale—a line in which the judge had to mark the degree of
a trait by a mark on the line. Degrees of the trait were indicated
by descriptive phrases underneath the line, but these phrases
did not belong to fixed segments of the line, but general
regions.   There were usually five phrases for each trait, but
the graphic scale was afterwards measured off as a ten-point
scale.

Mark a point on the line representing your opinion of the
subject:
How does his dress and appearance impress you?

---

slovenly and unkempt	somewhat indifferent and careless in dress	unnoticeable in dress	noticeably neat and clean	fastidious, almost a dude

There are various ways in which psychologists have tried to
make traits less ambiguous.

When we use a trait name in ordinary conversation, neither
speaker nor hearer knows exactly with whom the individual
is being compared, nor by how much he has to deviate from

what is ordinary, before he is considered to have the trait. Various devices have been tried for hardening the norm. In the U.S. army in 1917 Scott[7] designed a system of rating for officers called the man-to-man scale. When rating an officer for, say, leadership, the rater would be asked to compare him, not with some nebulous norm, but with five other officers selected by himself. The rater was asked to name five particular officers among his acquaintance to serve as examples of different levels of leadership—Highest, High, Middle, Low and Lowest, and the person to be rated had to be compared with these particular men. This was an effective way of crystallizing a fluid norm. Critics complained that everybody's norm was different, but this is always the case anyhow. A more serious objection is that judges find it hard to think of these representative people, and, in the kind of practical situations in which rating scales are used, it is difficult to get raters to take so much trouble. It must be remembered that most rating scales are designed to be used by acquaintances or superiors of the subjects concerned, or by subjects for themselves, and not by professional psychologists whose interest is scientific. The rating scale is merely a device for summarizing the rater's knowledge as it has been gained in the ordinary course of social relations, and reflection. Ratings cannot be any better than the insight and understanding of the rater. They can be dressed up in quantitative form and used as fodder for the calculating machine, but that does not make them into genuine measurements.

When one judge is rating a considerable number of subjects, it may be possible to induce him to use some fairly fixed pattern of distribution for his ratings. Most human traits when measured fall roughly into the form of a normal distribution curve; this is certainly true when we measure the height, weight or intelligence of a fairly homogeneous population, such as all the eleven-year-old girls in an English town; and it appears to be true also for other traits whose assessment is more subjective, such as introversion. In order to make the ratings of different judges comparable with one another it is, therefore, a common practice to tell judges the approximate proportion of ratings that ought to go into each compartment. The statistical assumptions that one makes are largely arbitrary. Symonds[8] gives percentages that should be allotted to different compartments depending on (*a*) the total number of persons in the group to be rated by the judge concerned, and (*b*) the number of classes into which they are to be divided. He assumes that a group of forty subjects will have a range of two and a half standard deviations above and below the mean, and a group of 150 subjects will have a range of three standard deviations.

It seems preferable, in view of the fact that ratings are usually discontinuous, to base the distribution on a binomial; and this has the advantage that one does not have to change the rule as the number of subjects changes. We should then require frequencies to correspond roughly with the following percentages:

Rating scale with: *should have the following percentages in different grades:*

2 grades	50 : 50
3 grades	25 : 50 : 25
4 grades	12 : 38 : 38 : 12
5 grades	6 : 25 : 38 : 25 : 6
6 grades	3 : 16 : 31 : 31 : 16 : 3

The logical basis for adopting one procedure rather than another is extremely flimsy, especially since the assumption that the subjects studied are a random sample of a homogeneous population is in most cases wildly untrue. Our situation is rather that of Lord Melbourne and his cabinet: it does not matter what we say so long as we all say the same thing. Ratings by several judges become much more readily comparable with one another when the proportions of different ratings are approximately the same, so that there is a strong case for adopting some convention. In the same way examiners marking scripts may adopt some convention about the frequency with which they will allot various marks. As the process of rating or marking goes on, however, certain assessments may come gradually to acquire an absolute meaning. Murray and his collaborators, working on the O.S.S. Assessment project,[9] used a six-point scale of rating, 0 to 5. At the beginning they intended to use these ratings in approximately the following proportions:

Rating:	0	1	2	3	4	5
Percentage:	7	18	25	25	18	7

In reality, however, a rating of 0 or 1 came to mean that a candidate was not recommended for acceptance by the Office of Strategic Services, so that ratings had come to acquire an absolute as well as a relative meaning, and their distribution could no longer be controlled by theoretical considerations. These difficulties can be avoided if judges arrange their subjects in rank order, instead of giving them ratings.

1. The 'halo' effect: to a limited extent one can diminish it by focusing attention on one trait at a time. If a group of subjects is to be rated on several traits, it is better to rate all on one trait, and then rate all on the next trait. Specific warnings against 'halo' are often included in the instructions. 'Halo' is nothing but a nuisance when one wants to use rating scales for studying the interrelation of traits; but when one is concerned with vocational selection the halo may be the most important trait to assess. Thus, in a rating scale used to summarize a foreman's opinion of the men working under him, there were several questions dealing with various more specific traits, manual skills, foresight, sociability, etc., and then a question directly asking for the 'halo':

If I were an employer, I'd be willing to take him on.	I shouldn't like to employ him,

The strength and persistence of halo effects is strong evidence of the tendency to judge personality as a whole, rather than to consider it as a collection of traits.

2. The problem of trait unity; this will have to be faced again when we consider the factorial analysis of personality measures. For the moment we are concerned only with practical procedures of test construction. When we ask 'Is he aggressive? Is he generous? Is he helpful?' we invite a definite judgment that assigns a certain amount of the trait; usually we do not leave any room for the judge to say 'partly', or 'in certain respects'; i.e. as we pictured the problem on pp. 40, 41 above, we are allowing for cases A, B, and C, but not for case D. If we are going to allow for the possibility of case D, we must do it by expressing a general trait in terms of a number of more specific items. For example, H. A. Murray[10] assesses the trait of dominance by means of the following ten items, each of which is separately rated on a six point scale:

	Below Average	Above Average
	— 3 — 2 — 1	+ 1 + 2 + 3

1. I enjoy organizing or directing the activities of a group-team, club or committee.
2. I argue with zest for my point of view against others.
3. I find it rather easy to lead a group of boys and maintain discipline.
4. I usually influence others more than they influence me.
5. I am usually the one to make the necessary decisions when I am with another person.
6. I feel that I can dominate a social situation.
7. I enjoy the sense of power that comes when I am able to control the actions of others.
8. I assert myself with energy when the occasion demands it.
9. I feel that I should like to be a leader and sway others to my opinion.
10. I feel that I am driven by an underlying desire for power.

When the subject rates himself, these items are not presented successively, but mingled with others. To decide how much genuine trait unity in respect of dominance is shown by one individual, we can calculate some measure of the dispersion of his self-ratings on these ten items. If the dispersion approaches that which would be obtained by a random distribution of self-ratings, then we can conclude that the trait possesses no effective unity for this person. Very little empirical study of trait unity along these lines seems to have been made. An approach that has been extensively employed, however, is the factorial method, by which the grouping of items can be studied in a population, though not in an individual.

One of the perils of the rating scale method is the deceptive ease with which it is possible to get results. It is easy to prepare a form asking for some kind of ratings, and hand it out to large numbers of subjects. It is not very difficult to induce subjects to give some kind of a rating, if all that he is required to do is to put a cross somewhere on a piece of paper. The record sheet will look much the same, whether it is the result of careful thought and study, or of a mere desire to get finished with the matter as quickly as possible. It is difficult to ensure that every judgment recorded on a rating sheet will be the expression of genuine knowledge. Some scales even invite trouble by requiring raters to answer every question. It is important that every scale should leave the rater an opportunity to say that he doesn't know, or the trait doesn't apply. It is also important that the experimenter should not make demands on his raters which they are unlikely to be able to meet. Some scales even require the rater to quote anecdotes about the subject in support of his rating. If one could induce the raters to do this, it would doubtless be an excellent way of ensuring that the rater does his job seriously, but too often circumstances are unfavourable to this sort of refinement.

Another way to reduce the effect of ignorance is to avoid asking questions to which the rater is unlikely to know the answer. Estes[11] asked his judges to rate various traits on the basis of a two-minute film, and compared their ratings with those of a group of psychologists who had studied these same subjects long and intensively. He found that his judges were rather successful in rating traits like inhibition, apathy, placidity, ascendance; but the evidence of the film did not help them much in judging objectivity, or desire for change or for play.

In a great many projects, the motivation behind the recording of judgments is so inadequate that the results cannot be of much value. But the psychologist whose main concern is to have a lot of figures to which he can apply his statistical apparatus may nevertheless be quite happy. It was the experience of the Admiralty psychologists, and also of the O.S.S. group in U.S.A., that ratings are most satisfactory when used for summing up the results of a group discussion among several judges. A hastily entered form by a bored or resentful executive is of negligible value. To hand out rating forms in large numbers, or to distribute them by post, is a characteristic device of the kind of psychologist who is afraid of people, or uncomfortable in dealing with them. He gets over the awkward personal part of his experiment as soon as possible, and settles down with relish to the manipulation of figures. After a couple of years another thesis is completed and on its way to limbo, to be unread and justly forgotten.

Instead of asking for a verbal assessment of a trait, we may try to observe it directly in action under controlled and measurable conditions. This is in some ways a more adventurous thing to attempt, and the problem has attracted a good many able experimenters. If there are stable traits of personality, one should be able to evoke and measure them in standard situations. This was the obvious procedure to adopt for the study of abilities, and has been extended to various other qualities; it is sometimes possible to present a task as a measure of ability, and then to use the results for measuring other qualities. Of the many attempts that have been made, we shall mention only a few as examples.

The English studies of perseveration form one of the

more resolute attempts to isolate a behavioural trait for experimental analysis.   The idea of perseveration, or mental inertia, was evolved from the speculations of various German writers, particularly Karl Gross,[12] and the work of the Dutch psychologists Heymans and Wiersma.[13]   Gross's 'cerebral secondary function' was a concept of speculative physiology for which there was little empirical evidence. According to this terminology, the 'primary function' of a sensory neurone is the reception of stimuli, and the 'secondary function' is the after-discharge, the continuation of the effect of the stimulus after the stimulus has ceased. Examples of the process could be found in a good many visual phenomena, for example dark adaptation, after-sensations, and the apparent continuity of discontinuous stimuli, as in cinema pictures.   It was supposed that each person might have a characteristic amount of 'secondary function' or 'perseveration' so that in some people the after-effects of stimulation would be more intense and prolonged than in others.

The notion was then extended to other regions—to motor activity, where it was expected that the 'perseverator' would show rigidity, difficulty in changing from one activity to another, while a non-perseverator would show more flexibility of behaviour, and to memory, in which the perseverator might find himself haunted by a tune or a phrase long after it had ceased to be relevant.   It was also supposed that the same trait might show itself affectively as rigidity of habit formation, unwillingness to adopt new practices, a preference for established routine and old custom.   Attempts were also made to connect variations of perseveration with psychotic syndromes, so that the schizophrene was said to be a perseverator, and the manic-depressive a non-perseverator.   Other workers identify mania with low perseveration, and depression with high perseveration.

This elaborate theoretical structure stood up poorly to experimental analysis.   Tests were devised for many of these supposed aspects of perseveration. Look first at the sensory tests. Individual differences in the perception of visual flicker were used as a measure. If we present a circular disc with two black and two white quarters, and rotate it at a gradually increasing speed, the black and white coalesce into an intermediate grey. At a speed where this coalescence is not perfect a flicker is perceived, as there used to be in the old cinema films. The speed of rotation at which flicker disappears can be used as a measure of the time required for the after-discharge to die away. Hence flicker should disappear for a perseverator at a lower speed than it does for a non-perseverator. Similarly, perseverators should find after-images recurring more frequently, and for a longer time, than non-perseverators; similarly, perseverators should adapt more slowly to darkness than non-perseverators, so that, for instance, they would require a longer time to read faintly illuminated letters in a dark room.

Motor perseveration was found experimentally to include two rather different notions. Some tests were designed to measure the ability to overcome a well-established habit—for example, to write ə instead of e; other tests measured the ability to shift from one familiar pattern to another, for example, to write *a b c* followed by *A B C*; these are sometimes spoken of as the 'creative effort' kind of perseveration, and the 'alternation' kind. The 'alternation' kind of perseveration is more or less the same thing that was studied by other workers under the name of retro-active inhibition. The idea is that in both cases the perseverator will find the shift of activity more difficult than will the non-perseverator.

Most of these measures have low reliability, and prove to be virtually uncorrelated with one another. Sensory perseveration can be discarded entirely; it is a notion of speculative physiology that has failed to establish itself. The idea belonged to a period when people hoped to find rather simple relations between properties of the nervous system and traits of personality. Such theories have one by one crept silently to rest and we can say with Byron, 'there let him lay'.

Of the motor perseveration tests, only the 'creative effort' type seems deserving of further exploration, and that seems to be just another symbolic act; the high perseverator, who finds it difficult to adopt a strange pattern of action, is symbolizing his rigidity and resistance to change. Work on perseveration has followed a course that is familiar in so much personality work. Research starts with the concept of a trait, a fixed quality of temperament, innate and firmly rooted in physical process. The trait first loses its physical basis, then its innateness, then its unity, and is dissipated by a series of debunking researches. If it recovers at all from this process, it does so as a trait not fixed by nature, but emerging in the course of social development; its unity is based not on physiology but on symbolism, and hence the trait organization may differ from one subject to another.

Other projects in which tasks that are ostensibly tests of ability are covertly used in the study of other traits, have included measures of oscillation persistence, suggestibility and caution. Oscillation (the '0' factor) is the variation of performance on a test with repeated trials. According to the English workers, some subjects show consistently more variation than others, whatever test is used. Not much seems to have been done about tracing the ramifications of this trait beyond the laboratory situation. Cattell[14] finds that it measures instability, and is negatively correlated with willpower or character integration. It seems rather a good trait to measure, because the subject would be very unlikely to press the purpose of the experiment, or to make regularity or irregularity of score an object in itself. Hence the experimenter is less at the mercy of his subjects' attitudes than commonly happens in these laboratory tests.

The opposite is true of experimental studies of willpower, persistence or endurance. It is easy to give one's subjects some tedious or unpleasant task, and then measure how long they will go on doing it; but whether the behaviour that a subject shows in the laboratory task is representative of his behaviour in the serious circumstances of life, is much harder to know. Whether a subject shows persistence or not depends in part on whether he is 'ego-involved' in the situation (to use a current barbarism), i.e. whether success in the task is important for his self-esteem. Since success in laboratory tasks is seldom of much intrinsic importance, the subject's self-esteem comes in only in so far as he takes the task to be in some way symbolic of his success or failure in other more important life-situations. So once more we come back to the fact that the meaning of the test result depends on the symbolism embodied in the act. The same general qualification applies to measures of caution and rashness, and of the level of aspiration. The bit of conduct that we are measuring—is it a valid sample? As Murray[15] and his collaborators have remarked, it is common to find psychologists careful of reliability (i.e. the inner consistency of the testing method) and yet remaining content with only the flimsiest evidence of validity (i.e. the confirmation of test results by external events). Among the multitude of laboratory measurements of personality traits, we find few in which there is any serious attempt to prove that the result of the measurement agrees with the daily conduct of the subject's life.

To escape from the artificiality of the laboratory situation, in which the subject knows that he is taking part in an experiment for the benefit of the psychological department of a university, some workers have tried to conceal what is happening. Examples of this are found in the famous studies of Hartshorne and May.[16] In one of their studies of honesty, for instance, they told the children that they were taking part in an athletic contest. They had to squeeze a hand dynamometer, make a long jump, and do 'chin-ups' on a horizontal bar. The experimenter privately noted his subject's performance on a trial effort, and then left the subject to record his own test result. Since he could be assumed to have tired himself in the practice trials, his performance when alone was unlikely to be better than when observed; and if he claimed to have done better, he could be judged dishonest. This is a very good kind of experiment, provided that no one guesses its purpose. The difficulty of concealment has perhaps been the chief reason why this type of test has not been seriously introduced into personality studies that are used for clinical or occupational purposes.

Another device of a somewhat similar kind is to use a rating scale not directly, as a fact about the person rated, but indirectly, as an act of the rater. For example, Sears[17] used a group of mutual ratings in a college fraternity to discover whether persons who were rated high on obstinacy, tidiness, and stinginess tended to project these qualities, i.e. to attribute more than the average amount of these qualities to other people. Cattell[18] used fluctuations in ratings to measure instabilities in the raters. Similarly, Hartshorne and May,[19] setting out to measure truthfulness, asked a series of questions to which an affirmative answer was almost certainly false (i.e. if you say yes, you're a liar). 'There are many specific acts of conduct (say the authors) which on the whole have rather widespread social approval, but which at the same time are rarely done. The questions revolve around situations of this sort.' There are two forms of the test, each containing thirty-six questions. Examples are:

5. Do you always preserve order when the teacher is out of the room?
19. Do you always obey your parents cheerfully and promptly?
29. Do you read the Bible every day?

Children were allowed to claim up to twenty-three out of thirty-six virtues before they were considered to have proved themselves liars.

Laboratory tests of the kinds described above have been very little used for practical purposes. Psychologists who have to use their understanding of a person for coming to some decision about him have not placed much reliance on these trait measurements. The reason seems to lie in the fact that the experimentalist has not usually analysed and controlled the meaning of the act for the subject, or the relation between the subject and himself. He has often behaved as if his subject were a decerebrate dog, and the results have been as trivial and confusing as might be expected. In spite of the somewhat disappointing results of this kind of work in the past, there may be many striking successes to look forward to when more adequate theoretical ideas are employed.

The complexities of the relation between the tester and his subject have led many investigators to prefer the definite information that can be obtained from physiological tests. It is often felt that the body cannot lie, or at any rate not so glibly as the speech mechanisms. People may make all sorts of misstatements (wilful or otherwise) about their attitudes, and it is difficult to convict them of falsehood, or to detect the truth; but a quality like blood pressure can be determined objectively, and there is no need to rely on opinions or impressions. With objective physiologically measured qualities the experimenter feels himself to be on solid ground. Physiological measures can be expected to test some universally human quality, in a way that psychological measures do not.

At one period, the physiological expression of emotion seemed to offer a fine route to experiments on personality. James' theories, and the experiments of Cannon exercised a wide influence, and suggested that the most reliable knowledge of the mind might come through the body. Lange's original notion, that different states of the circulatory system corresponded accurately to different experienced emotions, has not been confirmed by subsequent studies. There is no clear physiological distinction between fear and anger, and other more complicated conditions like envy, jealousy and hope show no distinctive physiological pattern. What can, however, be done rather well, is to find indicators of sudden

E

excitement.   Abrupt changes in blood circulation provide some reliable signs.   Several measures have been used—changes in the rate of the heart, in blood pressure, and in the volume of a limb.   One consequence of increased sympathetic activity is a contraction in the walls of the surface blood vessels. Changes in the volume of one finger can serve as a rather sensitive indicator of excitement.   Another indicator that has established its value is the galvanic skin reflex.   (In the days when men were still permitted to have souls, this was called the Psychogalvanic Reflex, later shamefacedly abridged to PGR.)   PGR is a fall in the body's resistance to a small electric current, in response to some exciting stimulus.   The current may go through the hand, or from one finger to another, and the circuit is balanced in a Wheatstone Bridge.   The more emotional a stimulus is, the greater the deflection of the galvonometer.   When Whately Smith[20] used a list of a hundred words with fifty educated subjects, he found among the words giving large deflections: 'kiss', 'love', 'marry', 'woman', 'wound', 'afraid'; while the words that gave the lowest deflections in the series were: 'flower', 'pond', 'pencil', 'swim'.   This ex- periment is an elegant demonstration that PGR means emotion of some kind.   Especially when used along with circulatory changes, it is a good record of sympathetic activity.

Various signs expressed through skeletal muscles are also good indicators of emotion.   The rhythm of breathing has often been used for this purpose.   The measure usually used is the Inspiration-Expiration ratio, the ratio of the time taken for breathing in to the time taken for breathing out.   In ordinary breathing the time taken for breathing in is less than that for breathing out; but, when excited, a subject tends to hold his breath, so that the I/E ratio increases.   This was the origin of the famous lie-detection experiment, which at one time seemed to promise so much for the physiological method in psychology.

A trembling hand has long been used by popular novelists as a sign of emotion.   The Russian psychologist Luria[21] used this as an index of emotional disturbance, and applied it along with word association tests as another variant of the lie-detector. He was able to apply tests to people under genuine stress, such as murderers on trial, or students waiting for a qualifying examination. The subject rested his hands on delicately balanced levers, which would show even slight movements; he was instructed to press a lever with his right when he responded to a word stimulus; the most useful part of the record for indicating emotion came from the involuntary movements of the left hand. Emotion showed itself as a disorganization, a loss of smooth functioning, similar to the delay in thinking of a suitable word to respond with. If our tests would reliably indicate which stimuli were significant for the subject, then we might use them for an objective study of the subject's private world. The limitations of this work were partly in the vagueness of the emotion indicated. Objective tests could not discriminate between guilt, shame, resentment and surprise, and thus helped little in determining the meaning of the stimulus. The tests we have just been describing were also defective in being too sensitive to momentary changes. They showed the figure but not the ground, the emotion but not the attitude from which it sprang. They were attractive to a fashion in psychology which split up experience into a sequence of brief discrete stimuli. We might do better if we combined these short-term variations, with others that vary over hours, like fatigue, or over weeks and months, like the basal metabolic rate, or various measures of endocrine activity.

The search for a physiological measure of fatigue has been well described by Bartley and Chute.[22] In the early part of the century it was confidently expected that some definite bodily process would be found to correspond to the experience of feeling tired. The exhaustion of a particular muscle-group was considered to be the typical way of becoming tired, and the accumulation of the waste products of muscular activity was expected to provide an explanation. It gradually became clear that there is no single physiological correlate of feeling tired. The condition arises not merely when a lot of physical energy has been expended, but under a variety of conditions, for instance when doing work requiring unfavourable postures, work that requires constantly pleasant treatment of other people, work that requires sustained alertness and watchfulness, or work that is felt to be useless.

Bartley finds the common element in a conflict of drives. Work produces fatigue when it is done against the influence of a strong drive urging one not to do it. In the study of both emotion and fatigue, there have emerged no simple correlations of bodily process with subjective attitude. Fatigue is a stance taken by the individual to situations that he confronts. It is an expression of aversion to the demands of the current situation, and a wish for escape and passivity. It can be the end-result of many factors, including the work just done, general bodily condition, physical conditions of work, and the meaning of the work for the worker. Although physiological changes may be precisely measured, these signs do not have fixed meanings. Thus, although physiological tests may give us valuable information, they do not have fixed meanings, but must be understood in terms of the total personality. There is not a fixed amount of work that makes a worker tired. Similar considerations apply to the influence of endocrine glands, or the effect of central nervous infections. The effects of personality can be very striking. But they do not, as earlier workers expected, produce the same traits in everyone. When an adult becomes infected with lethargic encephalitis, he may show mainly motor symptoms, without much disturbance of intellect or personality. But if a child has it, he is likely to grow up aggressive and unmanageable, and to be described as a psychopathic personality. Similar lesions may produce quite different effects.

REFERENCES

1, 16 and 19.   *Studies in the Nature of* New York, Macmillan,
HARTSHORNE,   H.   *Character, Vol I, Studies* 1930.
AND MAY, M. A.   *in Deceit.*

2. FROMM, E.   *The Fear of Freedom.*   London, Kegan Paul, 1941.

3. HEIDBREDER, E.   *Minnesota Personal Traits. Rating Scale Test Blank.*   Chicago, C. H. Stoelting, 1931.

4. WEBB, E.   *Character and Intelligence.*   Brit. J. Psychol. Monogr. Suppl. 1, No. 3, 1915.

5. ROGERS, C.   *Test of Personal Adjustment.*   New York, General Board of Y.M.C.A., 1931.

6. FREYD, M.   *Graphic Rating Scale for Teachers.*   Chicago, C. H. Stoelting, 1923.

7. SCOTT, W. D. AND CLOTHIER, R. C.   *Personal Management.*   New York, McGraw-Hill, 1923.

8. SYMONDS, P. M.   *Diagnosing Personality and Conduct.*   New York, Appleton Century, 1931.

9 and 15. O.S.S. ASSESSMENT   *Assessment of Men: Selection of Personnel for the Office of Strategic Services.*   New York, Rinehart, 1948.

10. MURRAY, H. A.   *Explorations in Personality.*   New York, Oxford Univ. Press, 1938.

11. ESTES, S. G.   *The Judgment of Personality on the basis of brief records of Behaviour.*   Cambridge: Harvard College Library, 1937.

12. GROSS, K.   *Die Cerebrale Sekundarfunktion.*   Leipzig, 1902.

13. HEYMANS, G.   *La Classification des Caracteres.*   Revve du Mois, 1911.

14 and 18. CATTELL, K. B.   *Description and Measurement of Personality.*   Yonkers - on - Hudson, World Book Co., 1946.

17. SEARS, R. R.   *Survey of Objective Studies of Psycho-analytic Concepts.*   Soc. Sci. Res. Coun. Bull., No. 51, 1943.

20. SMITH, WHATELY W.   *The Measurement of Emotion.*   London, Kegan Paul, 1922.

21. LURIA, A. R.   *The Nature of Human Conflicts.*   New York, Liveright, 1932.

22. BARTLEY, S. H. AND CHUTE, E.   *Fatigue and Impairment in Man.*   New York, McGraw-Hill, 1947.

CHAPTER IV

TYPES AND FACTORS

THIS chapter is concerned with various attempts to find a system of basic traits for describing human personality. Two main kinds of basic traits in current use amongst psychologists are *types* and *factors*. We shall begin by discussing *types*. Type theories have been predominantly a German pattern of thought, though they have also been used by French, Dutch and Swiss writers. Type theories are at present in an unsatisfactory state, because, like so much else in contemporary psychology, there is no one doctrine that commands general acceptance, or can be regarded as solidly proved. No firm conclusions can yet be drawn about the scientific status of any types. However confident the claims of their authors, acceptance does not often extend beyond a rather narrow circle.

A good deal of the work in this field is subjective in method; it has attracted every kind of crank, as well as many serious workers. One sometimes gets the impression that any German professor who wants a status in his subject feels it necessary to invent at least two types; and professors with very high aspirations may invent as many as six or eight. In the German-speaking world it seems not to be customary to apply rigid objective tests to geisteswissenschaftliche concepts. The Geisteswissenschaften are the moral sciences, or spirit sciences, like history and sociology. They do not expect to have the same degree of exactness as the natural sciences. Rather perfunctory experiments are published, without any of the statistical analysis that is considered obligatory in the English-speaking world. It often happened that the British and Americans dismissed a German as mystical and subjective, while the Germans considered the British and Americans shallow and lacking in insight. The migration of German scholars after Hitler came to power did much to make German ideas more accessible to the English-speaking world. Their diffusion has had an effect comparable to that of the Greek scholars who fled from Constantinople after 1453. This applied particularly to psycho-analysis and Gestalt psychology, both of which have now been absorbed into British and American thought. German characterology, and the various theories of types, have not been absorbed in the same way, because the leaders did not migrate. British and American scholars are often content with a very incomplete knowledge of the German literature, relying on some one text that has been translated. The elaborate development of statistical analysis (which the Germans have ignored) has attracted British and American scholars, and has perhaps led to an undue depreciation of the subjective methods popular in Germany.

There is no fixed and generally accepted meaning of the word 'type' that enables us to give it an exact definition. At least six distinct meanings occur in current psychological literature. We shall begin by trying to clarify these.

(1) **Types as invariant traits.** Types are generally considered to be basic traits, innate or constitutional, or at least established early in life, and not thereafter subject to a radical change. While many qualities might vary with circumstances, the personality type was thought to be an unchangeable core, that which is intrinsically the man himself, and not dependent on external events. In general, motivational traits show too much development in the course of a person's life to be satisfactory for defining types. Mostly the types have been defined in terms of subtler temperamental traits, which would not directly become part of the subject's motives. Qualities like Jung's[1] introvert and extravert, Kretschmer's[2] schizoid and cycloid, or Jaensch's[3] integrate and disintegrate types, are subtle variations of personal style, that would not usually be noticed by the person concerned, but nevertheless would colour much of his behaviour. Part of the search for types is then the search for

invariant elements in human nature. So much in a person changes with age, so much else varies with external circumstance, that the search for invariants is turned to ever more subtle and elaborately defined traits, secondary function, spaltungsfähigkeit, and so on.

(2) **Types as systematic classification.** Types are supposed to be mutually exclusive, and a person is ordinarily considered to belong to only one type. They are intended to provide a basic classification of the varieties of human nature, in the same way that plants or animals are classified in botany or zoology. The typologists have often been trying to do for men what Linnaeus and Cuvier did for plants and animals—to find out which principles of classification can be considered of fundamental importance. It might be worth while for psychologists to spend some time exploring the history of biological classification—to see what kind of errors they made, how they arrived at current practice, and how solid is its foundation. We find it written, for instance, of the sixteenth century botanist Lobelius, that he used the shape of the leaf as the basis of his classification, and so was led into various errors, such as putting ferns and certain monocotyledons into the same group. Have we in psychology any hope of arriving one day at a firmly established system of classification, or are we compelled to wander for ever in a limbo of subjectivity? From one point of view, typology is a search for order and stability in the description of human personality. It is often felt that scientific psychology cannot make much progress until it has an established and complete system of classification, in the same way that botany and zoology have. Current typological studies do not claim to be more than preparatory sketches for such a system. As things are at present, many psychologists are unwilling to claim more than a quite temporary and local validity for the basic traits that they isolate. Nevertheless, what they are searching for is a system of classification that will be based on the real, permanent and important differences between people. Theories of types are attempts to isolate and define such a classificatory system.

(3) Ideal types. When a German professor says that there are two types of men, A and B, he does not mean that every human being can be unequivocally sorted into one or the other. Similarly, if an anatomy text-book says that a man has thirty-two teeth, it does not mean that every man's mouth when examined will be found to contain exactly this number. The statement means something much more complicated, and is by no means easy to analyse accurately. It contains an allusion to what is ordinary or usual under certain (not clearly defined) circumstances, i.e. it is normal in the sense of being what mostly happens. It also contains an allusion to what is normal in the sense of being proper or healthy or ideal. This normal or ideal type may actually be rare in its pure form, yet it may be useful as a standard, or basis of comparison. The notion of ideal types has been used in psychology to describe pure patterns of character, which in real life are almost always somewhat mixed or adulterated. The economic man of nineteenth-century theory was an ideal type. Admittedly he never really existed, but it was a useful organizing idea for the purpose of analysing considerable regions of behaviour, to imagine a man whose actions were always rational and guided by his own long-term interests. Spranger's[4] ideal types of men have completely integrated systems of values, so that every act is expressive of the whole character, and not, as in real life, blurred by inconsistencies. The seventeenth-century character writers, when they described a flatterer, an old college butler, a sceptic in religion, were describing, not actual people, but ideal types, who showed a simplicity and consistency of character structure that is lacking in mere mortals.

This concept of ideal types is in effect what is used in botany and zoology, and it has proved exceedingly useful there. The biologist is so well accustomed to the method that it does not occur to him to defend or justify it. He takes such a classificatory system for granted, and forgets what centuries of confusion out of which the modern system grew. It may be that psychology will one day have a well-established classification that everyone accepts and understands. But this certainly does not exist at present. There is no general agreement about which ideal abstractions will give rise to the most convenient and effective classification. In fact, none of the existing classifications has solidly established its usefulness for anything more than local and temporary purposes.

(4) **Types as discontinuities.** A type is conceived as a discontinuity in nature—some real natural cleavage or boundary which provides a principle of classification. Among animals such discontinuities often mark out the boundaries of a species rather clearly, because animals of different species are commonly infertile with one another. Among human personalities we might be able to find contrasting reaction-types, responding in opposite ways to the same stimulus situation. In a quantitative measurement of the trait, this would appear as a bimodal frequency distribution, i.e. a distribution in which there are two modes, or regions of high frequency, separated by an intermediate region of lower frequency. Graphically represented, it looks like a dromedary, while the unimodal normal distribution is more like a camel. Sex is an example of such a natural discontinuity. Nearly every human being is either male or female, and there are very few intermediate cases. Handedness is another discontinuity, not quite so clear-cut, but still marked enough to give a bimodal distribution. Most people are either right-handed or left-handed, though there are some mixed cases. Race is another fairly well-marked group of discontinuities, though constantly liable to blurring and confusion through racial mixtures. At any rate in some regions of the world, negroes, Chinese and Caucasians are easily distinguishable physical types. There are other genetically discontinuous types, such as the blood groups, or rare pathological types such as the Frolich syndrome (a disease due to pituitary defect, it produces feeble-minded boys, who are commonly of sweet and gentle disposition), or Amanaurotic family idiocy (a hereditary disease of early childhood, ending in idiocy, blindness and death. It was formerly said to have been prevalent among Polish Jews,

but most of them have since died from other causes); but these are not for the most part of much psychological significance.

When we turn from physical characteristics to traits of personality, it has not been possible to find any discontinuities of personality, similar to blood-groups or handedness. Most traits of personality that can be quantitatively assessed fall into a continuous unimodal distribution, like intelligence, rather than into types. There is no trait of personality that has shown the desired kind of discontinuity or bimodality. Since, however, the units in which such a trait is measured are mostly quite arbitrary, and of unequal size, this is not a very serious objection. No one can tell what the true form of distribution is, so long as the trait is measured in unequal units. It is nevertheless remarkable that no discontinuous personality types have yet been identified, and many investigators are becoming discouraged by the fruitless search. Some American writers (e.g. Stagner[5]) have taken the view that the reality of personality types has been disproved because the expected bimodal distributions have not turned up.

Other definitions of the type concept have emerged from attempts to reconcile German thought with the methods of statistical analysis that are popular among British psychologists.

(5) Types derived from correlation of persons. Burt[6] has suggested that the relation between a trait and a type can be understood by the fact that a trait emerges from the correlation of tests, and a type from the correlation of persons. In the correlation of persons, a person's scores on, say, twenty tests are correlated with another person's scores on the same tests. If there is a high correlation between two persons on the tests, i.e. if they score high on the same tests, and low on the same tests, then they would belong to the same type. If there were a low or negative correlation between two persons, they would belong to different types. A type would thus be a group of correlated persons. While the concept has been clearly enough formulated, the data do not usually exist in sufficient elaboration

to enable the necessary calculations to be made. Thus the
identification of types by this means is a task for the future,
and not an accomplished reality.

(6) **Types as groups of traits.** A statistical interpretation
of types has been formulated in another way also. Eysenck[7]
regards types as 'observed constellations or syndromes of
traits'. He gives as an example the *introvert* type, in which the
traits of persistence, rigidity, autonomic imbalance, accuracy
and irritability would tend to accompany one another. In
Eysenck's view, a type is of higher generality than a trait. It
should be noted that, as Burt and Eysenck use the term *type*, no
requirement of discontinuity or bimodality is imposed. Eysenck's
use of the term is a statistically sophisticated formulation of
our second meaning, types conceived as systematic classification.
The main typologies in current use will be briefly enumerated,
though we cannot pretend to take them all very seriously.
Typologies have been based on external appearances and racial
origin, on gross bodily form, on various physiological processes,
on susceptibility to various functional psychoses, on perceptual
tendencies, and on choice of the life path. The first typology
was the classical theory of the four humours, attributed to
Hippocrates.

There were four cardinal humours of the body, blood, phlegm,
yellow bile and black bile. Upon the balance of these humours
depended the health of body and mind. The four temperaments
depended on an excess of one of the four humours. An excess
of yellow bile produced a choleric temperament, in which a
person was liable to sudden explosions of anger; an excess of
phlegm produced a phlegmatic temperament, in which he was
dull and unemotional (in extreme cases, withdrawn or catatonic);
an excess of black bile produced a melancholy temperament;
and an excess of blood produced a sanguine temperament, in
which a person was optimistic, energetic, and in extreme cases
manic. A healthy person had a proper balance of all four
humours.

Attempts to classify men by their bodily form have a long

history and a large literature. Usually characteristic temperaments and diseases are ascribed to different body types. Hippocrates distinguished two principal body types—the *habitus apoplecticus*, thickset, strong, and disposed to apoplexy; and the *habitus phthisicus*, thin, weak and disposed to tuberculosis. In the nineteenth century Rostan and other French writers established a three-type system, the digestive, muscular and respiratory-cerebral types (fat, middling and thin). Subsequent writers have used either the two-type or the three-type system.

Most descriptions seem to agree pretty well with one another, though there is a good deal of variety in terminology and techniques of measurement. According to Eysenck, over 100 different indices have been elaborated for expressing body types. Tables of Greek roots have been ransacked to provide new terms. The thin men have been called asthenic (Carus), hypovegetative (Pende), microsplanchnic (Viola), leptomorph (Eysenck) and ectomorph (Sheldon). The fat men have been called phlegmatic (Carus), hypervegetative (Pende), pyknic (Kretschmer), megalosplanchnic (Viola), endomorph (Sheldon) and eurymorph (Eysenck). Many attempts have been made to associate body-type with personality traits. The fat men have been described as extraverted, sociable, prone to marked swings of mood, and to manic-depressive insanity, and conversion hysteria. The thin men have been described as introverted, fanatical, preferring isolation, and prone to schizophrenia and obsessional neurosis. Kretschmer[8] and his followers, in an interesting series of studies, have sought to correlate habitus with type of psychosis. Kretschmer with the usual classification into three body-types, called them asthenic, athletic and pyknic. With this he associated a classification of psychoses that originated with Kraepelin,[9] and was developed by Bleuler and Jung. In its developed form, the notion is as follows: the functional psychoses (those forms of insanity that are not due to any definite physical disease) can be classified into two main groups, the schizophrenias and the manic-depressive insanities. These contrast sharply with one another, and are opposite extremes of the normal variation of temperaments. Less extreme forms of these pathological types are called schizoid and cycloid; and normal persons tending towards one end or the other of the distribution are called schizophrenic and cyclotheme.

According to Kretschmer's theory, schizophrenics, and schizoids in general, tend to be thin (of asthenic habitus) and manic-depressives, and cycloids in general, tend to be fat (of pyknic habitus). If his general theory were correct, it should mean that schizophrenes and manic-depressives are obviously and strikingly different from one another in personality traits, being deviations from normality in opposite directions. This is difficult to square with the hesitation that psychiatrists often feel in deciding whether to assign a patient to the manic-depressive or the schizophrene group. If the personalities are so extremely different, how can the symptoms sometimes be so similar?

Eysenck in a carefully designed experiment, was unable to validate the antithesis between cycloids and schizoids. He applied several tests which, according to Kretschmer's theory, ought to place schizophrenics at one extreme of a distribution and manic-depressives at the other, with normals in the middle. The tests that he applied did not arrange his subjects in this way, but mostly in the order normal, schizophrenic, depressive. He concluded that his evidence did not confirm the relation of psychosis to personality type. In another research the same author found some confirmation of a relation between body-build and neurosis: thick-set patients more often suffered from conversion hysteria, while thin people more often developed anxiety and obsessional neurosis. The tendency, though real, was rather feeble, and of little help in diagnosis. Eysenck used only two body-types, instead of Kretschmer's three, being unable to find statistical evidence for a separate third group.

Sheldon's[10] elaborate studies of bodily habitus, based on

measurements taken from photographs, have resulted in a three-type classification that is not strikingly different from Kretschmer's. With these types Sheldon associates characteristic temperaments within the normal range. On the basis of his own ratings Sheldon finds that the endomorphs (thick-set people) show love of comfort and relaxation, are dependent on social approval, and show a general predominance of visceral processes; mesomorphs are assertive and energetic and show a general predominance of muscular processes (somatotonia); the ectomorphs (thin people) are restrained, withdrawn and inhibited, and show a general predominance of brain processes. His results are interesting, but have not greatly impressed outsiders because of the lack of external confirmation. Sheldon's rating study lacks almost all the external controls that experience has shown to be so necessary. The body-types seem to have a limited validity as tendencies which occur more often than not, but they are certainly not the clear-cut discontinuities of the typologist's pipe-dream.

Other attempts to find a few clear-cut patterns of human character have also been based on the psychoses, particularly the so-called 'functional' psychoses. Kretschmer's system is one of these. Jung's introvert-extravert typology is another. Jung began by describing schizophrenia as an extreme and pathological form of introversion. This is a description with which most observers would agree, if it is considered merely as a description of part of the symptoms, and is not offered as a causal explanation.

One of the most striking features of the group of mental disorders known as schizophrenia is this process of introversion—a withdrawal of interest from the outer world, the world of events and things and other people, and a focusing of interest on the inner world of fantasy, meditation and private meanings. When you talk to a schizophrenic patient, he does not seem to take you seriously; other people's affairs are not very real or important to him. Freud describes schizophrenia as a narcissistic psychosis, in which the patient's love is withdrawn from others and concentrated on himself; and this agrees well enough with Jung's description.

In attempting to elaborate his typology, however, Jung developed another type called the extravert, whose pathological extreme he identified with manic-depressive insanity. This was not such a happy invention. It is true that manic-depressives, when not afflicted by their disease, are often friendly and sociable people, who make adequate contacts with others in a way that the schizophrene may fail to do. But it is not plausible to regard manic-depressive insanity as an exaggeration of extraversion. No one would have thought of such a theory except in the interests of a balanced and schematic theory. Rather it is plain that most insane persons are in some degree introverted. In mania or depression, especially in the more acute forms, interest is largely withdrawn from the events of the outer world. You cannot get a manic-depressive to take very much interest in anything you say to him, because he is too much wrapped up in his own thoughts. The inhabitants of a mental hospital never combine against the warders because insane people are too individual, too much the occupants of private worlds to collaborate effectively.

As we saw when discussing Kretschmer's scheme, the notion that schizophrenia and manic-depressive insanity are opposite extremes of a personality variable broke down over the difficulty of distinguishing the supposed extremes from one another. No doubt a typical depressive is different from a typical schizophrene, but anyone who has spent some time wandering around a mental hospital and talking to the patients will realize that most of them are not typical of any of the patterns described in text-books of psychiatry. It is not that the text-book descriptions are incompetent, but rather that the variety of real experience cannot be compressed into a few schematic types. The notion of a symmetrical antithesis of schizophrenia and manic-depressive insanity which fascinated Jung, McDougall and Kretschmer, has served for many years to obscure and confuse the picture of psychosis.

Apart from the writers whose thought was dominated by the contrast of schizophrenic and cyclic psychoses, there have been attempts to build a classification of personality types on the study of psychoses. The idea behind this approach is that pathological forms exhibit the true nature of the normal by exaggerating it. There are many parallels in medical science for an approach to normal physiology through a study of disease. The method is as old as Hippocrates who, when describing a habitus apoplecticus and a habitus phthisicus, was classifying normal people in terms of diseases they had so far managed to avoid. In modern times an understanding of the functions of the endocrine glands began with clinical studies of the symptoms of defective or excessive functioning of a gland. And it might well be that normal varieties of personality might be classifiable in terms of their pathological excesses. Thus we find psychiatric classifications of normal personality, in which various forms of insanity are taken as the pure or exaggerated forms of normal patterns. A well-known scheme of this kind is that of Rosanoff.[11] He spoke of three principal psychotic temperaments—(i) those showing chaotic sexuality (often described as schizoid, introvert, autistic, shut-in personalities); (ii) those with cyclothymic temperaments (these include three of the traditional Hippocratean temperaments, sanguine, meloncholic and choleric, corresponding to Kraepelin's terms manic, depressive and irascible); and (iii) those with anti-social temperaments, the psychopaths and criminals. The Humm-Wadsworth[12] questionnaire, based to some extent on Rosanoff's theory of temperament, classified people into five main varieties:

(i) normal, showing rational balance and self-control;
(ii) schizoid, lacking contact with reality (these are divided into an autistic phase and a paranoid phase);
(iii) hysteroid, with excessive self-interest, and lack of consideration for others;

F

(iv) the cycloid, showing excessive fluctuation in feelings (divided into a manic phase and a depressed phase); and
(v) the epileptoid, showing excessive ambition.

This is perhaps as good a scheme as anyone could be expected to invent during a social evening of parlour games, but it is a flimsy affair, lacking nearly all the evidence that would be required to establish its validity. Even more precarious is the grandiose scheme of Szondi,[13] announced as a synthesis and completion of the systems of Jung and Freud. Jeans' dictum that God is a mathematician was evidently taken seriously in the construction of this system. The varieties of human nature develop neatly in rising powers of two. There are four basic drives or vectors, eight kinds of mental disorders, and sixteen forms of social expression, consisting of each drive first in a direct form, and then expressed through its opposite as a reaction-formation. Each one has its characteristic occupations, value systems, forms of criminality and method of suicide. All these things are supposed to be revealed by the Szondi Test, in which the subject is asked to express preferences for photographs of various criminals and psychotics.

Many typological concepts have been built around perceptual processes. The brothers Jaensch[14] studied unusual and vivid kinds of imagery in children, and tried to associate these with endocrine disturbances. Many others have tried to establish the typological significance of preferences for form or colour. This is an interesting problem, which has attracted investigators ever since Kulpe[15] first read a paper on the topic in 1904. The usual attempt has been to link introversion and schizophrenia with a preference for form, and extraversion and affective psychosis with a preference for colour. This is a topic that has the merit of being open to objective experiment; but results have not been very gratifying. Rorschach[16] varied the usual antithesis by contrasting preference for colour with preference for movement responses.

German philosophical writers have often been interested in

classifying systems of values. It ⱱ   ⌐   Ɑlosophy
that a profound realization of ⌐   ⱸ-systems
spread through European ⱡ   ⱷd thinkers away
from metaphysics towards pⱸ   ⱨy and sociology. The
writings of Dilthey led the way ⱨ developing the relation between character and values. Spranger[17] did something to
systematize this kind of thinking when he described six contrasted types of value-systems. His *Types of Men* is explicitly
an example of *Geisteswissenschaftliche* thinking. Although the
zoological analogy is indicated by the use of 'types', the discussion is purely in terms of moral and social values. There
is no attempt to find a bodily basis for types, or to found them
on psychiatry, or to claim that they are innate. These types,
although they bear the same name, are not really part of the
same conceptual scheme as the other typologies we have discussed, and we shall not pursue them further here.

It is not easy to evaluate German typological thinking, especially for one who is accustomed to operating with other
concepts. No one could deny qualities of learning and insight,
and rich human experience to writers like Jung, Kretschmer or
Szondi. Yet it may be concluded that there are few fields of
human endeavour in which so much effort has achieved so
little. A bewildering variety of theories, and almost no well-
established facts or agreed conclusions; large concepts, and
miserable little results that vanish in the sand. Looking over
all the enterprises that have fizzled out, one is forced to the
conclusion that there is something wrong with the method.
Perhaps the reason is that there are no human types in the sense
required by these investigators. Animal species show certain
discontinuities which make classification possible. And even
within one species discontinuities may be developed by deliberate selection, so that a greyhound and a bulldog are recognizably different. But no such 'natural' or 'artificial' classification is available for humans, at any rate so far as personality is
concerned. No success has been achieved in relating personality
to race. Changes in the social or geographical environment are

often so potent that racial characteristics, if they exist at all, are overlaid and confused beyond recognition. Nor has personality any single and unequivocal relation to the categories of insanity, to body form, or to modes of apperception. Clearcut discontinuous types marked out by their original nature do not exist for the great majority of men. Perhaps the error has laid in treating people too much as separate entities, describing man in isolation without including in the description his relation to the environment.

TABLE 3: SOME WELL-KNOWN TYPE THEORIES

Primary Variable	Names of Main Types	Secondary Associated Variables	Author
predominant body fluids	choleric, phlegmatic, sanguine, melancholic	temperamental traits	Hippocrates
form of insanity	schizophrene manic-depressive	*normal personality type* extravert introvert further subdivided into types employing predominantly sensation, feeling reason and intuition.	Jung
form of insanity	schizophrenia and manic-depressive insanity	*normal personality type.* Schizotheme and cyclotheme *body form:* asthenic athletic pyknic	Kretschmer
form of insanity	(i) Chaotic sexuality. (ii) Cyclothymia, including manic, depressive, irascible and emotionally unstable. (iii) anti-social temperament.	traits of normal personality	Rosanoff

Primary Variable	Names of Main Types	Secondary Associated Variables	Author
form of insanity	5 main types, 2 of them sub-divided: normal hysteroid cycloid (manic phase, depressed phase) schizoid (autistic phase, paranoid phase) epileptoid	vocational suitability	Humm and Wadsworth
form of insanity	eight pathological syndromes: homosexual sadist epileptic hysteric catatonic paranoid depressive manic	vocation; mode of suicide; social goals of normal personality	Szondi
perceptual processes	primary and secondary function	wide-shallow and narrow - deep types	Gross; later Heymans and Wiersma
perceptual processes	preferences for colour or movement	extratensive vs. intraversive	Rorschach
perceptual processes	preference for colour or form	extraversion and introversion	Kulpe, Scholl Kroh, etc.
perceptual processes: eidetic images	integrate (B-type) and disintegrate (T-type)	endocrine dysfunction: hyperthyroid and hypoparathyroid; capillary irregularities	E. R. and W. Jaensch
body form	endomorph mesomorph ectomorph	temperamental traits described as viscerotonia (sociable, easy going, fond of eating) somatotonia (energetic, ambitious) cerebrotonia (withdrawn)	W. H. Sheldon

Primary Variable	Names of Main Types	Secondary Associated Variables	Author
values	six attitudes: theoretic economic aesthetic social political religious	vocational choice	E. Spranger. Used by G. W. Allport and P. E. Vernon

Factors. Although the aim of factor analysis is often similar to that of typology, the method and preconceptions are so different that the final products have little in common. Typology works with a zoological analogy, the classification of animals into species. Factor analysis works with a geometrical analogy, the location of points in a hyperspace. The typologist relies mainly on inspiration, the factor analyst mainly on computation. Factor analysis is a technique that developed out of an attempt to interpret the inter-correlations of intelligence tests as the expression of certain factors of the mind.

While we can give a general description of the aims and results of factor analysis, we cannot, in a book of this kind, give an adequate account of the methods employed; and it does not seem fair to the general reader to assume that he already knows all about them. This part of the book will accordingly be rather sketchy. Spearman[18] claimed to have shown that human abilities were composed of one general factor, present to some extent in almost every ability, and a large number of special factors, so narrow in their range that two tests seldom included the same special factor. If Spearman was right, 'g' or general ability, was obviously the quality that mainly mattered in a person, so far as his vocational performance was concerned. Spearman's claim stimulated a lot of research, and new methods were soon developed. Before long it became plain that there is no unique way of analysing a matrix of correlations into its underlying factors. To give a unique solution, some further condition has to be applied, and there is no agreement about what this further condition is to be. It is not anything that can be tested by reference to observed fact, but is rather in the nature of a logical or aesthetic criterion. In the analysis of intelligence, Spearman preferred to maximize the first, or principal factor; Thurstone[19] preferred to extract the smallest possible number of factors, assuming that none covered the whole field. Spearman regarded the general factor of intelligence as the cornerstone of the whole factorial theory. Thurstone denied its existence. Thomson[20] regarded it as a statistical artefact. Burt[21] accepted its existence, along with the other group factors which Spearman denied. In the analysis of other personality variables there have been similar divergences. Eysenck, employing Burt's method of simple summation, finds a general factor of neuroticism, which Guilford,[22] employing Thurstone's centroid method, denies.

There are signs, however, that the acuter forms of controversy about the factors of the mind are dying down, and workers may before long come to an understanding. Burt considers that disagreement on two large questions (the metaphysical status of factors, and the reality of the general ability factor) has obscured the large measure of agreement reached on other questions. The controversy about the existence of the general ability factor is now generally recognized to be the result of differing techniques of analysis, and not so much a disagreement about matters of fact. Spearman's extreme form of the doctrine of 'g' is generally considered to be no longer tenable. Thurstone's outright denial of a general factor is also now seen to be an artefact of his technique. A majority of workers on both sides of the Atlantic seem prepared to accept Burt's cautious and eclectic four factor theory.

According to Burt's account, the abilities involved in a test can be analysed into four factors: (i) a general factor common to all abilities, which might be called 'general intelligence'; (ii) group factors shared with many other tests, but not present in all; (for instance, 'spatial ability' or 'verbal ability'); (iii) special abilities, peculiar to one test, or a very small range of tests; and (iv) residual factors including various influences, such as day-to-day variations in performance, errors of measurement, etc. These four factors correspond to the Aristotelian description of genus, species, proprium and accidens.

It would be very gratifying if general agreement were found to exist on this formulation of the problem. But there is no reason to suppose that such agreement would extend to the assigning of definite weights to these four factors in any particular case. The fact is that mathematical considerations will not in themselves suffice to establish a unique solution to a factorial problem; they have to be supplemented by additional postulates to produce a unique solution and there is no clear guidance to the 'one best way' of selecting these postulates.

Doubts and disagreements that have arisen in the study of intelligence have extended to other qualities of personality. During the 'thirties in America when factor analysis was a charming new device new factors were two a penny on every bramble. This honeymoon phase came to an end in 1940 with Wolfle's[23] conservative review of methods and results.

It is now recognized that a hastily compiled questionnaire administered as a group test to a freshmen class, and pushed into the factorial sausage machine, is not likely to yield solid information about the ultimate variables of human nature. There is a tendency now to attach less weight to subjective evaluations like self-rating scales, and to rely more on objective measurements of specific response. It is also accepted that if the existence of a factor is to be securely established, it must be part of a systematic theory of personality. All the factors to be used must be established on the same population, and their relations to one another must be clearly shown. This means that a large number of tests and measurements must be obtained from a single group.

On the question of the metaphysical status of factors prevailing opinion is often positivist. There is a tendency among many workers to make rather modest claims about the objective existence of factors, to consider them, not as ultimate constituents of human nature, but as classifications that are convenient for some limited and temporary purpose. Vernon and Rodger use factor analysis as a guide to the choice of tests in an occupational selection programme. There can be no doubt about the validity and usefulness of factor analysis when used in this restricted way. But the more ambitious project remains. Investigators will not be content to go on indefinitely extracting factors, unless they can believe in the reality of the entities they discover.

Both the Illinois and the Maudsley schools (and these are to-day probably the two largest and most influential groups of factor analysts in the field of personality) are looking for real entities, which can be accepted as causally significant components of personality. Cattell feels strongly that the present confusion of psychological theory, the impression of a multitude of voices speaking discordantly across one another, is due to the lack of a system of basic variables. Almost anything can be measured, but it is important to know whether what we are measuring is a real and significant element of personality, or some trivial and transient by-product of testing procedure. Cattell looks to factor analysis to answer this question. Eysenck sometimes uses the common Continental analogy with classificatory biology, and speaks of his work as taxonomy; at other times he describes his work by the geometrical analogy common in Britain, and entitles his book *Dimensions of Personality*. The geometrical analogy is, indeed, fundamental to the factorial method, and many of those who use it do not seem to have given enough thought to its validity. To think of our classificatory concepts as dimensions rather than as types means abandoning the search for gross discontinuities, and accepting continuous variation between extremes. Undoubtedly this is in better accord with the facts.

But another assumption is covertly introduced, whose validity is more questionable. This is the assumption that everybody has a definable position on each dimension; i.e. that with respect to the basic variables, people differ from one another only in a quantitative way; the same variables are applicable to all. Our testing procedures are certainly likely to give the impression that this is so. If we construct a test to measure introversion-extraversion, then everybody who is tested will obtain some score, and so appear to have a definite amount of introversion. It might happen, however, that people varied, not merely in the quantity of a trait, but in the organization of their traits. Two aspects of introversion that are closely associated in some people, might be quite separate in other people. In a factorial analysis, such a result might be blurred, and treated as an inaccuracy that is inevitable in large-scale investigations, when it was in reality the image of a true and important fact. Investigators do not ask, are there any dimensions?; but rather, what dimensions are there? The methods of analysis that they have adopted commit them to the assumption that if one kind of dimension is wrongly conceived, then another must be right. The notion that there might be no dimension of this kind is rejected as an anarchist menace, and the possibility is not seriously considered. If no dimensions of personality, no fundamental variables can be established, then a science of personality is held to be impossible. A dimensional system is held to be the only alternative to chaos, to a behaviourist limbo of unlimited specificity. Either there are general traits, of which everyone possesses an ascertainable amount, in which case the scientific study of personality is possible; or there are no general traits whose provenance is the same for everybody, in which case behaviour is unorganized and specific, and personality is not amenable to scientific study.

There is, however, a third possibility. It may be that people have rather general and well-organized traits, but that these are not arranged on any single or universal principle. They develop not according to fixed rules, but in ways that are determined by events of the life-history. The organization of a person's traits would then depend on the meaning of his experience for him, that is, on the symbolic systems that he has developed. Such a method of describing personalities is possible, but it would not result in a system of traits, and we should not be able to develop a vocabulary for describing a person in isolation from his environment. The description of a personality would rather be a description of various relations (developing over a large part of the life-span) between a person and the environment in which he lives. The discussion of such methods belongs, however, to later chapters of this book.

REFERENCES

1. JUNG, C. G.   *Psychological Types.*   New York, Harcourt, Brace, 1923.

2 and 8. KRETSCHMER   *Physique and Character.*   New York, Harcourt, Brace, 1931.

3 and 14. JAENSCH, E. RIETAL   *Studien zur Psychologie.*   Leipzig, Barth, 1930.

4. SPRANGER, E.   *Menschlicher Typen. Types of Men.*   Halle, Max Niemeyer. 1928.

5. STAGNER, R.   *The Psychology of Personality.*   New York, McGraw-Hill, 1937.

6 and 21. BURT, C.   *Validating Tests for Personnel Selection. The Assessment of Personality.*   Brit. J. Psychol. 1943, 34, 1–19. Brit. J. Educ. Psychol. XV, 1945, 107–121.

7. EYSENCK, H. J.   *Dimensions of Personality.*   London, Kegan Paul, 1947.

9. KRAEPELIN,   *Text-book of Psychiatry.*   Leipzig, Barth, 1915.

10. SHELDON, W. H. ET AL.   *The Varieties of Human Physique: An Introduction to Constitutional Psychology.*   New York, Harper Bros. 1940.

11. ROSANOFF, A. J.   *Manual of Psychiatry.*   New York, Wiles, 1948.

12. HUMM, D. G. AND WADSWORTH, G. W.   *The Humm-Wadsworth Temperament Scale.*   J. Person, 12, 314–323, 1934.

13. SZONDI, F. L.   *Experimentelle Triebdiagnostik.*   Bern, Hans Huber, 1947.

15. KULPE, O.   *Versuche uber Abstraktion.*   Leipzig, Ber uber d. I Kungr. f. exp. Psychol., 1904.

16. RORSCHACH, H.   *Psychodiagnostiks.*   Bern, Huber, 1942 (original German edition, 1921).

17. SPRANGER, E.   *Types of Men.*   Halle, Max Niemeyer, 1928.

18. SPEARMAN, C.   *The Abilities of Men, Their Nature and Measurement.*   London, Macmillan,

19. THURSTONE, L. L.   *The Vectors of Mind.*   Chicago, Univ. of Chicago Press.   Revised Edition, 1944.

20. THOMSON, G. H.   *The Factorial Analysis of Human Ability.*   Univ. of London Press, 1939.

22. GUILFORD, J. P.   *Personality Factors S E & M—*   J. Psychol. 1936, 2. 109–27.
Personality Factors D R T & A.   J. Abn. Soc. Psychol., 1939, 134, 21–6.
Personality Factors N and G D.   J. Abn. Soc. Psychol., 1939, 134, 239–48.

23. WOLFLE, D.   *Factor Analysis to 1940.*   Psychometric Monographs No. 3, 1940. Univ. Chicago Press.

CHAPTER V

FORCES OF THE ENVIRONMENT

IN the last chapter we considered attempts to describe personality as a rigid, invariant structure, in large measure independent of the environment. This chapter concerns the antithesis—the description of personality as having no independent existence, but as providing a mirror of the environment. There are several variants of such a theory in the market. The Behaviourist version, popular just after the First World War, was a revised form of French eighteenth-century materialism. La Mettrie thought that man was really just a machine, and Condillac thought that he was really just a statue. The theory in either case was that nothing happened in a man until he was stimulated from the outside. A person has nothing of his own, but merely reproduces what is imposed on him from without. In the same way Pavlov's dogs were required to stand still in the harness until someone prodded them with something (tuning fork or revolving object), upon which signal they were expected to dribble. Since the development of modern positivist logic we have learned to look upon theories of this kind, not as statements of fact (true or false) but as expressions of a wish. The immediate motive of such a theory is usually anti-clericalism. There is no mystery, there is no God; I peeped, but there was nothing behind the curtain, it was all empty; don't let them frighten me again. Materialist psychology never became more than a programme. 'In principle, everything can be explained along these lines'; but in practice the detail was so complicated that nothing was explained at all. Behaviourists, not being seriously interested in problems of personality, were for the most part content to leave them like that.

Another attempt to dissolve away the personality was made by the apostles of pure sociology. Pure sociology is an attempt to derive some of the characteristics of human beings from their membership of groups, without the intervention of psychology. According to such theories, a man's actions are not the expression of his motives, but rather of the social situation in which he is placed. Karl Marx's theories are an example of such sociological thinking. Marx did not pay much attention to the analysis of an individual man's motives, being apparently satisfied with some general statement, such as that men always seek pleasure, or self-interest. He was rather interested in the way motives and thinking were determined from the outside. The chain of causes is taken to begin with techniques of production. The change from a feudal to a capitalist society was supposed to be due to the introduction of power-driven machinery. Changes in economic organization in turn produced shifts in the distribution of political power. Capitalists gradually replaced landlords as the dominant force in society; political initiative and leadership came mostly from capitalists. According to Marx, the further development of society could be inferred from the impersonal working of economic laws, without individual motivation. These economic laws were the law of increasing returns (that the larger business, with more division of labour, has an advantage over the smaller business) and the law of diminishing returns (that a crowded population of farm labourers is bound to be and remain poor, producing more mouths than it can feed).

Marx took these laws over from Ricardo and Malthus, and used them to prove what he expected. The poor, he deduced, would be more numerous than ever, but remain as poor as before, only just alive; the rich would become fewer and richer, as the smaller capitalists were swallowed up by the larger capitalists; the unbalance of productive power and consumer's power results in ever more convulsive crises of boom and slump, until eventually the whole show cracks. Marx did not go into any detail about what would happen after that. His imagination rested joyously on the time when capitalist throats were being cut, and he did not care to explore further. Prosaic details about the administration of the new state were disparaged as Utopian socialism.

If techniques of production are the first layer, and the political structure is the second, moral and religious ideas are the superstructure which exists as effect but not as cause. Most of the motives that seem, in a psychological view, to be the real causes of actions, are in reality unimportant. Since motives are fairly constant and universal in their action they can (according to Marx) be neglected, and attention concentrated on the variation produced by class structure. The class system will cause those who by their original nature are similar, to be mortally opposed in interest and purpose.

The psychologist whose system of causes is expressed in terms of motivated acts considers such a sociological theory to be obscure and paradoxical. If individual acts are purposeful, how can their aggregate acquire an entirely different meaning? How can a group show characteristics that are not derived from those of the individual members? How can there be a sociology that cuts itself loose from psychology? The fact that Marx's predictions were mostly incorrect need not invalidate the general notion. A group may have many properties that are not present in its members. There is nothing mysterious about this. Bertrand Russell long ago called attention to the syllogism: Men are numerous, and Socrates is a man, therefore Socrates is numerous. The fallacy in this is an example of what happens when the properties of groups are supposed to be identical with the properties of individuals. However queer it may seem to a psychologist, there is nothing intrinsically impossible in building up an elaborate structural account of society on the basis of a few simple assumptions about human nature. The economic man of the classical economists was such a model, whose conduct was treated in an abstract and generalized way for the purpose of elaborating structural relations. It is impressive how much of the social process can be expressed in these terms.

The description of society in terms of its structure need not take the form of an analysis into classes of the kind that we are familiar with in Western Europe. In uncivilized societies the social structure may be mainly expressed in a kinship system, as has been done by Radcliffe-Brown[1] and other British anthropologists. Alliances and conflicts may be the result, not so much of human nature, as of structural arrangements. One system of inheriting property may produce sibling rivalry; another system may produce alliances of children against the father. Other forms of social structure that turn up in every society are sex and age classifications. Structural rules within one society form a rather definite set of expectations about what people will do. When we pass from one society to another they vary in wild and unpredictable ways. Rules determining what is proper for men and for women often have only the vaguest relation to their physiological characteristics, and cannot be deduced from a psychology that is grounded in bodily process.

A sociology that confines itself to the study of social structure has some advantages in comparison with the sprawling promiscuity of the subject in its present condition. It no longer attempts to answer every conceivable question that might be asked about society, but confines itself to certain narrow and definite ones. In this way it hopes to attain the formulation of verifiable theories. This is a laudable aim. But it is doubtful whether social structure forms an intelligible field of study. Every science prompts questions that lead outside itself, into other people's departments. Structural sociologists have preserved the integrity of their subject by a rigid refusal to look over the fence, a determination to keep themselves unspotted from the world. It must be remembered that in Marx's time (or even Durkheim's) psychology had not been seriously or successfully applied to the study of motives. An orderly theory of motives was not altogether easy to formulate, and there were unresolved disputes between hedonist, rationalist and intuitionist theories. But all were agreed that they had covered the range of human motives, and that there would be no surprises to come. There was nothing much more to be done except to get them neatly written out. Characterology was mainly the tabulation of platitudes.

It was thus plausible to treat human nature as a constant factor whose influence could be neglected, and to throw the whole emphasis on the external situation. To-day this is not so plausible. Freud's work revealed unsuspected complexities about human nature, convincing people that there was still something to be found out. It also revealed explanatory principles of unexpected power, applicable to a great range of circumstances. To propose a sociology that would ignore individual motivation is not so plausible as it was 100, or 50 years ago.

There have been other attempts (more acceptable to psychologists) at adjusting the theory of motives and the theory of social structure to one another. Instead of denying individual causation, some have tried to reconcile the psychological and the social approaches by postulating some form of pre-established harmony between the life of an individual and that of his society. This idea was elaborately developed by Plato in the *Republic*. He described the structure of the individual soul by analogy with the structure of the State. The chief motives of the individual (lust, ambition and reason) corresponded to the main classes of society (the populace, the army, and the administrative class). In a well-organized soul reason would rule, just like the philosopher-kings in a well-organized society. In a disorganized soul reason is the slave of the passions like a State ruled by a tyrant. The attempt to find some link between sociology and psychology led to the revival of such theories.

During the nineteen-twenties the problem was constantly posed by advanced people in Europe and America, how can we reconcile the doctrines of Marx with the doctrines of Freud? At that time, it seemed obvious that two writers as 'progressive' as these must really be saying the same thing. The task of reconciliation was by no means simple. They seemed to have nothing in common except their contempt for

G

bourgeois institutions, and in Freud much of this contempt evaporated with advancing age. The attempt to build a theory that would utilize both was made by psycho-analysts of the Left. Horney and Fromm discarded much of Freud's instinctualism, and substituted theories of social causation. Horney traced the roots of the neurotic personality of our time to three conflicts attributable to the 'contradictions of capitalism'. The first conflict was that of co-operation and competition. People are urged simultaneously in opposite directions, towards success and towards love and sacrifice. If both goals are taken seriously, there is confusion and conflict. The second conflict is between the stimulation of desire and its frustration in practical experience.

Horney's[2] descriptions were aimed primarily at American society of the 'twenties and 'thirties, though they would apply in some degree to any part of the Western world, having been the common property of everyone who shared the influence of the French Revolution. The young were taught to expect and demand success, to work for it and claim it as a right, to base their self-respect on it. But since it was essentially comparative, it could be the lot of only a few, and the majority were bound to be disappointed. Gorer[3] and Mead[4] have stressed the conditional love given to the all-American child, the love that is the reward of success, and a stimulus to boasting. The promise that the career is open to talents, that the deserving young man can always find a way from log cabin to White House, may serve only to emphasize the bitterness of relative failure.

Lionel Trilling, in masochistic contempt, speaks of 'the well-loved child of the middle-classes, brought up on promises'. During the Great Depression of the 'thirties, when Horney's work was written, the failure of the American Dream seemed only too evident. And indeed there were many people who had permanently seen through the philosophy of progress, and were not prepared to be re-illusioned by the next boom. The American Dream might recover from the Age of Coolidge, but hardly with the old confident anticipation.

The third of Horney's contradictions is between the promise of freedom and its real frustrations. The American and French Revolutions had promised men Liberty; but true freedom is not easy of attainment, and does not always follow directly upon the proclaiming of a constitution. Marxists stressed the fact that much democratic freedom was merely formal—a freedom that could not be utilized in practice. Fromm[5] stressed the complementary paradox—that freedoms which men theoretically desire may in reality be expressed mainly as sources of anxiety. The modern man living in a democratic society is free to choose a wife, a religion and a career. The price of this freedom is isolation, the terror of being left alone in the world to sink or swim by his own exertions. Fromm pictured the German acceptance of Nazism as a defence against the anxiety of competitive isolation. Rather than be left alone and free, Germans preferred submission to the authoritarian father. In the same way an earlier generation had relieved the anxiety of business competition by a Lutheran consciousness of sin. The lower middle classes of the early sixteenth-century Germany, left isolated by the breakdown of the Guild system, and made helpless by the rise of competitive capitalism, turned to the doctrines of Luther, in which they were promised the hope of grace in return for a grovelling conviction of sin and worthlessness. Fromm underlined the anxieties of capitalist society by contrast with an idealized picture of medieval man, secure within his primary bonds, safe in the protection of manor, church and guild, and happy without the freedom he had never known. Horney pointed to the correspondence between microcosm and macrocosm. The same contradictory goals that are present on a large scale in society can be seen as conflicts within the individual. The neurotic person of our time is constantly (and unsuccessfully) striving to reconcile tendencies towards aggression and towards yielding; excessive demands on others, and fears of never getting anything; fantasies of boundless power, and feelings of utter helplessness. Thus the Platonic parallel of individual and society is worked out.

Horney and Fromm have sought to build a social psychology by neglecting the Freudian theory of instincts, and utilizing the theory of character defences. In doing so they have laid little stress on the stages of psycho-sexual development, or the theory of fixation, and have concentrated on the social situation of the adult. Other attempts to apply psycho-analysis have made use of the theory of instincts. In the first applications it was supposed that social processes could be considered as direct expressions of instinct. Thus the accumulation of capital was explained as a hoarding process due to the intensification of anal eroticism; war was taken to be the operation of the death instinct; and incest taboos were due to the unfolding of an inherited Oedipus complex. These crude applications of instinct theory to sociology had the effect of delaying the recognition of its value.

Malinowski, though on the whole unsympathetic to psycho-analysis, was the first to make effective use of analytic ideas in the description of an uncivilized society; and with Ruth Benedict's[6] *Patterns of Culture* the project of relating culture to personality was properly launched. A large body of literature (mainly American) has grown up around the subject. Most of these studies take the Freudian scheme of psycho-sexual development as their starting point. But they emphasize variations from one culture to another, instead of uniformities; and they relate fixation, not to mysterious inner properties of the libido, but to current practices of child rearing. If the analysts are right in saying that the pattern of adult personality is laid down in early childhood, this must hold, not merely between one child and another, but also between one society and another. In any one society there is a fairly uniform pattern of child rearing. Custom controls how a child is fed and held and kept clean, what demands are made on it, what prohibitions are enforced. A uniform pattern of child rearing throughout the society is likely to result in certain common traits in the adults of that society. These common traits are spoken of as the basic personality type, which is more or less the same as what used to be called national character.

Many correspondences have been described between methods of child rearing and basic personality type. In most of these accounts, the children come out with the same characters as the parents, so that a stable cycle has been set up. Among the Arapesh, as described by Mead,[7] children are long and affectionately nourished, they are not severely disciplined, and no high standards of efficiency are demanded. They grow up into gentle inefficient people, generous, co-operative and un-aggressive. The stability of personality pattern from one generation to the next is not due simply to imitation; the specific determining factors are the techniques of child rearing, which lay out the character patterns of the next generation. It is through these practices that the human animal is translated into a member of society.

The method of describing and accounting for basic personality in terms of childhood experience was first applied to uncivilized peoples, and the successes recorded there encouraged their extension to civilized societies. Mead and Gorer wrote on features of personality in the United States, Gorer[8] and Benedict[9] on the Japanese, and there have been other sketches of national personalities. The method of dealing with civilized people is not radically different from those used on Pacific Islands, except that more use is made of popular beliefs about history. The teaching of history in schools is an important element (both cause and effect) in the pattern of basic personality. Beliefs about Drake and Nelson must have played a vital part in determining British reactions to military defeat in 1940; and Gorer has similarly shown the meaning of the revolution in American popular belief. George III is the primal father of the American myth, the father whose death unites the band of brothers in an indissoluble union. The rejection of the European father, and the deliberate adoption of a new fatherland, has been repeated by each generation of immigrants, and once more by their children, who sneer at father's foreign accent and incompetent efforts to conform. With the rejection of paternal authority the way is open to the matriarchy. Studies of uncivilized societies draw less on history, partly because the facts are not easily available, and partly because popular conceptions of the national past are vaguer and less insistent than they usually are in a civilized society.

The cultural determination of personality is a theory that seems to apply rather well to simple and rather homogeneous societies living under stable conditions. From what we read, it sounds quite possible to describe a basic personality type for the Zuni or the Alorese. In an elaborately stratified society, and particularly in one where there is some degree of social mobility, this cultural determination cannot be so complete. If the possibility is open that a man may become a miner or a literary critic or an engineer, then action is not entirely a matter of external determination. Personality becomes an effect as well as a cause.

The 'culture and personality' field of study is at present in a stage of rich, amorphous growth. Ideas are crowding in thick and fast, and some of the new material makes exciting reading. What the subject needs at the moment is clearly some kind of discipline. Standards of evidence are low, and there is at present little notion of how to improve them. The whole field is infected with vagueness in two respects: there is no clear-cut notion of what constitutes personality, or of what features of culture are relevant to the study. 'Neo-Freudian' formulations of the culture and personality problem began by applying the Freudian theory of psycho-sexual development. They examined the trauma of birth, the first feeding experiences, weaning, cleanliness, attitudes to childish sexuality; opportunities to witness intercourse; castration threats and the relative power and importance of father and mother in the child's life. The outcome of these crucial experiences should give one a pre-formed pattern of adult personality. However, it would have been unrealistic for anthropologists to confine their observations to circumstances usually discussed in psycho-analytic works. Many other things forced themselves on his attention, including qualities that are not directly part of the social environment, though they have social consequences —for instance, the incidence of infectious diseases and the regularity of the food supply.

Kardiner[10] drew up a list of what he calls 'Key Integrational Systems'—aspects of culture and social structure that are important determinants of personality. The list extends to a page and a half, and includes such items as the position of women, the projective systems, arts, crafts and techniques, and many others that would appear more properly as effects than as causes of the personality pattern. In his anxiety to leave nothing out, he has robbed the hypothesis of all its original specificity. It has become inflated into a harmless truism—that many different circumstances influence personality.

Anthropologists have drawn on remoter and less obvious characteristics to supplement their original hypothesis. Gorer, finding a great variety of child-rearing methods being practised in the United States, finds a common element in the doctrinaire, theoretical approach of the American mother to her child. Benedict, finding little congruence between the experience of the small child and the character of the adult Japanese, postulates a kind of double nature—the chrysanthemum and the sword—in which opposites are allowed to exist side by side. By this time the doctrine has become so flexible that it will prove almost anything.

These writers have made brilliant use of the possibilities, but most of the points they are making are not really, under present conditions, open to scientific proof. They are skilful observations, similar to the best made by Lecky, Matthew Arnold or Tocqueville in an earlier generation, and collected in the same sort of way. There is no particular reason why we should think of them as Science (or that they would be better for being so) except that to-day it is commonly supposed that scientific knowledge is the only good kind of knowledge. To call a man unscientific is an insult, as in another age one might say of a Puritan that he was not in a state of grace. If we take a narrower view of science, and regard it as the application of certain verification procedures, then there may be good knowledge that has not been treated scientifically. This is the way that we should prefer to regard the matter; we should not expect all valuable knowledge to be scientific; but it is not essential to come to a decision on this usage. Gorer and Mead have marred their reputations still more by writing excellent and vivid English, and being read by a wide public. Had their books been written in the usual jargon, academic reputations would have been safer.

Murray[11] and Kluckhohn have attempted to bring some order into the 'culture and personality' field by their theory of the four determinants. These are constitutional determinants, group-membersip determinants, role determinants and situational determinants. Constitutional factors are not very satisfactorily described by their name. They refer not only to inborn or hereditary qualities, but to bodily processes operating at any stage. Endocrine processes, variations of blood pressure or blood chemistry, infective conditions and diet—all these would be considered under the heading of constitutional determinants. Group membership determinants are influences that come from the individual's membership of the group—influences that are common to the group as a whole. These would include extra-cultural influences such as the population density, and also cultural influences such as beliefs and practices common to the whole society—their food preferences, what time they go to bed, and so on. Role determinants are influences that reach a person because of his particular role in society, and thus do not reach all members in the same way. Role determinants are what we considered earlier under the rubric of social structure (though of course a really dyed-in-the-wool structuralist would not be prepared to admit that people have personalities at all). There are many influences that differentiate men and women, others that establish expectations for people at various ages. Similarly there are kinship expectations; ways in which an elder brother, aunt or grandmother is expected to behave. In addition, there are expectations based on occupation, and class and race membership. These approximate to what Linton[12] calls the 'Status Personality'. The fourth group are the situational determinants of personality—those which arise from the particular life-experiences of the individual's history, and which we need not expect to find repeated in other lives. These are the kind of material that a psycho-analyst studies.

Do these four determinants cover the whole field, or is there room for anything else? Murray and Kluckhohn take note of the possibility that habitat and scenery might play a part. Wordsworth certainly thought it important, and it may really be so, even though we cannot isolate the effect at the moment. There may be other influences too. Certainly we cannot close the book.

These influences cannot be neatly separated. An article of diet may have its primary effect as a constitutional determinant, but may also play its part as material for barter or bride-price, or as a delicacy reserved for one privileged group. The determinants are not four kinds of things, but four ways of looking at the environmental process.

The environment does not reach the individual as a mass of raw facts, but set in a framework of social meanings. Psychologists have always known this, but they have tended to assume, ever since Locke, that the associations with any one stimulus are so numerous and varied that nothing much could be done about describing them. Some recent work in social psychology, however, suggests that the process may be more orderly than was supposed. While there are some associations that are highly individual, most are fitted into rather stable reference frames. Some of these, such as those studied by Adelbert Ames, Jnr,[13] are not social, but are concerned with spatial orientation. Ames showed that when a framework was viewed at an unusual angle, impressive illusions of size or direction occurred. He used, for instance, a house built at $45° + 135°$ instead of the usual $90° + 90°$. Others have mainly social references, such as those studied by Sherif and Cantril.[14]

Sherif used for one series of experiments the autokinetic effect—i.e. the apparent movement of a spot of light in a dark room. He asked subjects to estimate the distance of this apparent movement. Since the room was completely dark, there was no background, and the answer could really be anything whatever. Judgments were first given individually, and afterwards compared. Sherif showed how widely diverging estimates soon converged on to an accepted Group norm. By virtue of their common situation the students soon formed a group, and the opinions of the others became a frame of reference for each. Although their judgments diverged widely at the beginning, they soon became closely similar to one another, all being controlled by group opinion. Some of these studies have a recognizable kinship with studies of social structure, and suggest ways in which the social psychologist may be able to link hands with the anthropological field worker. The time seems ripe for a major synthesis. These various disciplines should converge upon the individual in the social framework, and give us an effective system of concepts for placing him. But, however well developed these sociological descriptions may be, there will remain other tasks that are specifically those of the psychologist: physiological psychology, for the description of constitutional determinants; and biographical studies for the study of situational determinants.

REFERENCES

1. RADCLIFFE-BROWN, A. R. — *On Social Structure.* — Journal of the Royal Anthropological Institute, 70, 1940.

2. HORNEY, K. — *The Neurotic Personality of Our Time.* — London, Kegan Paul, 1936.
   New Ways in Psychoanalysis. — London, Kegan Paul, 1940.

3. GORER, G. — *The American People.* — New York, Norton, 1948.

4. MEAD, M. — *The American Character.* — Harmondsworth, Penguin Books, 1944.

5. FROMM, E. — *The Fear of Freedom.* — London, Routledge, 1949.

6.	BENEDICT, R.	*Patterns of Culture.*	Boston, Houghton Mifflin, 1934.
7.	MEAD, M.	*Sex and Temperament in Three Primitive Societies.*	New York, Morrow, 1935.
8.	GORER, G.	*Japanese Character Structure.*	Inst., for Int. Studies, 1939.
9.	BENEDICT, R.	*The Chrysanthemum and the Sword.*	Boston, Houghton Mifflin, 1946.
10.	KARDINER, A.	*The Psychological Frontiers of Society.*	New York, Columbia Univ. Press, 1945.
11.	MURRAY, H. A. AND KLUCKHOHN, C.	*Personality in Nature, Society and Culture.*	London, Cape, 1949.
12.	LINTON, R.	*Cultural Background of Personality.*	London, Kegan Paul, 1945.
13.	AMES, ADELBERT, JNR.,	*Binocular Vision as affected by relations between Uniocular Stimulus-Patterns in Commonplace Environments.*	Am. J. Psychol. LIX, pp. 333–37.
14.	SHERIF, M.	*An Outline of Social Psychology.*	New York, Harper, 1948.

CHAPTER VI

THEORIES OF BASIC MOTIVES

ONE of our main ways of understanding the meaning of an act is finding its motive. The motive of an act may be described from either end—in terms of the drive which initiates action, or in terms of the goal or end-result towards which it is directed. We might think in terms of the low level of blood-sugar, acting as a hunger drive, or in terms of the terminal activity, which is eating. Both kinds of interpretation can lead to an analysis of a great variety of behaviour into a limited number of basic motives. Many attempts have been made to find a principle for classifying all human motives under a few general headings.

In the seventeenth century moral philosophers like Hobbes and Spinoza gave general descriptions of the Passions and their origins. Seventeenth-century accounts of the passions cannot, however, be readily equated with modern lists of basic motives. They often contain emotions like joy, grief or hope, mixed with motives like curiosity or pride. It is only when we come to the work of Thomas Reid (Table IV, 1)[1] near the end of the eighteenth century that we find a treatment of motivation similar to that used by modern authors. Reid's term 'active power' corresponds closely to McDougall's (Table IV, 3) 'instinct' or Murray's 'need' (Table IV, 7). Towards the end of the eighteenth century in a systematic discussion of the active powers of man, Reid comments on the variety of theories in vogue. 'Some admit no principle but self-love; others resolve all into love of the pleasures of sense, variously modified by the association of ideas; others admit disinterested benevolence along with self-love; others reduce all to reason and passion; others to passion alone; nor is there less variety about the number and distribution of the passions.' The variety has certainly not diminished since 1788, nor have the descriptions and classifications employed changed in any radical way.

It is hard to find a compelling reason for thinking that one list is better than another. Yet the importance of the psychologist's goal is obviously great. If the enormous variety of human acts could be reduced to a few universal motives, the way would be open to a scientific description of behaviour. The parallel with chemistry has often been in people's minds. Chemistry made great advances when certain definite elements were identified; and the enormously various lot of substances found all about us was eventually reduced to a relatively small list of elements. If we could do the same with human motives, great advances could be made in psychology. The attempt to build a system of human motives has been similar to the search for basic traits, and has attracted people for the same reasons.

But it must be emphasized once more that the meaning of the procedures is quite different. A trait is a quality of a whole person, and one expects it to be reasonably durable as a description of him. A motive is a term used for describing a particular action. If a motive constantly recurred in one person, it would become more or less the same as a trait. But ordinarily we should find motives appearing in relation to a particular kind of stimulus situation. In a description of a personality, a basic motive would not appear in isolation as a trait, but rather as a thema, in relation to some kind of stimulus or *press* (in Murray's terminology). The environment as it appears in a psychological description occurs not as a physical or chemical agent impinging on the body or sense organs, but in terms of its meaning for the person—an injury, a gift, a threat, a promise.

The same stimulus may have many different meanings, and many different stimuli may have the same meaning. It is the meanings that are important, and not the stimulus in its own nature as a physical or chemical process. However, it might be possible to group human motives under a small number of heads, and if this could be done it would undoubtedly make behaviour much more coherent than it is now. A doctrine of basic motives would not necessarily imply an emphasis on heredity or innate traits or biological determinism. It is compatible with a good deal of environmental flexibility, because it imposes a limitation only on the kind of motives that will appear. The kind of situation that will evoke the motive may have some original definition in terms of its physical properties, but this will early become overlaid by the meaning of the situation for the person. This was clearly understood by McDougall when he formulated his doctrine of instincts, for he recognized that in human behaviour instincts appeared not in a pure form, but in the form of sentiments, tied to some object in the environment. We find, not anger in general, but hate towards a particular person.

Various eighteenth-century writers had realized that the concept of instinct might provide a clue to the original nature of man. James and Reid developed the idea, stressing parallels between human and animal instinct. But for Reid *instinct* was only one of several principles of action. It was a 'mechanical principle', contrasted with the 'animal principles' (comprising appetites and desires) and the 'rational principles'.

'By instinct,' says Reid, 'I mean a natural blind impulse to certain actions, without having any end in view, without deliberation, and very often without any conception of what we do.'

In James's[2] *Principles of Psychology* a century later, instincts appear in much the same way, as one of several principles of action, and applying only to some segments of behaviour. But in McDougall's[3] *Introduction to Social Psychology* the concept of instinct was used in a more ambitious way, as the source of all motivation. McDougall's book was the source of a great deal of British and American discussion of motivation. His theory was an attempt to establish psychology on evolutionary principles. He set out to establish a definite and complete list of basic motives identified by objective criteria. The criteria set up by McDougall were principally four: (i) Instinctive behaviour must appear without learning. (ii) It must be universal, or nearly so, in a species. (iii) Parallels should be discoverable in other species. (iv) Each instinct is served by characteristic structures, adapted to the functions that it serves.

By the use of these criteria he set up a list of thirteen major human instincts, which accounted for most of human behaviour. Each instinct had four aspects—(a) perceptual aspect, readiness to notice certain stimuli (b) a conative aspect, characteristic response patterns (c) an emotion belonging to the arousal of the instinct, as anger belongs to combat, and (d) an impulse to action, a goal or desire typical of the instinct. Out of deference to the Aristotelian trilogy of thinking, feeling and doing, impulse and emotion were sometimes grouped together, though they are better kept separate. As McDougall's doctrine developed through criticism and controversy, it was the impulse to action, the doctrine of basic motives, that he regarded as the most important part of the instinct theory. In the last revision of his theory[4] he dropped the term *instinct* so far as humans were concerned, and introduced the term *propensity* to stress the fact that his doctrine of instincts was mainly a doctrine of basic motives.

McDougall's theory, like most other psychological theories, was an armchair system. The theory as a whole was not directly available to investigation. The controversies about it did, however, stimulate real discoveries in some directions— chiefly Gesell's cinematic studies of motor development in young children, and detailed physiological analyses of certain animal drives, such as feeding, sex, migration and hibernation. Investigations were less successful in demarcating the various social drives. McDougall recognized seven social instincts— mating, parental and gregarious instincts, appeal, combat, self-assertion and submission; in some discussions he hesitatingly admitted an eighth—primitive passive sympathy. Of these, only mating, parental and combat could be related to characteristic anatomical structures; and although some innate basis for all of these was certainly recognizable, it became hopelessly confused and overlaid quite early in the course of development.

It is often quite unrealistic to try to allocate segments of behaviour to one of these propensities rather than another. Some psychologists thought they could get along with a shorter list of basic social motives, and the criteria of identification were so vague that nobody could be sure who was right. Some proposed additional basic motives; for instance, W. I. Thomas's desire for response, and for new experience, do not fit exactly into McDougall's list, nor do Murray's defendance or abasement or exhibition.

McDougall's books were very popular, particularly among teachers and general readers. While his doctrines were not of very much practical use, they were inoffensive and accorded well enough with common sense. But among psychologists— they were attacked from several different points of view. There were materialists, who feared that McDougall was trying to smuggle God and the soul back into psychology; there were environmentalists, who thought that he was trying to deny man's right to be new, different and better; there were writers like G. W. Allport, who denied the continuity of development, and asserted the functional autonomy of motives; and there were the psycho-analysts and the followers of Adler, who held that things are not always what they seem.

The environmentalists and the materialists we shall not discuss here at more length, because their arguments are familiar, and do not settle anything. The question of the functional autonomy of motives is more deserving of careful analysis. Allport (Table IV, 5) considers that the whole attempt to reduce all motives to a brief list of fundamental motives is a mistaken one. He points out that the motives of an activity may change over the course of years, while the activity may remain more or less the same. For instance, a man who goes to sea originally to earn a living, may remain there because he likes the sea. This argument begs the question. The question is, not whether the motivation of an act may change, but whether every act is referable to one or another of a short list of basic motives. Liking the sea may itself be analysable into some other more general basic motives that have been present all the time in a latent or disguised form. The sea may symbolize to him the mother to whom he returns. or it may be the freedom of open spaces, escape from the dark enclosing womb, or perhaps some subtle combination of the two that satisfies both inconsistent needs. The doctrine of the functional autonomy of motives, while it contains an acceptable principle, may often act to restrict and inhibit perception of the connections between things. If there is anything that we do well and truly know in psychology, it is the continuity of personality.

Freud, while making the fullest use of this continuity, has not attempted to draw up a detailed list of basic motives. He has preferred to use a few very general principles, each of which can be asked to explain a great deal. In the German tradition, a principle that did not explain everything at once would hardly be worth having.

The Anglo-Saxon way is more scrappy, piecemeal, step by step, often less perceptive, but also sometimes less silly. Freud began with a contrast of sexual and ego motives, those which serve the preservation of the race, and those which serve the preservation of the individual. Later he reformulated his fundamental polarity as that of the sexual and the aggressive drives—the goals of life and of death. Life instincts included both sexuality and self-preservation; death instincts included both self-destruction and externalized aggression. Freud was content with such a broad classification, because he wanted to describe personality in terms of its inner conflicts, and not, like McDougall, in terms of a number of detailed separate principles. So long as motives worked amicably in alternation, or side by side, Freud was content to describe them by one

H

vague comprehensive term, whose meaning could be left undefined. Since he was searching for principles of conflict, for general descriptions of the kind of situation that brings a man up against himself, Freud could not use more than a small number of general principles without creating an intolerable complexity. It might be possible to reconcile the detailed analysis of particular instinct-patterns, each belonging to a few characteristic situations, with a much more general grouping into two or three types of conflict situation. Freud's doctrine of basic drives does not so much contradict McDougall's, as attack a different problem.

If we examine the lists of basic motives prepared by Reid, McDougall, Dunlap, Cattell and Murray, (Table IV, 1, 3, 4, 6, 7) we shall find that there is a large measure of agreement between them, and only minor points of disagreement. But at the same time we shall see that with present techniques there is no way of deciding definitely on the correct list. No clear-cut criterion exists, corresponding to the atomic weight of an element. Basic motives are convenient ideas, and their existence seems solid enough, but their edges are indistinct. Their boundaries are poorly marked, their number indeterminate. Some motives are fairly well localized in definite physiological processes. Eating, drinking, migration, copulation occur under conditions that are fairly definite and well understood. It is the 'brain drives' that give more difficulty, the social motives that have no localized seat in the organism, and little known physiology.

Several alternative sets of terms for describing these seem about as good as one another. What we need is a classification that will correspond in some deeper and more intimate way to the workings of human thought, particularly in its more impulsive and less deliberate modes. Our description must somehow conform with the situation as it is perceived by the actor at the moment, and not in terms of long-term effects interpreted by an outsider. An example would be the use of the old term 'procreative impulse' to describe sexuality.   The impulse is certainly not from the animal's point of view a desire to have offspring.   A real beginning of the new kind of analysis has been made with Lewin's[7] 'topological* psychology', or 'field theory'. This is an application of Gestalt psychology to the study of motives. 'Field theory' is an attempt to describe actions in the same terms in which the situation is perceived by the agent.   The description of an action is not in terms of its function or long-term effect, but rather in terms of its immediate spatial relations.   If spatial metaphors are the real stuff of thinking, then a description of motives in these terms will get close to its real nature.   It may thus be that the description of motives by a geometrical analogy as 'vectors' will increase our powers of empathy into otherwise remote and inaccessible processes.

Many philosophers have commented on the spatial metaphors underlying so much of our thought.   The description of desire in terms of motion goes back to Democritus and the Epicureans. Medieval descriptions of motivation in terms of movement of the vital or animal spirits are a speculative physiology based upon this mode of thought.

Hobbes described desires as *voluntary motions*, 'These words appetite and aversion we have from the Latines,' says Hobbes (*Leviathan*, Ch. 6); 'and they both of them signify the motions, one of approaching, the other of retiring.   So also do the Greek words for the same, which are horme and aphorme.   For Nature itself does often press upon men those truths, which afterwards, when they look for somewhat beyond nature, they stumble at'.   The Kantian theory, that space and time are forms through which the outer world is perceived, is part

---

*(Topology in its original meaning is a kind of geometry which does not employ any form of measurement.   It has been described as the geometry of the surface of a rubber sheet; there are no fixed distances or directions; nevertheless, certain spatial relations remain.   There is no difference between a circle and a square; both are closed figures, or 'Jordan curves'.   But being inside a closed figure is always different from being outside it.   The logic of human instinct seems to be similar to that of topological geometry.   Vector analysis is a legitimate extension of topology.)

of the intellectual ancestry of Gestalt psychology. Carlyle also stressed the metaphorical nature of thinking.

'Examine Language; what, if you except some few primitive elements (of natural sound) what is it all but Metaphors, recognized as such, or no longer recognized.... An unmetaphorical style you shall in vain seek for: is not your very *Attention a stretching-to?*' (*Sartor Resartus*, Book I, Ch. XI.)*

We quote these examples from earlier literature to show that the spatial nature of our thinking has long been recognized. Topology is a universal language that transcends culture, and can be used to describe the inevitable experiences and goal of humanity. To be inside, to get out, to enter or penetrate, to enclose or retain or exclude—these are the basic and universal metaphors of our thinking. The use of a topological rather than a functional classification of human motives may enable us to achieve a system which is no longer arbitrary, but is firmly based on the real nature of our motives.

Kurt Lewin, who did so much to expound and develop this mode of thinking, did not himself make a list of basic vectors; but various such attempts have been made, and two are described in our Table (those of Murray and Tomkins, Table IV, 7, 11). It may seem that they add little to existing formulations, and are little more than new and odd ways of stating familiar facts. If we look only at present achievements, this may be true enough. But the vectors seem to be opening new possibilities for defining a universal human language of action that may in time supplant the language of function in psychology. We may thus arrive eventually by this route at a 'real' or 'true' list of human motives, which will have an intimate correspondence with the basic metaphors of our thought. In the meantime, however, a system like that of McDougall has considerable value for the description of personality. Even though it cannot claim any ultimate validity, it is unlikely to lead us far astray. In this respect, the basic

---

*It is unsuitable here to give an orderly historical account of concepts of space. We cannot manage more than a few arbitrary examples.

motives are in a much better state than the basic types. A comparison of Tables III and IV will make this plain. The types are extremely various, and the evidence for many of them is very flimsy. In contrast, basic motives are concerned with known and accepted qualities, and disagreements are mainly concerned with the breadth or narrowness of sub-division, and the utility rather than the validity of the descriptions.

A large number of separate principles of explanation cannot all operate at once unless some relation between them is also given. From McDougall onwards, the list-makers have compiled their lists without much attempt to show their relations to one another. Maslow[5] has stressed this point in two interesting papers. He points out that no drive can be described in isolation from others; it can be understood only in relation to the satisfaction or dissatisfaction of other drives. He proposes to meet this defect by arranging needs in a hierarchy of prepotency. The most insistent are the physiological needs—hunger, thirst, pain, fatigue, etc. He attempts no detailed psychological description of these, grouping them together under the general title of homeostasis. After these, in order of prepotency, come safety needs, love needs, needs for esteem, and needs for self-actualization. Each group of needs has to be fairly well satisfied before a later group can emerge into prominence. Man is a perpetually wanting animal, and new needs emerge as prepotent ones are met. Ordinarily, a man who is starving, or suffocating, will not concern himself much with collecting stamps or joining a club, when there is any chance of satisfying a prepotent need. Maslow describes some circumstances in which exceptions to this hierarchy occur: there are some people in whom needs for self-esteem seem to be more important than needs for love (some of these may be a result of early frustrations); there are others who, as a result of well-established basic satisfactions in childhood, are able to tolerate large frustrations of basic needs, in pursuit of ideals. Nevertheless, over a long period, and in general, the hierarchy is maintained. This principle has been obscurely recognized for a long time; and examination of the order in which principles of action are arranged in Thomas Reid's work will show that the order closely resembles Maslow's. But no theoretical importance was given to this idea. Any future enumeration of basic drives must take account of this hierarchical principle, and of the exceptions.

McDougall recognized that his instincts usually appeared in the form of sentiments. Murphy[6] has given this process the useful name of canalization. Basic motives appear not in a bare instinctive form, but interwoven with learned experience. What McDougall did not sufficiently recognize or stress was the fact that motives also undergo many other transformations. They may be changed into their opposites, or they may shift their objects in the most surprising way. While Freud was interested in tracing the vicissitudes of instincts, he later came to consider that the principal task of psychology was not the tracing of actions to their instinctive origins, but rather the study of the shifts and disguises that motives undergo. Thus mechanisms of defence, rather than instincts came to be the main principles of explanation in psycho-analysis. These are the topics that will occupy us in the following chapter.

TABLE IV: SOME SYSTEMS OF BASIC MOTIVES

Name and Author and Date	List of Basic Motives	Characteristics
'active powers'	I.	'By instinct, I mean a natural blind impulse to certain actions, without having any end in view, without deliberation, and very often without any conception of what we do' (p. 99).
1. Thomas Reid. *Essays on the Active Powers of the Human Mind.* 1788.	*mechanical principles of action:* (1) *instinct,* e.g. sucking, swallowing, crying when hurt, fear of the dark. (2) *habit.*	

II.
animal principles of action:
(1) *appetites:* hunger, thirst, lust, activity and rest.
(2) *desires:* of power, of esteem, of knowledge.
(3) *affections:*
    (*a*) *benevolent:* towards children, parents, benefactors, the distressed, the wise and good; friendship; public spirit, an affection to any community to which we belong.
    (*b*) *malevolent:* emulation, resentment of action.

III.
rational principles of action:
(1) regard to our good on the whole.
(2) duty, moral obligation.

'Both (habit and instinct) operate without will or intention, without thought, and therefore may be called mechanical principles.'
'Animal principles are such as operate upon the will and intention, but do not suppose any exercise or judgment or reason; and are most of them to be found in some brute-animals, as well as in man.'
(p. 117): 'Appetites are a particular class of desires, distinguished by the following marks: first every appetite is accompanied with an uneasy sensation proper to it, which is strong or weak, in proportion to the desire we have of the object. Secondly, appetites are not constant, but periodical, being sated by their objects for a time, and returning after certain periods.'
(p. 125): desires are distinguished from appetites by this: that there is not an uneasy sensation proper to each, and always accompanying it; and that they are not periodical but constant, not being sated with their objects for a time, as appetites are.'

Name and Author and Date	*List of Basic Motives*	*Characteristics*
Instincts 2. W. James, 1887.	sucking, biting, spitting out, clasping, pointing, carrying to the mouth, crying, smiling, holding head erect, sitting up, standing, locomotion, vocalization, imitation, emulation, pugnacity, anger, resentment, sympathy, hunting, fear (including fear of noises of strange men and animals, of darkness, of high places, of the supernatural), acquisitive instinct, constructiveness, play, curiosity, sociability, shyness, secretiveness, cleanliness, modesty, shame, love (sexual and parental).	Instincts are actions done with no prevision of the end; but instinctive acts, in an animal with memory, cease to be blind after being repeated. Man has more instincts than any other animal. Instincts are transient; if not exercised, at the right time, they fade away. If exercised, they are replaced by habits. James regards instinctive actions as innate and as the source of some, but not all, later goals.
Instincts 3. W. McDougall. *Theory First Formulated in* 1908. Revised 1923. In 1932, the term was changed to 'propensities'.	Parental instinct, combat, food-seeking, repulsion, escape, gregarious, primitive passive sympathy, instincts of self-assertion and submission, mating, acquisitive, constructive instincts, instinct of appeal; some minor instincts, e.g. scratching, coughing, laughter.	'an instinct is an innate disposition which determines the organism to perceive (to pay attention to) any object of a certain class, and to experience in its presence a certain emotional excitement and an impulse to action, which find expression in a specific mode of behaviour in relation to that object.' Distinguishing features of an instinct are (i) found in all or almost all of a species, (ii) parallels in other species, (iii) based on characteristic bodily structures. Every motive is held to be derived from one or more of the instincts.

Name and Author and Date	List of Basic Motives	Characteristics
primary desires 4. Knight Dunlap, 1925.	alimentary, excretory, protective, activity, rest, amatory, parental, pre-eminence, conformity.	primary desires are those which are important everywhere, and main-tain their general char-acteristics through the ages, secondary desires are derived from them. Primary desires have an organic basis, and typi-cal forms of excess, defect and perversion.
prepotent reflexes 5. F. H. Allport, 1924.	starting and withdraw-ing, rejecting, strug-gling and yielding, hunger reactions, sensi-tive zone reactions, sex reactions.	these reflexes are sup-posed to be the physical basis of social responses.
ergs 6. R. B. Cattell. *General Psychology.* Sci-Art Publishers, Cambridge, Mass., 1941.	I. organic needs: air, water; avoiding pain, heat, cold, to urinate and defaecate. II. propensities which are organic, viscerogenic: rest, food - seeking, mating, protecting the young, avoiding noxi-ous substances. III. propensities showing no clear organic rhy-thm; escape by means of (*a*) flight or (*b*) 'freezing'; deference; seeking help; collec-ting; exploring strange places; seeking com-pany of which com-ponents are: primitive passive sympathy, tend-ency to evoke emo-tional responses from others, and imitation; self-assertion; aggres-sion; laughter; and per-haps construction.	'an innate psychophy-sical disposition which permits its possessor to acquire reactivity to cer-tain classes of objects more readily than others, to experience a specific emotion therefrom, and to enter on activity which ceases more com-pletely at the attainment of one specific goal than at other specific goals. The goal satisfactions may be defined either externally by the parti-cular relation between the organism and an environmental situation, or internally, by some physiological condition. There are, further, in-nately preferred ways of behaving in reaching the innately preferred goals.

Name and Author and Date	List of Basic Motives	Characteristics
Needs 7. H. A. Murray, 1938.	Abasement, succorance, harmavoidance, infavoidance, counteraction, defendance, autonomy, dominance, aggression, rejection, deference, affiliation, nurturance, sex, sentiance, play, achievement, exhibition, understanding, order.	an overt or manifest need is distinguished by these indices: 1. A typical behavioural trend or effect. 2. A typical mode (actores or sub-effects). 3. The search for, avoidance or selection of, attention and response to, one of a few types of press (cathected objects of a certain class). 4. The exhibition of a characteristic emotion or feeling. 5. The manifestation of satisfaction with the achievement of a certain effect (or with a gratuity), or the manifestation of dissatisfaction with failure to achieve a certain effect.
vectors 8. H.A. Murray, 1938, based on work of E. Homburger.	(1) adience vector, approaching desirable objects. (2) ingression vector, seeking and entering an enclosed space or haven and staying there. (3) adherence vector, clinging to a supporting object. (4) contrience vector, attacking external objects. (5) abience vector, fleeing from disliked or feared objects. (6) encasement vector, holding one's ground against intruders by erecting a wall. (7) egression vector, breaking out of an enclosed place. (8) locomotion vector, moving rapidly through space, including exploration.	an alternative terminology to that of needs. 'The advantage of vector analysis is that it is based on readily discernible, spatial changes, and for this reason there is apt to be good agreement among those who make the initial observations'.

Name and Author and Date	*List of Basic Motives*	*Characteristics*
	(9) manipulation vector. (10) construction vector. (11) reception vector, sucking or passively taking things into the body. (12) acquisition vector, aggressively acquiring objects. (13) ejection vector. (14) retention vector. (15) injection vector, sticking an object into something.	
'Drives' 9. E. C. Tolman, 1941.	A. *Biological Drives* (i) appetites: maternal drive, nest building drive, thirst, hunger, sex, general activity, exploratory, rest, urination and defaecation, play, aesthetic. (ii) aversions: cold - avoidance, heat - avoidance, danger - avoidance (fright) obstruction-avoidance (aggression).	The identifying feature is a specific and characteristic consummatory response. Each appetite is set in motion by some peculiar internal metabolic condition. This metabolic condition occurs in apparently more or less regular cycles due to combinations of internal and external conditions. And when it is in force the animal is driven until an approximate consummatory object is found. . . . each of these aversions is set off, not by an internal metabolic condition (as is an appetite), but by an evoking environmental object or situation.
	B. *Social Drives* gregariousness, loyalty to group, imitativeness, dominance submission, competition, acquisition, sharing with and soliciting from others, co-operation tendencies.	Any of these driving tensions, while it is in force endows the environmental consummatory or evoking situations with value — consummatory situations with positive value and evoking situations with negative value.

Name and Author and Date	List of Basic Motives	Characteristics
'needs' 10. A. H. Maslow, 1943.	Basic needs are arranged in a hierarchy, as flows: (1) physiological needs. (2) safety needs. (3) love needs (for affection and belongingness). (4) esteem needs. (5) need for self-actualization.	Physiological drives are rejected as a centering point. Many drives, e.g. fatigue, maternal drives, are not localized in the body. The appearance of one need usually rests on the prior satisfaction of another, more prepotent need. Man is a perpetually wanting animal. No need or drive can be treated as if it were isolated or discrete: every drive is related to the state of satisfaction or dissatisfaction of other drives. classification should be based on goals rather than drives or behaviour, should be human-centred, rather than animal-centred. . . . The theory of homeostasis, plus recent work on the relation of appetites to bodily needs, means that it is now impossible as well as useless to make a list of fundamental physiological needs.
Vectors 11. S. S. Tomkins, 1947.	I. 'on': to depend upon objects. II. 'from': to acquire positive valences from objects. III. 'toward': to approach or enjoy objects. IV. 'with': to share experience.	'by *vectors* we mean the psychological direction characteristic of behaviour, striving, wishes, cathexes or feelings'. 'They may have as their objects other persons, the self, social institutions, physical objects, ideas, in short, any object of human interest'.

Name and Author and Date	*List of Basic Motives*	*Characteristics*
	V. 'for': to bestow positive valence upon objects.	
	VI. 'over': to govern objects.	
	VII. 'under': to be governed by objects of negative valence.	
	VIII. 'by': to be governed by objects of positive valence.	
	IX. 'away from': to avoid or escape objects.	
	X. 'against': to attack objects.	

REFERENCES

1. REID, T.	*Essays on the Active Powers of the Human Mind.*	1788.
2. JAMES, W.	*Principles of Psychology.*	London, Macmillan, 1890.
3. McDOUGALL, W.	*Introduction to Social Psychology.*	London, Methuen, 1908.
4. McDOUGALL, W.	*The Energies of Men.*	London, Methuen, 1933.
7. LEWIN, K.	*Principles of Topological Psychology.*	New York, McGraw-Hill, 1936.
5. MASLOW, A. H.	*A Preface to Motivation Theory.*	Psychosomatic Medicine 1932, 5, (85–92).
	A Theory of Human Motivation.	Psychol. Review (50), 1943 (370–96).
6. MURPHY, G.	*Personality: A Biosocial Approach to Origins and Structure.*	New York, Harper, 1947.

CHAPTER VII

PATTERNS OF MATURATION AND MECHANISMS OF DEFENCE

SOMEWHERE a system of basic regularities must be found, if there is to be a science of psychology at all. We have looked at systems of basic traits, designed either as types or as factors. We have looked at accounts of personality in which the basic regularity is found in the unity of the culture; and at those expressed in terms of a system of basic motives. Two other approaches remain to be considered—that in terms of developmental stages, and that in terms of psychodynamic mechanisms.

The idea of finding laws of development that would analyse human growth into a sequence of predetermined stages has been in the air for quite a time. Darwin and Haeckel are the sources of many such ideas. Wilhelm Roux and the embryologists made notable advances in the latter part of the nineteenth century in the precise description of developmental stages. The psychological study of development was pursued by several different methods that were largely independent of one another.

Without attempting to review this great body of work in detail, we can recognize four main lines of investigation, which can be symbolized by four famous names—Binet,[1] Gesell,[2] Piaget[3] and Freud.[4] All set out with a similar problem, to analyse the typical patterns of child development, to determine the directions of mental growth, and the order of their appearance. A technique leads to a more precise measurement of the intelligence quotient (I.Q.), by which the adult's performance is predicted. A description of maturational patterns is an account of how children develop, using among other things the mental age at any stage.

It is not easy for the present generation of psychologists to remember that Binet's work began not as a technique of measurement, but as a description of maturational patterns. The main business of the early work on intelligence was the allocation of tests to certain years. At the age of three and a half a normal child can say what to do when he is hungry, at the age of four he can string beads, and so on. If he cannot do these things at the normal age, then he is defective. Tests were used primarily at the age for which they were designed, and only in special cases were they used at other ages. Binet phrased his assessments of development in the form of abilities, i.e. he described what children did in terms of success and failure, and chose problems in which children usually showed an improved performance from year to year. In France the work that Binet began continued to be a study of development. At the Institut Jean-Jacques Rousseau the analysis of children's thinking continued with increasing depth and subtlety, especially in Piaget's studies on the development of children's philosophies of moral conduct, of space, of causation, and so on. The quantitative assessment of abilities did not attract the French, and they soon dropped it in favour of analyses of children's logic and metaphysics, interpreted as a kind of maturation.

Meanwhile, in America the use of testing for the study of development was gradually superseded by the use of testing for the measurement of ability. Terman continued, even in the 1937 revision of his scale, to allocate tests to years, as Binet had done, but from the psychometric point of view this is an anachronism, and does not enter into the scoring. A test passed is a point credited, and from the psychometrist's point of view it does not matter to what year of development the test belongs. In later American versions the Binet tests become little more than a point scale, in which the original interest in development was lost. American pressure on competitive achievement gradually turned the testing programme into an attempt to predict success or failure in the adult world. The significance of childhood testing became restricted to the estimation of the I.Q., and the mental age, originally a far more interesting and valuable concept, fell into disuse.

Gesell, although (like Binet) phrasing his tests mainly as the assessment of unfolding abilities, never became deflected from his primary purpose of interpreting growth. He did not use the concept of general intelligence, but described growth in four fields of functional organization—motor behaviour, adaptive behaviour, language and personal-social behaviour. Gesell always kept the human being in the foreground, and was not so dominated by a passion for scores that he felt it necessary to combine the four aspects into a single developmental quotient.

The Freudian description of stages in psycho-sexual development[4] differs from those of Binet, Gesell and Piaget, in that it was not derived from the direct observation of children, but reconstructed piecemeal from the reminiscences of adults. It is also distinctive in that the patterns of maturation with which he is concerned are mainly motives, and not abilities or techniques or beliefs. Most of the original suggestions about psycho-sexual development came from Freud himself, though many elaborations were due to Jung, Rank and Abraham. Freud's account of the matter was in the main a description of the progressive unfolding of drives from an inner source; but at every stage he recognized the intervention of the environment. In the earlier stages the environment acted in rather simple and stereotyped ways, so that it would reinforce the effects of the inborn pattern of maturation. The prenatal environment—warm, soft, wet and cushioned—must be in its main features the same for everyone. So also must the process of birth, though we can imagine a great difference of infant opinion beginning there, between those who are glad to be free of oppressive restrictions, who like wide open spaces, fresh air, freedom, adventure and new experience, and those who spend their lives searching for security, the dark safe place, the wall at one's back, the rock of ages cleft for me, the island refuge where birth and death are brought together again, and peace is restored. This cleavage may itself be either temperamental or environmental—the anti-claustral adventurous pattern might be due to a more active and vigorous constitution, or to a severe and prolonged birth trauma, a threat of suffocation which required an intense effort from the child to ensure survival.

Psycho-analysts have never been at pains to distinguish the effects of true heredity from those of a universally experienced early environment. (Analytic theories have always inclined more to epigenesis than to preformation.) Each stage of childish development would leave its mark on the personality. There would be certain possible variations in the primary pattern, producing long-term effects on personality. The first feeding experiences seem to exert a permanent effect, and so does the amount of affectionate cuddling that the infant received in the earliest part of life after birth. Children who are undernourished, or who cannot absorb their food properly, may develop grasping, demanding ways, as though they anticipate having to fight for everything they get. In the second year attitudes towards authority begin to consolidate themselves. Patterns of submission or defiance may be established, and the appropriate occasions for the display of each.

In the Freudian scheme these are particularly associated with the control of defaecation, and the child's interest in its own excrement. The notions of excrement as something valuable to be retained, like gold, or as something dirty with which to defile and destroy a hated enemy—both are fantasies that seem to be spread over most of the world, though different techniques of cleanliness training give them a varying importance. In the subsequent period also there are certain universal situations to which every child has to respond in some way, though the responses chosen may vary widely. In the myth Oedipus was exposed as a child by his father. When he was grown up he killed his father (in

I

ignorance), gained a rather easy eminence by solving the riddle of the Sphinx, and afterwards married his mother. Of course, trouble came after this.

For Freud the Oedipus complex is the prototype of family emotions, though this is a somewhat strained comparison. The term 'Oedipus Complex' as it is used to-day, refers to at least five different kinds of problems that the child may have to meet from the fifth year onwards. These are: (i) Masturbation practices, and the related castration fantasies. (ii) Fantasies about the mother's body, and the meaning of birth and sexuality. (iii) Anxieties about jealousy, possession and hatred, which may involve father, mother and sibling. (iv) Problems of authority and discipline. (v) Fantasies about growing up, and preparation for adult roles. All of these will come into prominence in some period of childhood, and any two of them may be closely connected, or may be separate. The connections between these phases may be partly due to customs of child rearing, and partly to accidental experiences. For instance, fantasies about sexuality and the mother's body may be vividly stimulated if the child watches the parents in bed together, as most children do at one time or another. But if a child is very carefully brought up, and has no opportunity to see anything really naughty, then the knowledge acquired in later childhood about other people's sexuality may be quite disconnected from personal experience, and he may grow to adulthood with only very dim archaic memories of the mother's body, and a vague feeling that something is being kept back from him. If he has been specifically punished for masturbating, then sexuality may mean to him a defiance of authority, and a peril of castration. But for other children authority may be much less concerned with sexuality, and more concerned with freedom to move about, or ownership of property or attitudes to work.

All the four schemes of maturation began by emphasizing uniformities and regularities; and for Gesell and Piaget these have remained the central themes. Binet's work was gradually transformed in the direction of differential psychology, and Freud's into a psychology of personality. Psycho-analytic writing has recognized more and more variations within the universal sequence, more and more points of choice where crucial and lasting decisions are made.

Disputes about the universality of the Oedipus complex are now less prominent than they were. If by the Oedipus complex is meant the problems we have listed and their solution, their universality can hardly be questioned. In one form or another every child must come to terms with them. The 'classical' Oedipus complex is, however, a much more specific affair. Here the protagonists are (i) a stern domineering father, who is immensely efficient and strong, orders mother about and bullies her a bit, and threatens his child with castration as a response for masturbating (ii) a gentle loving mother, somewhat afraid of father, making obedience to him a condition of her love for the child; unwittingly over-stimulating her son by trying to get from him the kind of affection that her husband fails to give her; and (iii) a son who fears his father as a tyrant, and hates him as his mother's lover; envies his power and success and wishes to be like him when he grows up.

This is one of several possible family patterns, and few people to-day would assert that this is a phylogenetic memory, recurring in fantasy without the aid of experience. In his earlier discussions, Freud relied on heredity to account for the universality of the Oedipus complex; and so long as psycho-analysis was mainly German, these notions were generally accepted. But as psycho-analysis was transplanted to the English-speaking world, some means had to be found of accounting for universality without offensive notions of phylogenesis. There really are some rather strange facts to be accounted for. People make use of universal symbols, without knowing what they mean, and yet so appropriately that they seem to have some previous familiarity with them. The symbolism of dreams and of neurotic symptoms both seem to have a generality that could hardly be due to similarity of individual experience. And yet the notions of phylogenesis, which Freud presumably derived from Haeckel, Hering and Semon, and which seemed quite acceptable in the German world, are not so to us. The appearance of inherited symbols is accounted for by a combination of the following facts: (i) The use of spatial symbols is universal and precultural, a world-wide system of metaphor, not because of any special inherited structures, but because spatial metaphors are a true mirror of the process of thought, and have some intimate correspondence with the dynamics of the brain. This is the Gestalt theory which we have already described, and will not labour further here; (ii) There are many situations which are almost inevitable, merely by virtue of being human and belonging to a society; (iii) Many symbols, although genuinely obscure to the person who used them, are nevertheless quite well known to him in another context.

Anyone who has spent a few hours leaning on a bar counter listening to dirty jokes will have heard, in con-scious form, all the sexual symbols that Freud 'discovered' in *The Interpretation of Dreams*.[5] With the leer in the voice and the gleam of glasses to define the context, it is not difficult to inter-pret most of the symbols, which at other times would be deeply hidden. A man dreamt that he came into the kitchen and, on opening the oven of the electric stove, saw that there was a bun inside on the tray. The dream seemed to him completely meaningless. But when a soldier said to him 'My wife has a bun in the oven', he had no difficulty in understanding the man's meaning. Without having heard the idiom before, he was able to interpret it immediately merely by the similarity of the spatial forms—the small object enclosed in a larger cavity; (iv) Many symbols are culturally transmitted, in the conventional language of poetry, but presented in 'nice' and respectable forms, without the gross directness of the psychoanalyst.

These facts together may be enough to understand symbolism without requiring the phylogenetic hypothesis.

Of the four systems of maturation that we have described, it is really only the Freudian that has had any important application to the psychology of the adult personality. Gesell and Piaget are genuinely child psychologists, intent upon interpreting the childish world as it is, rather than upon guessing at its meaning for adult life.   The mental testers following on Binet came to view their developmental studies more and more in terms of the I.Q. as a static terminus, to be predicted by the tests. For Freud the process had far more significance. He observed the development process through the wrong end of a telescope, and events of childhood were never considered for themselves alone, but always in terms of their significance for the adult. The fact that certain memories had been repressed, but nevertheless retained their force and influence on adult symptoms and dreams, showed that they must have been originally important for the child.   These fixated experiences are thus a guide to the most important drives or instincts of childhood, and also to their later significance. In Freud's view, neurosis always involves regression to an earlier level of fixation; so that the fixation in childhood is the principal cause of the neurotic breakdown. The occasioning cause is some setback to present hopes, which discourages the forward view. Commonly it resembles in some way the situation around which the original fixation was built, and this resemblance of the present to the past is what gives the current setback its pathological force.

A man employed as a country storekeeper was found to have stolen a large amount of money from his employer. Although he was not prosecuted, he developed a depression, and became incapable of work for some time. His speech was slow and dull, and he spent long periods avoiding people and walking by himself. He had been involved in a similar episode a few years earlier, when he had also taken money from the firm he worked for. At that time he had also been drinking heavily. His wife had taken charge, and insisted that he must pay over his wages to her. She intended to give him an allowance, but he never asked for it, telling her that he was winning money at the races.

He had preferred stealing to asking his wife for a part of his wages. This irrational behaviour could not be understood except through the past. His father had been a drunkard, and had often left his mother without the money to buy food for the children. The father had also beaten her. He (the son) remembered quarrelling bitterly with his father when he was nine or ten years old. He had an elder brother who also drank, and he feared that this was an hereditary taint, though since the first disaster, he had succeeded in giving up drink entirely. Much of his behaviour was a repetition of the same conduct for which he reproached his father. Beneath a façade of conformity and obedience to his wife, he had harboured fantasies of rebellion against her over-strict rule, and lacking courage to express his rebellion directly, he had obtained his revenge by ruining himself a second time. An obscure recognition of the compulsive and irrational nature of his conduct was expressed through the fantasy that it was hereditary and predestined. In this way he identified himself with his father, and perhaps also in some degree freed himself from guilt by denying responsibility.

It is thus only through the history of childhood that the adult life gets its meaning. Freud's first cases showed how some sexual experience in puberty might emerge as a neurotic symptom perhaps ten years later. Subsequent studies pushed these crucial episodes further and further back into the past; Rank[6] emphasized the traumatic significance of birth. According to him, birth is an experience from which most people never recover. You are never quite the same again, there is always something. Klein[7] added other early developmental stages in the first and second years, building up a sinister dream-world of naughty little babies. One continuing tendency of later psychoanalysis has been to extend the developmental history towards the past.

In analytic theory, present symptoms contain allusions to remote past events, and this indicates that fixation has occurred. In this sense fixation presumably means that the subject continues to think about or respond to some episode of the past because it has not been satisfactorily closed. In the famous Zeigarnik[8] experiment, subjects are given a number of small tasks, some of which they are allowed to complete, while others are stopped before the subject has had time to complete them. When subjects are subsequently asked to write down a list of the tasks they did, more of the uncompleted tasks were remembered. We may suppose that this is an elementary model for one kind of fixation. An episode remains as a persistent nagging memory because the problem or conflict that it represents has never been resolved. Related to this kind of fixation we get the repetition compulsion, in which a subject repeatedly becomes involved in the same kind of misfortune, in spite of apparent efforts to avoid it.

The unfortunate storekeeper whom we have just described was this kind of 'fate neurotic'. There are also other kinds of fixation described in analytic literature. Freud's early hysterics had fixated some traumatic experience belonging to puberty, and although they forgot it soon afterwards, the effects of the trauma continued to be active, and to have a decisive influence on future development. The disturbing experience was a rape or attempted rape, and the meaning of the experience seemed to be that it was both alarming and alluring. The patient's own description emphasized the external threat or injury, but it was plain that this was usually not of central importance, and in some cases lacking altogether. The alarming quality of the experience came from the pleasure it had given to the victim. The fact that the girl had forgotten the experience which was so important to her meant that it had been repressed, and this repression or denial meant that the danger came mainly from within, not from without. The danger from within was the strength of the instinctive drives in herself that had been aroused by the incident. And according to Freud's account of the matter, it was the repression that produced the fixation. The incident continued to be important because it had been denied, and not worked through. There is some similarity to the first example of fixation that we discussed, in which an uncompleted task insistently demands completion. Here the 'uncompleted task' is the sexual desires that have been aroused but not sated.

A third variety of fixation is that in which one phase of development has proved so satisfying that there is no desire to go further. We speak of a man's having a mother fixation when he is so well satisfied with the love of his mother that he has no wish to transfer it to other objects. Such a fixation seems to occur always when a period of deep satisfaction is followed by one of insecurity and frustration. All the later life is spent looking back to a Golden Age, located in the irretrievable past. Any step towards a new love-object, or a new technique for dealing with the environment, arouses so much anxiety that there is a quick return to well-tried ways. In this sense fixation is equivalent to perseveration, or rigidity of disposition, a self-imposed narrowing of object-choices. There are shifts of interest and affection which seem appropriate to each age—stages through which we expect people to grow, without casting too many lingering looks behind. When the expected shift does not occur sufficiently, we speak of fixation. Such fixation may be overt and continuous, as when a man does not marry because he loves mother too well; but very often the normal shifts of attachment appear to occur, and may really do so to some extent, but inadequately and insecurely. When some reversal of fortune occurs, some check or failure that disappoints forward-looking ambitions may revive forgotten desires, so that the fixation appears in the form of a regression. The son who has made an unsuccessful marriage comes back to live at his mother's home. This sort of regression is a voluntary retreat into the past. The other kind of regression, in which one returns again and again to some unsolved problem, is mostly evoked by some circumstance which resembles the first one. There is usually some external event that initiates the neurosis; but to the outside observer the importance of this event may not be at all obvious. It is not the event itself that matters, but its meaning for the person. Some hidden similarity between a present and a past situation revives an ancient anxiety, and leads to a neurotic breakdown. McCurdy describes cases in which a father's death evoked a revival of Oedipus fantasies in the son, which led to a psychotic breakdown. This is Freud's concept of the 'return of the repressed'.

The psycho-analytic account of the stages of psycho-sexual development was put to use in the theory of fixation and regression. It was in this way that the link was established between adult symptom and early experience. There can really be no further doubt that many adult symptoms contain archaic references to very early experience, and long-forgotten episodes of childhood. This is attested by a great mass of detailed observations that leave no room for doubt in those that know the evidence properly. Freud's account of psycho-sexual development can be described as intimations of immorality from recollections of early childhood. His accounts were not drawn from direct observation, but were reconstructions from the reminiscences of his adult patients. They have since been confirmed by many first-hand studies of small children.

The continuity of experience is one of our most important principles for understanding behaviour. We must accept this in general, even if we regard as doubtful much analytical speculation about relations between stages of fixation and varieties of neurosis. It may well be that current classification is too unstable to bear the weight of so elaborate a theory, particularly when we are dealing with the psychoses. But the practice of looking before and after is essential. The idea of defence mechanism is one of the most fertile and instructive to be found in psycho-analysis, but it is also distressingly elusive. Freud never drew up a list of defence mechanisms, but simply invented terms whenever they seemed useful. The idea that symptoms and syndromes can be understood as regressions to an earlier stage of development is one of the great organizing ideas of psycho-analysis. The concept of defence mechanisms is another. Freud took the behaviour of neurotics seriously, instead of merely dismissing it as irrational. He realized that many absurd actions, which were quite contrary to the real interests of the patient, had a real function and purpose, if they were understood in the patient's terms. Many acts had to be understood as the result of the patient's inner conflicts. Acts that were queer and irrational as ways of dealing with the external world, might be intelligible as ways of defending oneself against dangerous and forbidden impulses from within. If a man felt an uncontrollably strong desire to kill his father, but also knew that this was a naughty thing to do, and would get him into serious trouble, then much of his behaviour might be organized around the need for avoiding this fatal act. The devices he adopts for avoiding the direct expressing of his forbidden impulses are his defence mechanisms. They are compromises which seek to combine protection against internal and external threats.

The names of the various defence mechanisms (Table VI) (repression, isolation, projection, and so on) are descriptions of apparently absurd bits of behaviour which are seen to have a logic of their own when their hidden motivation is understood. One of the obstacles to understanding is that the person who is behaving queerly often does not know the meaning of his own behaviour. As the logic of the unconscious became better understood, more defence mechanisms were gradually added. There are all sorts of inconsistencies in current usage, and these cannot be repaired piecemeal. Some of the variations in current usage are analysed in Table VI. We must nevertheless do the best with what we have, because, however slippery they may be, these notions are the most valuable we have for the description of personality. In the rich and suggestive interpretations that are made possible by the use of these ideas we seem to be doing justice to the possibilities of human nature, instead of remaining bound by the desiccated trivialities of association psychology or behaviourism. The mechanisms have not been developed as 'laws of human nature' in general, or in the abstract. They were originally defined in relation to particular situations. For instance, introjection is originally the act of swallowing, which becomes symbolic of many relations with the external world, and later becomes the way in which a child takes over rules of family conduct and makes them its own. The parental admonition 'don't do that' later becomes the child's own warning to himself 'it would be naughty to do this'. This becomes a pattern of many later acts of introjection. The analyst does not think of defining in the abstract what causes introjection. He rather thinks of the mechanism as originally bound to particular situations of early development, and used later in situations that are in some respect repetitions of the original.

Every mechanism is thus traced back to some situation of family life, and ultimately to the language of the body itself, to those spatial metaphors which constitute the universal heritage of symbolism. Freud's defence mechanisms are devices which people adopt to deal with impulses that are dangerous, and likely to get them into trouble. Anna Freud[9] distinguishes four kinds of defence mechanisms according to the circumstances that evoke them—those arising from guilt feelings, those arising from fears of the external world, those arising from fear of the strength of instincts, and those arising from conflict of instincts; they show, in an unsystematic form, the meaning of alternatives that are open to people when a direct response becomes blocked or stifled. It is difficult to keep these distinctions sharp, or to be sure which we are dealing with at any one time.

They are perhaps best described in more general terms as various attempts to reconcile inner demands with outer reality. Ordinarily we do not recognize the presence of a defence mechanism unless there is something queer or abnormal about it. If A slaps B, we should consider it normal that B should be angry with A or afraid of A or perhaps both; but if he were angry, not with A, but with some other man who had done him no harm, or if he were not angry at all, but liked it, we should consider this abnormal, and requiring explanation in terms of some mechanism. Freud's defence mechanisms were all described against a background of 'normal' psychology. He never attempted to define this 'normal' behaviour in detail, but we are assumed to know it for purposes of contrast with the 'abnormal' conduct that he is describing.

Freud thus had no intention of producing a 'complete' or exhaustive list, because this would have to include the various 'normal' reactions which he took for granted, and never tried to enumerate. His descriptions include processes which are queer for two reasons. Some are so because the motivation is apparently distorted in some way, and they become intelligible when we have recognized the situation that the subject is defending himself against. If a man believes that he is eternally damned, and when asked why this is so, replies that he forgot to clean his teeth this morning, the situation is not intelligible in itself, because the cause does not seem adequate to the effect. But if we can show that failure to clean the teeth is a substitute or disguised expression for some much more serious act, then we shall have 'explained' the delusion by means of mechanism involved. With many mechanisms we can make the situation intelligible by seeing that the solution adopted by the subject did have some effect in reducing his anxiety, and defending him against some danger, even if the danger is mainly illusory. But many other devices are not defence mechanisms, but examples of the peculiar logic of the Id.

This was what Freud described as the 'primary process', a useful term used occasionally in his works, and reappearing in his unfinished *Outline*.[10] The 'primary process' includes a variety of oddities described elsewhere under the names of dream-work, symbolism, condensation and representation through the opposite. These are mechanisms, but not defence mechanisms. The only reason why they occur is that that is the way people think. If we want to understand dreams, fantasies, and neurotic symptoms, then we have to learn the rules of this illogic. The Freudian mechanisms (or dynamisms) thus include a good many processes that are not defence mechanisms. And several that are at times quite clearly defensive in nature may at other times be used without any defensive intention. For instance, projection, as Freud[11] described it in the Schreber case (Schreber was the classic case of paranoia, who projected his guilty feelings of homosexuality on to supposed 'bod-rays' and other displacements). is undoubtedly defensive. The ideas which the paranoiac ascribes to others are ideas which he has, but which he cannot tolerate himself. But projection as it is seen in projective tests is not defensive, or at any rate not primarily so. When Xenophanes remarked that the gods of the Ethiopians are black, he was illustrating the process of projection in this more general sense.

In the later analytic writings, all descriptions of defence mechanisms are phrased in terms of ego, id and super-ego, so that it becomes hard to explain their meaning in other terms. Psycho-analysis is firmly committed to the acceptance of the three little men inside your head who deceive one another, quarrel and make friends again, form alliances, offer bribes, and shut a knowing eye to an indiscretion. Often there seems to be only a vague recollection that these are metaphors whose proper field of application is a very restricted one, and there is a danger of making an Athanasian mystery out of a useful distinction. Some attempts have been made to systematize this fascinating but disorderly body of ideas about defence mechanisms. Anna Freud,[12] following a suggestion in Freud, considered the possibility that particular defence mechanisms are associated with particular neurotic disorders.

Thus repression is particularly associated with hysteria, isolation and undoing with obsessional neurosis, projection with paranoia, and so on. It was not, however, proved possible to carry through a scheme like this in any complete way. Nor can the plan to connect particular defence mechanisms with particular developmental stages permit any neat organization of the material. Any systematic treatment of the defence mechanisms would have been foreign to Freud's method. This was to throw out a series of powerful generalizations, with one or two illustrative examples; and before his bewildered followers had grown accustomed to them, he would try out some new ones, without explaining whether or not he had discarded last year's lot. To include them all in one vast gothic structure is perhaps more than even so admirable a systematizer as Fenichel can achieve.

The defence mechanisms are not a general theory of psychodynamics, but a number of inductive generalizations describing repeated observations during the process of analysis. They form a clue to the meaning of symptoms, and the more such clues you know, the better is your chance of interpreting the next one. The practising analyst thinks of them, not as abstract forces, but in relation to particular persons or events, that have a common meaning. Each mechanism has its prototype in certain familiar experiences which the analyst is accustomed to look for in the life-histories of his patients; and when these mechanisms occur during analysis, in relation to the analyst, they are taken to be repetitions of these early experiences. The interpretation of these repetitive devices is a large part of the business of psycho-analysis. The analyst needs to know a good many of these devices in order to practise his trade, but he sees no advantage in systematizing them, or closing the list. What to the academician is an irritating vagueness, a perilous fluidity of thought, is to the clinician a way of preserving flexibility, a guard against premature calcification.

We cannot expect to extract a schematic or symmetrical theory of dynamics from psycho-analysis. The fact that the defence mechanisms exclude from discussion all 'normal' reactions itself warns us against looking there for a complete or systematic theory. In accounts of the subject the the various mechanisms simply lie there side by side held together by an inglorious *undverbindung*. There is no general theory that tells one: under such and such circumstances there will be projection, under these there will be reaction-formation, and so on. No attempt has been made by analysts to formulate the mechanisms as psychodynamic laws, or to generalize about the occasions on which they occur. Which of them are alternatives to one another, which include others as special cases, which arise under such disparate circumstances that they are not comparable?

There are various ways in which we might set about ordering the field. Tolman[14] once suggested that the mechanisms could be reduced to three—repression, fixation, and displacement, or 'sign-magic'. There is indeed a large group of mechanisms that can be considered as varieties or special cases of displacement: projection is displacement from oneself on to another person; transference is displacement from the parents to the analyst, and so on. There is also a group of mechanisms that are not displacements, but are rather various forms of rejecting an unwelcome impulse. Repression was earlier used as a generic name for these, but later it was used as one of several, the others including isolation, undoing, denial, reversal and reaction-formation.

These observations suggest that a careful analysis and classification of the defence mechanisms in current use might enable us to 'rationalize' terminology (in the economist's sense). No doubt this is true, but it is essentially an academic criticism, an outsider's comment. The defence mechanisms in their pure form are not exactly the daily stuff of the analyst's thinking, but rather abstractions invented afterwards to describe and explain the conclusions he has reached. The analyst may think: 'My patient was offended by the interpretations I gave him yesterday, yet now he is being specially nice to me, expressing his concern that I may be feeling the cold weather; probably this concern marks a hidden hostility.' Or he may observe, 'Here the patient is ashamed and apprehensive about arriving five minutes late, exactly as if the analyst were a schoolmaster, or a stern father, and the patient a naughty child.' The analyst directly recognizes the meaning of the process he is observing, and notices that, while the patient's conduct is in some way strange or irrational, it can be made to appear ordinary and natural if a certain transposition is effected. The recognition of the defensive process is this transposition that the analyst has to make, and this constitutes his interpretation. He may if he wishes afterwards generalize these transpositions as reaction-formation and transference, but the names are not essential to his understanding of what has happened. The more intuitive kind of psychologist may interpret these transpositions many times before he ever thinks of giving a general name to the process. The object of his interpretations is to learn to recognize the patient's technique of dealing with situations which for some reason arouse anxiety in him. The well-known defence mechanisms are techniques by which people have dealt with these anxiety-arousing situations, but there is no fixed range of these, and probably there are many other common devices that remain to be interpreted. Humour is not usually listed as one of the mechanisms of defence, yet it often has this function. To know a person means to know what kinds of situations are most likely to arouse anxiety in him, and what techniques he has available for dealing with them. When we can see a few characteristic techniques of manipulating and placating other people used repeatedly from childhood into adult life, then we have discovered the element of continuity which gives meaning and unity to a personality.

Unity may sometimes lie more in the situation that the person has to resolve, than in the solution adopted. Anna Freud describes a girl who pestered everyone with her insatiable demands ('me-too'). At a later stage as a result of the anxiety aroused by criticism she surrendered all demands for herself, and became exceptionally unselfish; she projected her ambitions on to her men friends and her sexual desires on to her women friends, and tried to satisfy herself by identifying with them, and vicariously enjoying their successes. In terms of a trait psychology, her personality would have shown a meaningless discontinuity. Yet as a technique for dealing with certain inner stresses and external frustrations, this conduct may show a clear relation to what has gone before. A characteristic device for dealing with certain kinds of threat may serve as a clue to organize large regions of character. Such an organizing principle may be variously known as a defence mechanism

(Freud),[13] dynamism (Healy),[15] life goal (Adler),[16] character resistance (Reich),[17] neurotic trend (Horney),[18] mechanism of escape (Fromm),[19] unity thema (Murray).[20] Each of these writers has given a vivid description of certain patterns of organization.

The kind of psychological thinking that grew out of the theory of defence mechanisms led on to the description of various types of character. Adler described neurotic characters, Reich, La Forgue, Horney, Fromm, etc., have added others, and gradually a rich and varied portrait gallery has been built up. While there is no system, no complete enumeration or closed list of characters, a wide enough range of descriptions is now available to provide the psychologist with patterns of a great many of the people whom he is likely to meet. In the later developments of psycho-analysis, emphasis has shifted from the study of symptoms to the organization of personality as a whole. In Fenichel's[21] view, this corresponds to a real change in the patients whom the analyst studies. The neurotic symptoms commonly described fifty years ago were mostly 'ego-alien' intrusions into what appeared to be a normal personality. For instance, a facial paralysis of hysterical origin might suddenly appear in a person who was not particularly disturbed or upset in general; or a respectable and self-disciplined person might find himself expressing impulses (quite against his will) to shout out obscenities. The typical disorders of to-day (says Fenichel) are disorders of character. The symptoms are no longer bizarre and isolated, but are so woven into the personality that the patient accepts them as part of the self, and does not recognize them as symptoms. It is difficult to know just what to make of this. Are the changes due to the external world or to the methods and concepts of the analyst? Certainly some kinds of case that were known fifty years ago are unknown to-day. The multiple personalities described by Janet[22] and Morton Prince[23] have returned to single life, the grand hysterics of Charcot no longer pass through their predestined stages. One suspects that many elaborate symptom-structures were partly due to a desire in

K

patients to accommodate themselves to the expectations of a doctor for whom they felt a warm, if misguided, affection.

The fact that other types of personality structure are now commonly described may be because psychologists are now capable of recognizing them. Neurosis is no longer rare and strange, but is seen to be the general condition of mankind. Child-rearing is usually in some respects a difficult business, and the crises that children meet unsuccessfully turn up many years later in adult neurosis. The type of neurosis depends partly on the age when the child first meets his big trouble. It is possible that (as Halliday has suggested) changing patterns of neurosis are an indirect result of changing customs of child-rearing. During the Victorian age, in Britain and America, the child-rearing patterns of the first three years were rather easy-going. Children were commonly breast-fed on demand, and adults were not so fussy about cleanliness. The main trouble began later when the child was regarded as a responsible human being, capable of absorbing Father's views on God and duty. The commonest disorders would thus relate to the phallic or early genital phase. These disorders are built around the Oedipus situation, and their favourite mechanism is repression, giving rise to hysterical symptoms. In the twentieth century the emphasis has shifted. The Oedipus period is no longer so anxious. Fathers and other adults are less solemn with five-year-olds about duty and virtue, threats about masturbation are less common and less severe, so there is not the same degree of castration anxiety. The main anxieties now come earlier. Feeding by the clock and excessive cleanliness give rise to anal characters, whose characteristic disorder is the compulsion neurosis.

While the principal cause of change is due to changing social customs, we can recognize another and subtler cause, due to the improved technique of the psycho-analyst. New disorders are recognized as concepts become more adequate. A considerable shift of emphasis has occurred in the objectives of analysis. At first analysis was mainly concerned with uncovering instinctual forces that had been repressed.

The analyst's interpretations consisted in saying, 'of course this or that is really sexual', in getting the patient to recognize and accept the buried instincts, and to trace them back to childhood origins. It was in this phase of analysis that the emphasis on the psycho-sexual stages of development was greatest, and the location of libido in various erogenous zones formed a large part of the analysis. In its later developments analysis has been less concerned with the hidden instincts, and more with the devices by which they are hidden.

The analysis of defences is the interpretation of habitual devices which a patient uses for warding off anxiety. The analyst finds examples of these devices by showing how they occur in the course of the patient's relations with the analyst. A patient pays his bill early, a few days before it is due. He brings the money on the day after the analyst has made an interpretation that the patient considers particularly foolish. The analyst is able to convince him that the early (or over-generous) payment is a reaction-formation covering a protest against having to pay at all; this in turn is an allusion to the resentment that he feels about having to contribute to his mother's keep, although he says that he can never repay her for all she did for him when he was young. . . . Even the most trivial incidents are interpreted as specimens of pervasive tendencies. Character can show itself in any activity at all.

In a true-blue Freudian analysis we trace an illusion to childhood, and identify the stage of sexual development from which the original instinct came; we then trace the defences against the instinct, and link the defence to some repetitive pattern that has already been identified in the large affairs of the patient's life. Analysis is complete when every episode can be shown to contain some meaning, both of the main instinctive drives of childhood, and of the patient's typical character defences against them. Abraham and Reich, elaborating suggestions by Freud, described pattern characters resulting from fixations at various stages of psycho-sexual development. Fixations occur when some intense experience is repeated again and again, so that the child fails to develop into a fully adult person. In a paper of 1908 Freud[24] described certain traits of character that arise from fixation at the anal-sadistic level of development. The qualities of the 'anal character' are mostly reaction-formations against aggressions at the anal level—orderliness and conscientiousness, stinginess about money, and obstinacy, which under pressure may develop into rage and vindictiveness. The characteristic pattern of illness is the compulsion neurosis.

Following on suggestions by Abraham[25] about the oral character, a variety of patterns has been elaborated by anthropologists with a psycho-analytical background. Abraham described one type of oral-erotic character, who was easy-going, dependent, fond of sweets and of talk; but with increased knowledge it has become plain that many different characters are possible. Du Bois' Alorese[26] who are left behind when their mothers go to work, and consequently trust nobody, and do not believe in love; Gorer's Americans who are fed by the clock, and learn to expect love to be conditional on performance; Mead's Arapesh, who are long and affectionately breast-fed, and develop into trustful, untidy, easy-going adults—these are all varieties of 'oral character' in the sense that the adult traits seem to be based on crucial experiences of early feeding. In analytical descriptions, the characteristic disorder of oral fixation is depression. Those who control the daily life of depressed patients can easily find instances where mouth disorders of various kinds are noticeable, such as refusal to eat, silence, persistent sucking or biting, and fears about starvation. Other character patterns have even been related to the experiences of birth.

In the analytical methods developed by Adler and by Horney, the instinctual aspect of the conflict dwindles. The general term 'anxiety' is used to cover everything that the neurotic is afraid of, and all attention is focused on the patient's devices for dealing with this anxiety. The structure of personality is shown in the devices adopted for overcoming anxiety. In her first book Horney, while recognizing many possible defence mechanisms, described four possible ways in which a neurotic personality could be built around stereotyped defences against anxiety. The basic anxiety that all of them have to meet is loss of love, the child who does not get warm and genuine affection from his mother. One child may meet this fear by making every effort to please others and be loved; may strive for popularity, feel deeply uneasy if he is disliked, even by someone who is of no importance to him. He may feel an unlimited craving for love, make repeated demands for reassurance that he is really loved, combined with a jealous suspicion that this is really impossible. ('I'll love mother more and then she'll love me.')

An alternative response to the same situation is that of the moral masochist, the submissive man who will always turn the blame on himself; he is determined to be perfect, to see to it that he does nothing for which he could be blamed or criticized. He feels deeply apprehensive if he is five minutes late for an appointment. He is afraid of success, because it will bring on him the envy of competitors, so always draws back at the moment when success is near; wins the first four games of the set, loses the last six, and congratulates the winner with a friendly smile. ('It's naughty to be angry, or to grab things; mothers love good children.')

A third pattern is the child who meets the threat of loss of love by a determination to be strong and successful, rich or famous. He wants these things either as a condition of love ('if I am a success I shall be loved') or as a way of compelling love ('if I am strong I can make her love me') or as a substitute for love ('if I am tough then mother won't matter any more'). This is the true Adlerian character, endlessly competitive, who will run in the race only if he can be front horse.

Another solution to the anxiety aroused by loss of love is the technique of withdrawal and encasement ('if I can do without love, then I shall be free'). Such a person may

continually retreat from personal relations, feel anxious
about incurring any obligation, distrustful of being loved.
He may similarly be unwilling to settle in a safe and permanent job, and refuses to undertake a psycho-analysis unless
he can arrange beforehand the date when it will terminate.
In her original accounts of these personality patterns, Horney
saw the neurotic element in the rigidity, the undiscriminating
and unconditional quality. Wanting to be loved is not neurotic,
but it is so if one has to be loved all the time, and by everybody.
So too with compulsive need to be perfect, or to be front horse,
or to be free.

In later discussions she takes the view that the personality
is neurotic because two incompatible goals are sought at
the same time. Where Freud saw the central meaning of
neurotic suffering in the conflict between instinct and culture,
Horney sees it in the simultaneous use of incompatible
solutions. The person who wants to be loved, but at the same
time to incur no obligations, or wants to be powerful and also
to be good, is asking for things that cannot come together.
Horney sees these conflicts within personalities as a mirror of
contradictions within Western society as a whole. Her descriptions of neurotic personalities were markedly influenced by the
effects of the economic depression of the early 'thirties.

Table V—Psycho-Analytic Mechanisms

References to the following processes are scattered through
Freud's works. They were collected by Healy,[27] Bronner and
Bowers, who give the following list of what they call the
'established dynamisms of psycho-analysis'.

Displacement: this has two meanings: (a) A process by which
one idea may surrender to another the whole volume of its cathexis.
This process may often be a defence mechanism, in that the new
goal may be more acceptable to the ego. 'Displacement from
below upward' (as when anal and genital interests are replaced by
oral and visual ones) is an example. In this sense displacement is
used as equivalent to sublimation, as in Anna Freud. (b) A shift of

instinctual energy from one pathway to another, without any implication of a defensive purpose.

Transference: shifting of feelings of love from one person to another; nowadays mainly restricted to transference from parents to analyst, though the attitude transferred need not always be love. This is not usually defensive, and is not listed by Anna Freud as a defence mechanism.

Symbolization: in psycho-analysis this term is reserved for symbols whose meaning is unknown to the user and, in part, stereo-typed. It refers mainly to male and female sex organs, and to processes of birth, copulation and death.

Condensation: a process by which several distinct ideas are fused into one, as in a dream, where one dream-figure combines parts or aspects of several persons. This is not a defence, but a general characteristic of dream thinking.

Unconscious fantasy: fantasies are substitute gratifications; it is in the main a displacement of aim motivated by external frustration, rather than a defence against the instincts. Although mainly under the Pleasure Principle, they may include any of the other defence mechanisms.

Repression: the exclusion of painful and unpleasant material from consciousness and from motor expression. Repression was at one time a general term for all defences, but was later treated as one among several, though it may be supposed to enter into every defensive process in so far as it is unconscious.

Reaction-formation: the development of conscious socialized attitudes and interests which are the antithesis of certain infantile unsocialized trends. 'Anal' traits like orderliness and cleanliness are supposed to be reaction formations to desires for dirt and smearing; bashfulness may be a reaction against a desire to exhibit oneself; sympathy and vegetarianism a reaction against aggressive impulses. (First mentioned in *Three Contributions to the Theory of Sex.*)[28]

Projection: thrusting forth on the external world unconscious wishes and ideas which would be painful if accepted as part of the self. In this original sense projection is a defence mechanism, particularly typical of paranoia. Freud says that a paranoiac is an unconscious homosexual, whose thoughts go through the stages 'I love him', 'I hate him', 'he hates me'. (First mentioned in paper on anxiety neurosis 1894.)

Isolation: a process by which the memories of unpleasant experiences are deprived of their effect. (This appears to be identical with the concept of dissociation used by Janet and McDougall.) (First described in *Inhibition, Symptom and Anxiety*.)[30]

Undoing: an attempt through a symbolic act to abolish or will out of existence some past painful experience. (Commonly found in obsessive ceremonials.) (First described in *Inhibition, Symptom and Anxiety*.)

Conversion: the symbolic expression by means of physical manifestations (motor and sensory) of both repressed instinctual wishes and the defence set up against them. A paralysis of the arm can signify both an intended aggression and the defensive struggle against it.

Introjection: the assimilation or incorporation of another object or person into the self. (First mentioned in *Jealousy, Paranoia and Homosexuality*.) The term seems to be interchangeable with *identification*, though Healy, Bronner and Bowers attempt to make some distinction. This is not usually defensive in nature. (First mentioned in *Interpretation of Dreams*.)

Sublimation: the exchange of infantile sexual aims for interests or modes of pleasure-finding which are no longer directly sexual, and which are on a higher social level. Anna Freud and Fenichel use this as a general term for healthy or successful solutions to conflicts. (First used in *Three Contributions to Theory of Sex*.)

Rationalization: an unconscious manipulation of our opinions to evade the recognition of forbidden impulses. (First described by Ernest Jones.)[29]

Idealization: over-estimation of the love-object; displacement of primary narcissism on to an ego-ideal.

Dream work: the means by which latent dream thoughts are converted into the manifest dream. These are not so much defences as aspects of primary process. Dream work includes displacement, condensation, symbolization, dramatization and secondary elaboration.

First mentioned in *Interpretation of Dreams*. Healy, Bronner and Bowers regard their task as one of description and tabulation, and do not attempt to reorganize the data.

These authors discuss regression separately, and do not include it among the dynamisms, because it is a characteristic of libidinal activity. Freud describes it as a defence mechanism in *Inhibition, Symptom and Anxiety*,[30] along with four others, repression, isolation, undoing, reaction-formation.

Symonds[31] describes the mechanisms as 'defences against anxiety', and classifies them as follows:

1. *Repression* (blocking of discharge of an impulse). This includes among its expressions laziness, passivity, inactivity, social withdrawal, secretiveness, taboos and scruples, indecision.

2. *Escape or Flight* from Anxiety-Arousing Situations. This includes phobia, regression, flight to fantasy, play, curiosity, desire to collect objects, hyperactivity, flight to reality.

3. *Disguising the Source of Anxiety*. This includes displacement, introjection, projection, aggression against the feared object, rationalization, character defences such as narcissism (overcoming fear of not being loved by presenting to the world a picture of strength and confidence); masochism (humbling oneself in order to please others); perfectionism (trying to escape criticism by leaving no opening).

4. *Modifying Expression of Impulse*. This includes sublimation, reaction-formation, obsessional trends, laughter, compensation, symptom formations—disturbances of eating, elimination, speech and sleep, stereotyped acts.

5. *Testing Reality*. Trying to make a fantasy danger in order to see how dangerous it is.

6. *Paying a penalty*. This includes acts of self-injury and of restitution.

7. *Auto-erotism*.

Symonds admits that this classification is tentative, and allows for a good deal of overlapping. He makes no further use of it in the chapter headings of his book. It has the merit of comprehensiveness, but does not appear to be an entirely successful rearrangement of the material, which remains somewhat untidy.

Anna Freud[32] mentions ten established defence mechanisms: *regression, repression, reaction-formation, isolation, undoing, projection, introjection, turning against the self*, and *reversal*: all these are in some degree pathological. The tenth, which is not pathological, is spoken of as 'sublimation or displacement'.

The main differences from Healy's list are (*a*) turning against the self is added; (*b*) reversal is distinguished from reaction-formation and undoing, whereas Healy treats reversal as identical with reaction-formation. Further mechanisms described are denial in fantasy, denial in word and act, restriction of the ego, identification with the aggressor, and 'a form of altruism' (projection of one's wishes on to others). Several of those listed by Healy are not mentioned: transference, symbolization, condensation and dream work are evidently not considered as defences. It is not clear why rationalization and conversion are omitted.

Fenichel[33] distinguishes (*a*) successful defences, which bring about a cessation of that which is warded off, and (*b*) unsuccessful defences, which necessitate a repetition of the warding-off processes. Successful defences are collectively called sublimation, though Fenichel remarks that it does not designate a specific mechanism, but may include various devices, such as a change from passivity to activity, or a reversal of aim into its opposite. Pathogenic defences include: *denial, projection, introjection, repression, reaction-formation, undoing, isolation, regression.* (Rationalization and Idealization are discussed later in another section.) The above mechanisms of defence are described as defences against instinctual drives. Fenichel also described various defences against effects. These are for the most part the same as the first group. His queer and rather clumsy classification appears to be a compromise to include the earlier view that all defences are against the instincts, and the later view that they are against 'anxiety' in general.

REFERENCES

1. BINET, A.	*La Mesure en Psychologique Individvelle. Etude experimentale de l'Intelligence.*	Rev. Phil., 46, 113–123, 1898. Paris, 1903.
2. GESELL, A.	*The First Five Years of Life.*	New York, Harper, 1940.
3. PIAGET, J.	*The Language and Thought of the Child.*	New York, Harcourt Brace, 1926.
4. FREUD, S.	*A General Introduction to Psycho-analysis.*	New York Garden City Publishing Co., 1943.
5 and 13. FREUD, S.	*The Interpretation of Dreams.*	London, Allen & Unwin, 1942.
6. RANK, O.	*The Trauma of Birth.*	London, Harcourt Brace, 1929.
7. KLEIN, M.	*Psycho-analysis of Children.*	London, Hogarth Press, 1932.
8. ZEIGARNIK, B. AND LEWIN, K.	*Über das Behalten von erledigten und unerledigten Handlungen.*	Psychol. Forsch., 9, 1927.
9, 12 and 32. FREUD, ANNA.	*The Ego and the Mechanisms of Defence.*	London, Hogarth Press, 1937.
10. FREUD, S.	*An Outline of Psychoanalysis.*	London, Hogarth Press, 1949.
11. FREUD, S.	*Psycho-analytic Observations concerning an autobiographically described case of Paranoia.*	Jahrbuch fur Psychoanalyt. Forsch., Vol. III, 1911.
14. TOLMAN, E. C.	*Motivation, Learning and Adjustment.*	Proceedings of the American Philosophic Society, 84 (1941), 543–563.
15. HEALY, W.	*Personality in Formation and Action.*	London, Chapman and Hall, 1938.
16. ADLER, A.	*Understanding Human Nature.*	London, Allen and Unwin, 1932.

17. REICH, W. — *Character Analysis.* — New York, Orgone Institute Press, 1945.

18. HORNEY, K. — *Our Inner Conflicts.* — London, Kegan Paul, 1946.

19. FROMM, E. — *The Fear of Freedom.* — London, Kegan Paul, 1941.

20. MURRAY, H. A. — *Explorations in Personality.* — New York, Oxford Univ. Press, 1938.

21 and 33.
FENICHEL, O. — *The Psycho-analytic Theory of Neurosis.* — London, Kegan Paul, 1946.

22. JANET, P. — *L'Evolution Psychologique de la Personalite.* — Paris Editions A. Chahine, 1929.

23. PRINCE, MORTON — *The Dissociation of a Personality.* — London, 1906.

24. FREUD, S. — *Character and Anal Erotism,* 1908 (*Collected Papers, Vol. II*). — London, Hogarth Press, 1933.

25. ABRAHAM, K. — *Selected Papers.* — London, Hogarth Press, 1927.

26. DU BOIS, C. — *The People of Alor.* — Minneapolis, Univ. at Minnesota Press, 1944.

27. HEALY, W., BRONNER, A. AND BOWERS, A. M. — *Structure and Meaning of Psycho-analysis.* — New York, Knopf, 1930.

28. FREUD, S. — *Three Contributions to the Theory of Sex,* 1905. — From Basic Writings of Sigmund Freud, E. A. Brill, New York, Modern Library, 1938.

29. JONES, E. — *Papers on Psychoanalysis.* — 4th Ed., 1938. London, Baillière, Tindall.

30. FREUD, S. — *Inhibition, Symptom and Anxiety.* — London, Hogarth Press, 1936.

31. SYMONDS, P. M. — *Dynamics of Human Adjustment.* — New York, Appleton-Century, 1931.

CHAPTER VIII

PSYCHODYNAMICS

THE concept of defence mechanisms, developed in one direction, gives rise to descriptions of neurotic characters. Developed in another direction, it initiates the project of constructing a system of psychodynamics. Writers on psychodynamics are not primarily interested in personality. Some indeed would like to do away with the concept altogether and replace it with something more 'scientific'. They aspire to treat action, purpose and conduct in terms of genuinely abstract laws. The shortage of general laws in psychology has been a distressing thing to them. It must be emphasized that there are at present no psychological laws in most regions of behaviour, in spite of the immense efforts that have gone into formulating and testing them. This is not usually made obvious because psychologists do not like running down their subject. But it tends to emerge at meetings of parent-teacher associations, when someone gets up and asks: 'Will Johnny go on biting his nails if I beat him for it?' or 'Will my children stop quarrelling if I give them the same of everything?' The psychologist who is set up to answer questions has really only one answer—'that all depends'—followed by one or two illustrative anecdotes. The public expects the psychologist to possess general laws of a cause-and-effect kind. The way in which psychology has been boosted as a natural science has encouraged the public to suppose that such laws exist, where in fact they do not. Nor does the psychologist's difficulty depend merely upon the fact that the situation happens to to be a complex one. The behaviourist attempt to make laws in terms of habit and conditioning broke down mainly because of a misconception of the nature of a stimulus. It was supposed that the stimulus could be defined in terms of its physical and chemical properties, without bothering about how it appeared to the observer. The generally recognized failure of the habit psychology has encouraged psychologists to be receptive to other ideas.

The first steps in formulating psychodynamic laws have been taken by three groups of workers: by those who start from the defence mechanisms aspiring to tidy up the Freudian mess, and to have some neat experiments with unequivocal results: by behaviourists who want to enlarge the scope of learning theory to include conflict situations: and by Gestalt psychologists who want to extend their subject from the study of perception to that of conduct. These groups are, of course, likely to overlap, but they do indicate three considerable fields of psychological activity. Indeed, psychodynamics is absorbing most of the old rat psychology and for humans most of 'learning', 'memory', 'association', and 'expression of emotions' as they appeared in the earlier curricula. The learning experiment was a situation in which rats' behaviour could conveniently be classified into two kinds, which the experimenter called 'right' and 'wrong'. For instance, a variety of paths was provided through a maze, and at every corner one turning was 'right' and one was 'wrong' and it was hoped that the rat would confine itself to those two kinds of behaviour. In any event, no notice would be taken of anything else that the rat did, because in terms of the learning experiment all other aspects of his behaviour were ignored. If he stopped to comb his whiskers, or sat down and looked at the view, the experiment was considered unsuccessful and was re-designed. The American maze experiment (that typical product of pre-depression behaviourism) was made by an energetic purposeful people who believed in progress. They knew what was good for their rats, and liked to see them get on with it. The maze experiment was refined to the point where automatic records sufficed to classify turnings into 'right' and 'wrong', and it was not necessary to look at the rat at all. Of course there can be no science without abstraction, and to find any meaning in behaviour one must observe it from some definite point of view.

The defect of the maze experiment was that the aspects chosen for observation were only moderately instructive. Psychodynamics began when experimenters were willing to observe other aspects of behaviour than rightness and wrongness. Experimenters began to cheat in various ways—secretly alter paths in the maze, block them all up, administer unjustified shocks or air-blasts, frustrate well-established expectations, establish insoluble conflicts. They were also prepared to observe many aspects of behaviour instead of only one, to set up open situations in which many different lines of action were available to the subject, and to interpret anything that turned up. The effectiveness of this procedure depended on having adequate and fertile concepts about the meaning of behaviour. Two kinds of experimental design were commonly used. One was to set up some situation which was dubbed 'frustration' or 'conflict', or 'privation', and then classify the responses evoked. The other was to try to find the conditions that would evoke a particular mechanism, such as Repression or Projection.

If an abstract formulation is given to the concepts of psychoanalysis, they may be divided into the Genetic Propositions and the Dynamic Propositions. The Genetic Propositions are the stages of psycho-sexual development and theories of fixation and regression. The Dynamic Propositions are the defence mechanisms, which, as we have seen, can be classified into varieties of repression, and varieties of displacement. Psychodynamics has been a good deal concerned with attempts to get these into forms where they are available for experimental analysis. Quite a number of experiments have produced passable analogues of situations described in analytic work. Something reasonably resembling fixation and regression can occur in animals. A well-known experiment is that of Hunt,[1] who found that if rats are starved in the first few weeks of life, they will hoard food later on, whereas rats that have always been well fed are less likely to hoard food. This has a recognizable resemblance to the concept of 'oral fixation'. Similarly it has been possible to produce experimental analogues of some of the defence mechanisms.

Projection is a process that has proved somewhat more accessible to experiment and it has been possible to produce projections in a controlled situation. An example is the often quoted experiment of Sears: he took as his subjects a group of American students who lived in a fraternity house, and all knew one another well. They were asked to rate themselves and one another on three traits—neatness, stinginess and obstinacy. These traits were selected because they are supposed to be typical of the anal character, and in analytic theory paranoia and projection are supposed to be in some way connected with anal erotism. For each person three scores become available on each trait: a self-rating, an average rating given to others, and an average rating given to the self by others. Insight was measured by the amount of agreement between self-ratings and the average ratings given by others. Where insight was low, Sears found a slight tendency towards projection; i.e. those who rated themselves lower than others rated them, tended to rate others high.

There is room for a lot more experimentation of this kind, and it is likely to be more effective with people than with animals. Not much behaviour has been noticed in animals recognizably similar to the human defence mechanisms. And even with humans it is not easy to produce unconscious processes to order. Repression in particular has proved difficult to demonstrate in any clear-cut way. Many experiments that were supposed to show examples of repression have failed, or given indecisive results. Some of the experimenters seem to have been content with a rather dim notion of what repression is. It does not, incidentally, mean that unpleasant experiences are more readily forgotten than pleasant ones. Sears justly observed about these experiments that they are interesting but not usually decisive.

Rather in reproducing the conditions of special mechanisms, the experimenter may be better employed in trying to build a general psychodynamics. The defence mechanisms were specifically intended to describe unconscious mechanisms which were in some degree pathological. They were not intended to provide a complete description of the motivation of behaviour. Psychodynamics has to include all kinds of behaviour, 'normal' as well as 'abnormal'. Psycho-analysis, though broadened by a general theory of instincts and of mental structure, retains many traces of its origin as a psychopathology. Both Fenichel and Anna Freud, while treating the pathological defence mechanisms in considerable detail, lump together healthy reactions under the blanket term 'sublimation', and do not consider them further. In psycho-analytic descriptions various defence mechanisms are mentioned, without any supposition that they are exhaustive.

Psychodynamics will also have to diverge from the analytic treatment of the defence mechanisms by being a closed system. It must begin from a classification of the possibilities that is logically complete. An attempt of this kind is that of Rosenzweig,[2] who classified responses to frustration into three kinds —extrapunitive, intrapunitive and impunitive. Even if only moderately illuminating, this has the merit of being a closed system, in which any further classes introduced would be subdivisions of existing ones. A general psychodynamic theory would have to fit in all the defence mechanisms somewhere and also a good many other forms of behaviour that do not come anywhere into Freud's descriptions. The abstract treatment of psychodynamics is sometimes spoken of as a synthesis of psycho-analysis and learning theory, though it is not yet clear that such disparate systems can be effectively synthesized. Nor is it clear that 'learning' is the concept from general psychology around which we can most usefully organize our ideas about personality.

What prevents the Behaviourist from developing a theory of personality is mainly the demand for an objective stimulus.

L

Hull, the leading theorist of behaviourism, has repeatedly emphasized that psychology must have nothing to do with 'anthropomorphic subjectivism'. (An outsider might consider that a theory concerned with men's actions would rightly be anthropomorphic. This is, however, an elementary error.) If the stimulus is to receive objective treatment, then it must be considered to be the same for everybody who receives it, and the particular meaning that the stimulus has for the person will not be emphasized. The Behaviourist feels that he has made his bow to Gestalt contributions when he has acknowledged that the 'stimulus' is not an isolated physical process like a beam of light, and that one must consider the 'total situation' perceived in an organized way.

In addition to learning theory, there have been attempts to found a general psychodynamics on topological and vector concepts. Gestalt psychologists have been able to tackle new problems and initiate techniques in dynamic psychology which bear witness to the power of Gestalt concepts. The professional scientist tends to evaluate concepts operationally, in terms of their fertility in suggesting experimental designs, or therapeutic techniques; and from this point of view Gestalt psychology stands high. These workers do not (as Behaviourists often do) treat men as disguised rats. Life space has room for expectations, aspirations and other qualities that seem to Professor Hull dreadfully anthropomorphic. The level of aspiration experiment opened the way to the experimental analysis of the ego values, the needs for prestige and success, the easily wounded narcissism, that Adler's writings described so vividly. In this experiment a subject is given repeated trials in some simple task, such as typesetting; after each trial he is asked to estimate his next performance; and efforts are also made to find out whether he was pleased or otherwise with the previous trial. We can thus study whether the subject's performance tends to exceed his anticipation, or to fall short of it, how easily he is satisfied with what he has done, and how flexible his later judgments are under the influence of success and failure. Does he set himself difficult goals (like Robert Browning) or is he satisfied with an easily attained achievement?

An individual subject under the eye of an observer will readily turn an experiment like this into a symbol of his own success and failure, and thus reveal significant aspects of his personality. The situation can be complicated in various ways by arranging the trials to produce success or failure, or by introducing a commentator. Most of Lewin's experiments, of which this is one example, provide open situations in which a variety of responses is available; often too a situation is repeated, so that progressive or regressive trends are available. In his Principle of Contemporaneity Lewin[3] stressed the fact that the experimentalist studies the present action of forces at the moment of the experiment, and is not primarily concerned with their history. In its application to human situations, this has resulted in a sharpened awareness of personal relations in momentary processes. It has coincided with a similar trend in the technique of psycho-analysis, whereby transference (in the broader sense) becomes the main theme of the analysis. The analyst is not so much concerned with a step-by-step reconstruction of the patient's past, as with a demonstration of the social techniques exemplified in the course of his relations with the patient.

Thus it is not easy to say how much is due to developments within psycho-analysis, and how much to Gestalt influences. The Gestalt influence is noticeable in the study of a variety of situations, ranging from the rigid arrangements of an orthodox learning experiment to the fluid processes of a leaderless group. (These techniques will be further discussed in Chap. X.) A distinctive feature of Gestalt concepts is the attempt to describe the subject's relation to the field in which he is acting. In ordinary speech we distinguish firmly between a person and the things round about him. But if we consider a person as a physical and chemical process, we know that it can exist only as a continuous interaction, in which the boundaries are fluid and shifting. Angyal[4] has pointed out the impossibility of defining physical boundaries for a person. The air in his nose or lungs, in-digested food in the stomach, urine in the bladder, a loose tooth—which of these is part of the person? The person exists only by virtue of a constant material interchange with the environment. So too in terms of the 'life-space'. The life-space is those parts or aspects of the environment to which the subject responds. A page of print is quite a different stimulus to one who can read and to another who cannot. Angyal has suggested that what distinguishes psychology from physiology is the symbolic aspects of stimuli. As long as we are dealing with a stimulus in terms of its physical and chemical properties, that is physiology. When the stimulus is considered as a symbol, we are in the realm of psychology.

Social psychology is concerned with defining the frames of reference within which facts are perceived, when such a frame of reference is shared by a group. In the study of personality we have to consider peculiarities of the individual life-space de-veloped from the circumstances of personal history. Although a person shares frameworks with others belonging to his commun-ity, each individual in some respects carries around his own life-space. Having insight into a person means getting inside his life-space, perceiving the world in his terms. What is import-ant or unimportant, what is friendly or hostile must be for that moment the same for both persons. Realizing the importance of spatial thinking, Lewin tried to systematize ideas of the life-space by applying topological concepts. Knowing that much of the measurement carried out in psychological ex-periments was meaningless, and amounted to little more than window-dressing, he hit upon the ingenious idea of using a non-metrical geometry for the representation of life-space. The idea is an attractive one, because it enables one to use some of the spatial thinking that is so important and universal, without falling into logical absurdities, like asking whether the three angles of an emotional triangle are equal to two right angles. He was able to use genuine topological concepts to represent certain relations. The basic relation for topology is that of being inside or outside a region; and this is obviously a metaphor of great importance for our thinking. In childish imagery the process of birth is mainly a topological change, from being inside to being outside. Another basic image is built around feeding at the breast. Oral incorporation is the prototype of the mechanism of introjection or identification, taking another person into oneself. The anal imagery of retention and ejection can also be described in topological terms, as Alexander has shown.

The idea that two regions are connected or disconnected is a natural and convenient metaphor for describing such processes as McDougall's mechanism of dissociation, or Freud's isolation. Janet long ago used it in a rather literal way to describe some of the supposed phenomena of multiple personality. Much of our spatial imagery, however, cannot be described in purely topological terms. It requires something more like a projective geometry, in which directions, or vectors, are important. Horney has made effective use of these concepts when she classifies social relations as going towards people (demands for affection), going against people (aggression) and going away from people (withdrawal). Our inner conflicts are represented as occurring between these alternatives. It is true that the difference between going towards a person and going against a person cannot be expressed purely in vector terms, nevertheless the spatial imagery is important.

Other concepts suggested by Lewin involve quasi-metrical notions, like the thickness of boundaries between regions or the restricted space of free movement; and mechanical notions like the fluidity of a situation, elasticity, plasticity, and permeability. The fluidity of a medium is the ease with which locomotion through the medium is possible. It is possible to apply the metaphor to a social group where relations may be 'stiff' or 'free and easy', i.e. more fluid.

Similarly, we may suppose that a society is more easily changed, as in pioneer America, and more rigid in a caste society where a person's status is mainly determined by his birth. The same concept can be applied to the structure of an individual personality. A rigid person would be one who tended to remain the same in spite of a great change in his circumstances. Different regions of the life-space have different degrees of fluidity. Those parts of the life-space that are considered 'real' are more rigid than those that are under the control of fantasy and wish-fulfilment processes. The elasticity of a region is its tendency to return to its original state after having been changed. The concept could be applied, for instance, to the conduct of released prisoners of war. Those who have a high degree of elasticity are not permanently affected by their imprisonment, and are easily able to abandon their 'barbed-wire mentality'. Others who have a low degree of elasticity show prolonged after-effects, are deeply suspicious of anything that emanates from authority (however well-intentioned), and inclined to self-pity, passivity, and obstructive tactics. They continue for a long time to show the deformity initiated by imprisonment. We can also assess the elasticity of a whole society, for instance, its ability to recover after foreign conquest or exile. Lewin's concept of elasticity resembles in some respects the older idea of preservation, but is applied to a much wider range of circumstances.

A notable feature of the later development of Gestalt thinking is the boldness with which transition is made from group to individual, and back again. This is a thoroughly 'psychological' psychology, in which there is no attempt to translate psychological descriptions into physiological terms. There is, of course, no desire to establish an autonomous realm of mind in which a transcendental ego could disport itself freely, liberated from the humiliations of the body (that poor relation). Gestalt thinking was not an attempt to find a vitalist loophole for religion. It is rather, like psycho-analysis, an attempt to take psychology seriously. Lewin always insisted that his geometrical descriptions were not metaphors, and must be taken quite literally. This was a valid reply to naïve critics who supposed that physical space is somehow 'out there', but that life-space is 'in your head' and therefore 'not real'. A sophisticated understanding of modern geometry enables one to understand that any space is 'real' in which a suitable system of relations is consistently maintained.

The question is rather whether the relations found within a life-space reveal the consistency and systematic unity that enable topological or other geometrical concepts to be effectively applied to them. The answer is not yet clear. It is hard to say whether Lewinian topology should be viewed as a *tour de force* or as a *jeu d'esprit*. There is no doubt that Lewin's theory has inspired much of the most effective work in social psychology of the last decade. The achievements of the W.O.S.B. (War Office Selection Board) group in Britain and the O.S.S. workers in America are attributed largely to his stimulus. But in their published work Lewin's geometrical concepts are used only sporadically (as in the attempt described by Harris[5] to devise a 'topological' obstacle race). They turn up more as metaphors to which an occasional appeal is made than as organizing ideas. Nor is it clear that images drawn from mechanics are susceptible of any more systematic development. Every psychologist trying to describe states of anxiety, emotion or conflict makes use of the concept of *tension*; and it is not difficult to show that anxieties may be expressed by an actual increase of muscular tension (measurable, if you like, in foot-pounds). Yet the concept of tension, as currently used, is no more than a term that is used all over the place, and it has no single consistent and identifiable meaning.

If we are going to use geometrical analogies to organize our psychological ideas, we should begin from the image of the body and its spatial relations. We want to construct an ego-centric space, in which the relations inside and outside, up and down, towards and away from, are primarily important, and the body is the centre of reference. The lifespace can be developed outwards from the body, and in relation to its axis, as the Ptolemaic universe was developed in relation to a man standing.

REFERENCES

1. HUNT, J. McV.   *The Effects of Infant Feeding - frustration upon adult hoarding behaviour.*   J. Abnorm. Soc. Psychol, 36, 338–360, 1941.

2. ROSENZWEIG, S.   *An Outline of Frustration Theory.* Ch. XI in Personality and Behaviour Disorders; Ed. J. McV. Hunt.   New York, Ronald Press, 1944.

3. LEWIN, K.   *Principles of Topological Psychology.*   New York, McGraw-Hill, 1936.

4. ANGYAL, A.   *Foundations for a Science of Personality.*   New York, Commonwealth Fund, 1941.

5. HARRIS, H.   *The Group Approach to Leadership Testing.*   London, Routledge and Kegan Paul, 1949.

CHAPTER IX

PROJECTIVE METHODS

THEORIES and techniques usually grow up together. If questionnaires and rating scales are the appropriate techniques of a trait psychology, projective methods are appropriate to a theory that emphasizes a fluid interchange of self and environment. The term 'projective test' or 'projective technique' (due to L. K. Frank) is a general description of certain indirect approaches to the study of personality. The intention is to get the subject to give an appreciation of his own qualities without his being aware that he is doing this, or at any rate without being aware of how much and in what respects, he is doing it. When we say that a person is projecting himself into a story, we mean that he is thinking of the story as if it refers (in some degree) to himself. One way of doing this is to suppose (or imagine) that one of the characters in the story is oneself, so that what happens in the story is, in a pale sort of way, happening to oneself. If a boy is excited when reading *Treasure Island*, that is because he imagines that he is really doing the things that Jim Hawkins is said to do. In this case we can say that he has identified himself with Jim Hawkins, or that he has projected himself into the story. There are, however, many instances of projection in which no specific identification is involved.

In Murray's experiment, children were shown pictures of sinister faces before and after a game of 'murder', and asked to rate them for malice. The faces looked more malicious when the children were frightened. We can say that the children had projected their fear into the picture, even though there is no clear character with whom they are identifying. Identification is thus one variety or sub-class of projections. Freud originally used the term projection to describe a defence mechanism by which unacceptable ideas about the self are pushed out on to the external world. The somatic prototype is spitting out something that tastes bad.

In the present context projection is used in a wider sense, to include any quality of the self that is attributed to the external world, or, even more generally, any way in which some individual or private mode of perception is revealed. It is only in this latter vague sense that a test like the Rorschach can be considered projective. Common to all projective techniques is the use of stimulus material that is in some respect unstructured or ambiguous. There is a contrast with the intelligence test, in which, as far as possible, each problem has a single definite answer. In a projective test every question has more than one possible answer, and the answer chosen is expected to express something distinctive about the person who answers. The value of a projective test depends partly on the extent to which it admits of and encourages individualized responses, and partly on the rules of interpretation. It is only after such rules are established that the test has any meaning at all. It is not difficult to think of activities that may have some projective significance, and it is a favourite activity of the brighter honours students in their final year to fiddle about with a new projective test. The difficulty of the task lies in the establishment of secure rules of interpretation, and in validating them.

An immense amount of patient and accurate work has to be done before a projective test is transformed from something interesting and suggestive to a reasonably objective and valid tool. Many people who have published bright ideas have not followed them up with the necessary spade work; and others have evidently been unwilling to subject their butterfly notions to the anvil of validation. Only a few tests, such as Word Association, Rorschach[1] and Thematic Apperception Test[3] have been extensively explored. Even with these, procedures of validation have been rudimentary.

It is not worth while to try operating with a strict definition of projective testing. Free painting, finger painting, and play therapy can all be considered varieties of the method. Any situation in which the perception or handling shows some expressive individuality in the user may be used as the basis of a projective test. The methods in current use vary in two directions—the stimulus may be more or less structured, and the response may be simpler or more elaborate. The less structured the stimulus, the greater the scope for self-expression. A Rorschach ink-blot or a Stern[2] cloud-picture is less structured than a Murray[3] picture. With a Rorschach blot far more alternative interpretations are possible, and the subject is only to a small extent controlled by external reality. Schwartz's[4] pioneer project, the Social Situations Pictures Test (designed for the study of delinquency) showed his subjects a variety of situations relating to delinquency, carefully drawn to eliminate any possibility of misunderstanding. On the bank of the river where the truant is sitting, there is a sign saying NO FISHING, and the good people's road is marked TO CHURCH. There is very little room for individual interpretation of the picture. In Koffka's[5] words, the external forces of organization are so strong that there is little room for the internal forces of organization to reveal themselves. When Schwartz made his test it was not generally recognized that ambiguity is an asset, and not a liability. A picture that left no room for misunderstanding would also leave no room for self-expression.

We cannot assume, however, that increased vagueness is always or unconditionally an advantage. An increased variety of response is helpful to the psychologist only in so far as it can be interpreted. It may happen that by increasing the vagueness of the stimulus we have increased the range of available responses without adding anything to the inferences that can be drawn about the subject. In any projective test there is a good deal of 'dead wood', variations that may possibly be significant, but cannot be utilized with existing techniques. In a test like Jung's word association, where there is a great variety of possible responses, only a tiny fraction of the variability is interpreted. Especially in the early days of this kind of testing, one was impressed with the contrast between the rich variety of responses, and the miserably poor conclusions drawn. It was often plain that testers did not know what to do with the results they had collected. A picture providing a narrower range of alternatives might prove to be more fruitful in interpretation. Thus the first T.A.T. picture (the boy with the violin) for which there are only three or four common stories, is easier to interpret than the eleventh, for which the interpretations are more various. This is a romantic landscape, dimly drawn; some have stressed the great cliffs, others have supposed ruined castles above them; sometimes the pterodactyl or the bull is the main figure, sometimes a minute human being in flight. In others the story is treated symbolically, suggesting the disasters of war, or is taken to be a painting or a dream.

The first direction in which projective tests can be classified is thus the vagueness or definiteness of the stimulus. The other direction is the simplicity or complexity of the response. The simplest kind of response is choosing among a fixed set of alternatives. A multiple choice Rorschach has been constructed, similar in design to items of many Intelligence tests. The subject merely has to indicate which of various responses seems 'most appropriate'. Other simple responses are found in the Word Association test, where the subject has to name the first word that comes into his head; or the Szondi,[6] where he has to state preferences among portraits; or the Rorschach, where he has to name the objects suggested to him by the ink-blots. At the other extreme are complex responses like the protocols of the Thematic Apperception Test, in which the subject composes a five-minute story, or Homburger's Dramatic Scenes,[7] in which the subject is required to arrange a complex scene with toys and model furniture, or free paintings in which elaborate compositions may be prepared. As the content is reduced, the responses become emptier and more scorable.

As they gain in meaning and richness, they become less easy to score, less readily classifiable. Kent and Rosanoff built up a scoring system for their Word Association test, by counting the frequency of the various responses given by a thousand subjects. For the crude statistics that were acceptable thirty years ago, this was considered an adequate method of scoring. By comparing the responses of a subject with this standard list, it was possible to determine how many common or popular words were used by the subject.

In the America of that time, being normal or ordinary meant the same as being healthy, and neuroticism was measured by the tendency to produce individual responses. Pressey's[8] cross-out test was scored in a similar way. A sufficiently impoverished system of responses could thus be susceptible of exact scoring. The ink-blot test as used by Rorschach was rather too elaborate to be exactly scored, and still further notations have been added by Beck,[9] Klopfer[10] and others. Rorschach workers have never been willing to publish norms in the ordinary American sense; but they do indicate certain responses as popular, and others as original; and Rapaport[11] has used this method to distinguish normals and psychotics, in the same sort of way as Kent and Rosanoff[12] did. Rorschach reports have always hovered uneasily on the border of quantitative methods. They publish what they call scores, but refuse to attach to them any clear-cut significance. When responses become more complex than those of a Rorschach test, scoring becomes altogether out of the question except in some rather trivial sense, like counting the number of words in T.A.T. stories. As responses become richer in content, so interpretations become less objective. We cannot say that one method is in principle better than the other. Fortunately it is not necessary to choose between them. Projective tests are not very difficult or laborious to apply and we can use both kinds if we want to. Often they supplement one another usefully. The main thing is to see that we get the best out of the material obtained. There is no urgent need at present for new varieties of projective test. What we really want is better ways of understanding the rich material that we can now collect.

L. K. Frank[13] has described projective methods in terms of the kind of response that is required from the subject, and the tester's purpose in asking for it. He speaks of five kinds of methods. Constitutive methods are those in which the subject is required to impose some structure or organization on unstructured material. The Rorschach test is a well-known example of this kind. The subject is shown an ink-blot, and asked 'what could this be?' Since it has no clearly stated meaning of its own, the meaning is constituted by the subject's choice. Constructive methods require the subject to arrange material into larger configurations. For example, Lowenfeld's[14] mosaics test requires the subject to arrange pieces of various colours and shapes into patterns. Interpretive methods elicit from the subject an interpretation of some composition. For example, in Morgan and Murray's Thematic Apperception Test,[15] a picture is shown to the subject, who is required to make up an exciting story about the scene depicted. He does twenty stories altogether, usually about ten in an hour on each of two test days. Usually the story is spoken, and the tester copies it down. The pictures in Murray's series give some indications of a story, but are not definite enough to yield one single story which is *the* correct answer. Several quite different interpretations are equally plausible, and the choice between them gives some indications about the storyteller. Frank also speaks of cathartic methods of projective testing. These not only reveal subjective processes, but also encourage affective release. Much of children's play therapy has this dual purpose, working off emotions as well as expressing them. Throwing stones at dolls may provide the needed object for permitted aggression, in addition to revealing to the therapist the source of anxiety. Frank's last class are the refractive methods, in which the way of using material throws light on the user. This vague description could really apply to any of the projective methods, but is intended to apply particularly to detailed analyses of peculiarities of style in habitual activities, like handwriting or speech. This has elsewhere been called the study of expressive movement.

This classification is only moderately satisfactory. The compartments are not wholly watertight; some are concerned mainly with what the subject has to do (for instance, the contrast between constitutive and constructive methods); others are concerned mainly with the kind of meaning that will be applied by the psychologist to the subject's material. Nevertheless, his description is useful in reminding us that there is some common thread running through this great variety of methods.

Any projective test approaches its subject obliquely. Psychologists have become deeply discouraged about the truth-value of the answers they usually get to their questions. Gone are the days when one expected to be able to take answers at their face value. During the 'twenties the American public was ruthlessly battered with inquisitive forms, psychological, sociological and educational. Do you ever listen to your parents quarrelling? Do you get fits? Have you given up wetting your bed? (It is not surprising that psychologists are accustomed to speak of a *battery* of tests.) The American public defended itself by gross deception. Partly the answers to questionnaires were simply lies; and partly they were honestly intended, but gave a false result because of repression or other defence mechanisms. Anyhow, it gradually came to be realized that a frontal attack on problems of personality by means of questionnaires and rating scales was not likely to produce results of lasting value.

A self-rating scale is not even the roughest approximation to a true picture of the person. It is a picture of how one person (the subject) intends to appear to another (the experimenter). We cannot properly assume that he would give the same answers to another experimenter, or that any of his answers would be true. In rather superficial relations, such as attitude and interest scales, and public opinion polls, there might be a rough approximation of truth, but as soon as one began to touch on values that were central to the personality, the direct approach was useless. Projective techniques were devices that grew out of disillusionment with questionnaires. If people will not answer truthfully when put on their guard, let us try to catch them *en deshabille*.

In a projective test we do not question a subject directly about himself. Rather we ask him to do something quite different, and hope that in doing it he will unwittingly reveal something of himself. What he reveals in this way is more likely to be true than what is directly reported. The less obvious the relation between the manifest and the latent meaning, the better the chance that the subject would be off his guard, and would reveal aspects of himself that he had not intended. An attractive aspect of a test like the Rorschach is that it would be impossible for the uninitiated to guess how the results are interpreted. It was not merely, however, that psychologists were trying to protect themselves against deliberate deception. It also came to be realized that people, even when trying to be honest, have very little effective knowledge about themselves, and cannot be trusted even on simple matters. A test that can tell us no more than a man knows about himself is a poor thing.

Any projective material can be interpreted from two points of view, which have been called form and content, but would perhaps be better spoken of as process analysis and projective analysis. The point can best be understood through an example. In the fourth picture of Murray's T.A.T. series, a man is standing tensely, staring in front of him, and a woman is looking at him. On the wall at the back there is a picture of a woman only slightly dressed. One storyteller says: 'This man cannot make up his mind what to do. He doesn't know which girl to marry—the one who will look after his home, or the one who will take him to artist parties.' Another storyteller says: 'This may be a picture about a missionary, and the man is angry because the chief won't let him come into the tribe. . . .

No, perhaps the girl has been captured by cannibals and he is coming to rescue her. . . . Can you tell me if there is another girl at the back, or is it just a pin-up?'

In both stories there is indecision, but in different ways. In the first the uncertainty is projected on to the hero; we are analysing the projected content of the story. In the second the indecision is in the process of story telling, and never reaches the stage of projection. In interpreting form, we are treating the subject's productions, not as projections of his own experience, but as expressive or symbolic acts. This helps to show us the meaning of the projective process. The act of projection is often an attempt to master some difficulty, to arrive at a meaning or interpretation for one's own behaviour, to look at oneself from the outside. Murray's interpretations of T.A.T. are mainly concerned with projected content. The first task he sets himself is the recognition of the hero. The hero is the character in the story with whom the storyteller has identified. One then goes on to use facts about the hero as evidence for corresponding facts about the storyteller. It is often easy enough to see that an identification is being made just as one is accustomed to look for the hero of a novel.

The hero usually comes at the beginning of the story; events are described from his point of view, in terms of his thoughts and feelings about them; the outcome affects him closely; the story is felt to be completed when something decisive has happened to the hero. The difficult task is not to see that an identification is being made, but to decide on its precise meaning. An identification is usually not complete. In the interpretation of a T.A.T. picture, part of what is said comes from the picture, and part from the storyteller. In response to the first T.A.T. picture, a subject produced the following: 'This child has been learning this piece here, been trying, going over it several times, can't manage to fathom it out, just sitting there, wondering what to do next about it; been given it to learn for the next lesson, can't learn it. I should think he would try it again; if he had been given it to learn, he would

M

make an effort—to show that he had tried.' The facts that the hero is a boy, and that his task concerns music, come from the picture, and do not tell us anything about the storyteller. They are part of the 'external forces of organization'. But there is much besides that is an identification of the figure in the picture with the storyteller, and a projection of her situation as she perceived it. We notice the discouragement and passivity, listless submission, willingness to try again half-heartedly without expectation of success. It is taken for granted that the pattern of the situation is imposed by others, that there is little room for one's own initiative. The description of the hero does in fact closely reflect the life history of the storyteller. She had just failed an important examination, and was wondering whether she could summon up the resolution to sit again. This is an identification with 'me as I am' and, in some degree, 'as I was'. The storyteller, who is in reality twenty-one years old, is extending the submissiveness of the past into the present. She readily accepts the role of a helpless child who has no alternative but to obey. At other times the identification may not be a literal, factual one, but a wish-fulfilment, concerning 'me as I should like to be'. Here is an example of such a fantasy, by a schoolmaster of twenty-four years (unmarried, and living with his parents).

'This boy has a violin and is sitting thinking what makes sound and how he would like to play the instrument. He would like to have one himself. When he is grown up one day he would like to have crowds at his feet listening to him. Hopes to be an important man.'

This begins as a realistic identification, and develops into a wish-fulfilment fantasy, in which the reality-check lapses. We notice how he alters the story as he goes along. At the beginning the violin is his, but a little bit later he would like to have one for himself. As he slides into the identification he remembers that there are a lot of things he would like to have, of which he feels deprived (such as a home or a wife of his own perhaps). 'Play the instrument' may also contain a hidden metaphor for sexual powers, the great exhibitionist gesture, with the crowds at his feet. So the fantasy drifts along, and the original dull reality is forgotten. The identification is with 'myself as I should like to be'. On occasions the identification figure may be 'myself as I fear that I may become'. Here is a story about T.A.T. picture No. 13 (a woman with exposed breasts is lying on the bed, and a man standing with face concealed in his arm). 'This is another sad story. The man and the woman were in the bedroom. They had a quarrel. The man was very quick-tempered and we can see that he has just murdered her. He looks very distressed and we can see that he has evidently just realized what he has done. He went and reported himself to the police.' This story is by the same man who made the previous one. It expresses the fear of the strength of the instincts, both sexual and aggressive, which is the expected counterpart of the earlier wish-fulfilment fantasy. There are various other minor variations of the relation between the self and the identification—figure, and the precise definition of the meaning of this relation is of the greatest importance for interpreting the story. The meaning of the story (from the point of view of projected content) can be summed up in a wish, moral, maxim or warning which expresses the inner purpose of telling the story. Most stories, of course, are ambivalent, and could be expressed by various conflicting maxims. The last one could be interpreted as: 'I am a fierce sort of fellow; people must be careful of me' (a wish-fulfilment fantasy); or as: 'I am not very impressive to most people, but there are hidden fires' (a compensatory gesture); or 'My instincts are dangerous' (a warning to aid restraint); or 'I can obtain for-giveness through suffering' (a reparation fantasy). Perhaps all these strands are really present, though the context would enable one to decide which was the most prominent line of thought.

There is no fixed way of analysing a T.A.T., no set of signs or symptoms that have a constant, invariable meaning. All that can be said beforehand is that we expect to find the story-teller projecting himself and his situation into the stories, and

we usually start our interpretations by noting his identifications. But there is no one set of psychological categories in
terms of which the stories have to be evaluated. Murray and
his co-workers at the Harvard psychological clinic were the
people who developed the test, and since they also developed
an elaborate system of basic variables for describing personality
many people thus tend to think of the T.A.T. in connection
with the Murray variables, but there is no intrinsic connection;
and other systems for describing the basic variables of personality, such as those of Tomkins[16] and of Henry,[17] can be
satisfactorily used with T.A.T. material.

Content analysis is applied not merely to the hero, but also
to other characters in the story, and to the recurrent circumstances and situations of the stories. Tomkins has shown
admirably the possibilities of this kind of analysis. He lays
little stress on identification, and much on the selection of
situations, and the comparison between stories. He takes a
few broad regions of experience—the family, love, sex and
marriage, work and crime, and shows that it is easy to assess
in a rather objective way the weight given to each of these
regions in a series of stories. For instance, if eight stories deal
with work situations where people are considered as striving
and failing, rather than as sinning or loving, then we may
consider this region of experience to be of great importance
for the storyteller. In most circumstances the relative importance of a region is very well indicated by the choice of subjects for stories. Tomkins concerns himself less with the
identification than with the storyteller's judgment. For
instance, Picture 8 BM depicts a group of men in overalls
lying in the ground. One story about them says: 'These men
are a lot of loafers who should be sent to work.' Another story
says: 'These men have had a hard morning's work, and are now
enjoying a well-earned lunch-time rest. They will soon be
back on the job again.' Although their interpretations are
quite different, both stories emphasize the moral importance
of work, and suggest that the storyteller would be uneasy

under enforced leisure, and incapable of enjoying it. Tomkin's method emphasizes the moral, or judgment that the subject makes about the situation, rather than the allusions to actual experience. He does not attempt to define the precise identifications that have been made, but rather the meaning of situations for the storyteller.

This is a modified application to waking fantasy of Freud's principle that a dream is a wish-fulfilment. When Freud wrote the *Interpretation of Dreams*, he was occupied with the contrast of nature and convention. The unconscious was the real person, the conscious person was artificial and somehow unreal. So the *real* meaning of the dream was the wish, and the defences against the wish were considered something secondary, and of lesser importance. In his later writing Freud considered convention to be of equal importance with nature, the defence against instinct to be as real and important as the instinct. So if he had cared to reformulate his dream theory, he might have said (as Rivers did) that a dream is a conflict, or that it is a judgment on a situation, in which a balance of forces is represented.

Such evidence about attitudes or judgments is the kind of information that we can expect to get from a test like the T.A.T. We should not expect it to supply a lot of factual information about the storyteller. To try and guess from T.A.T. protocols how many children the storyteller has, and whether he has ever been to Hong Kong, can be an amusing pastime, but not an economical use of one's resources. The most fruitful use of projective analysis is the interpretation of attitudes. The same analysis can be applied to certain other kinds of projective material, such as play interviews with young children, free paintings, and verbalized reveries to music. Any situation will do in which fantasy is projected on to some material, and communicated to an observer. Analysis is made easier if the subject's choice of material is restricted, and a standard set is developed. Lowenfeld's[18] World Game is one such semi-standardized play situation. Each child is given a sand tray and a set of toys, and asked to make a 'world'. There are human figures (adults and children) animals, and inanimate objects, such as trees, motor-cars, small houses and fences. There is an element of constancy or identity in the standard set of materials, which is the same for every child; and an element of variation or individuality in the use which the child makes of it, which is always unique. Play is interpreted on the assumption that the child projects its own experience and problems on to its use of the play materials. While Lowenfeld's World Game has been widely imitated, most Child Guidance Clinics with research interests have developed their own variants. Standardization is not carried to the length of attempting to formulate scores or norms, like an intelligence test. The field-worker is too distrustful of finality to be satisfied with a score instead of a living person. He is not convinced that an adequate set of fundamental variables has been formulated, capable of dealing with every situation that arises. Thus he is unwilling to abandon the freedom of his receptivity. Once a fixed scheme of analysis has been adopted, the observer tends to become blind to anything that does not fit in.

Children show a marked tendency to represent in their play the kind of situation that appears to them as a problem or an anxiety. Patricia, eight years old, lied and showed off a lot, and was keen on dressing up in fine clothes. When she came into the play-room at the Children's Centre, she chose a toy snake immediately and described it as a bead necklace. Directed questioning revealed her wish to be a boy, for which she compensated by demands for finery. Choosing a snake, and then using it as a necklace, was a way of getting the best of both worlds. Children do not, however, always directly represent their anxieties in play. Denials and omissions may be equally expressive. Noelle, aged six years, referred to the Centre for night-fears, repeatedly played a game with dolls which tended to develop into a theme of sleep and bed-time. But each time this point was reached the actual night was omitted, and play began again at breakfast time. The source of anxiety is represented by a gap in the story. Another variety of denial was shown by Ian, who began the interview by taking out the gun, tank and aeroplanes; then hurriedly replaced them and spent the rest of the interview playing in a bored way with the blocks. He had been referred to the Centre for aggressive behaviour, sullenness and fears. The sequence of the play expressed the thought that anger is too dangerous, and cannot safely be released.

In one way or another children manage to project a great many of their important attitudes into their play. They can express wishes, fears and defences more readily through symbolic play than through verbal abstractions. The practice in our Children's Centre is to use a play interview with standard materials with children up to the age of nine or ten years, and for older children, whose play has ceased to be expressive, to use free painting or T.A.T.

The varieties of interpretation that we have been describing so far have been primarily concerned with projected content. It is also possible to apply interpretation to the actual process, without applying notions of projection. In the interpretation of the Rorschach Test, for instance, very little use is made of the mechanism of projection. Rather the psychologist takes the subject's behaviour in the test situation as a sample of his method of dealing with a variety of situations. It is the act of responding, and not the projected meaning of the response, that is interpreted. The subject is shown an ink-blot (there are ten in all) and asked to say 'what this could be'. He is given no guidance about the best way to set about the task, so that there is room for a good deal of variation. If he gives a response he is asked if there is 'anything else', and encouraged to go on until there is nothing to add, but he is not told whether he is doing well or badly, nor is he told about other people's answers. It is the sort of situation for which custom and good manners are no preparation.

Rorschach did not use the responses in the way that we should use a T.A.T.—worrying one's way into the subject's identifications and projections. He was interested in the subject's responses only in certain abstract ways, and to emphasize this made use of conventional abbreviations for the classes to which he allocated responses. Each response is considered from five different points of view. (i) The area; does the response refer to the whole blot (W), or to some part of it (D)? (ii) The aspect (or determinant) that is used. Does the subject consider the shape of the blot (F), the colour (C), the shading (K), the movement perceived (M), or some combination of these? (iii) The quality of the response (+ or −); a sensible and intelligent response is +; a response that is vague, absurd or far-fetched is −; one indicating insanity may be confabulated or contaminated. (iv) The content; this is considered only in a general way, such as animal, human, anatomical, architectural, etc. (v) Whether the response is commonplace or original. This scoring category is entered only for the twenty or so commonest responses (P), or else for something markedly original (O). In addition, if there are several responses on one blot, their order is considered. When the responses to all ten blots have been completed, they are classified in various ways: the total number (R), the number and percentage in each category, etc.

Rorschach's interpretations were originally concerned mainly with the differential diagnosis of various forms of psychosis. He wanted to be able to decide from the study of his perceptual processes whether a patient was depressive, paranoid, suffering from organic brain disease, and so on. It is often useful for revealing psychotic processes, because the task is one for which no prepared defences are available. He originally used normal people mainly as a kind of control group, but later workers have extended its use in the description of positive qualities.

Rorschach's thinking was mainly in typological rather than dynamic terms. In spite of the immense popularity of the Rorschach test in America, the use of it has never been integrated with the dynamic concepts that are otherwise widely used in American psychology. In many respects it remains an intrusive foreign body, with a terminology of its own, and private cult-membership. In Britain the test has not been so popular, and its use has been mainly psychiatric. In Holland and Germany the typology has been congenial. The interpretation of the area responses follows lines that are familiar among typologists. A large proportion of whole responses is supposed to indicate tendencies to abstract, generalized thinking and large views. The opposing preference for detail indicated practical tastes and immediate goals. It is assumed, without very much effort at direct validation, that the subject's way of perceiving the blots will be typical of his behaviour in a great variety of situations. The most significant ideas in the Rorschach test occur in the account of the determinants. The contrast between preferences for form and for colour has often turned up in German psychology. Colour is usually supposed to represent extraversion or hysteria and form, introversion or obsessional neurosis.

Rorschach complicated the usual interpretations by introducing the movement category. M indicated strength of natural endowment, and also (when considered in relation to C) tendencies towards introversion. There is no doubt that M responses of good quality are indications of a high level of mental functioning. Along with other indications, it can give a fairly good estimate of I.Q. The connection with introversion is less clear. There are several signs that serve as anxiety indicators (cloud or smoke responses, tiny details, 'colour shock', anatomical responses involving gross mutilations, loathsome animals, etc.), and the validity of these interpretations has in some degree been confirmed by objective studies. The order of responses is used by Rorschach to place the subject on a scale from 'rigid' through 'orderly' to 'disorganized'. The order is rigid when the subject always begins a blot with a whole response, goes on next to mention common details, and then to rare details. If the order is too rigid, it indicates that the person is inhibited, that he cannot express his impulses freely, that his spontaneity is restricted by an obsessional need to be correct and exact. At the other extreme is a disorganized order of responses, in which they appear higgledy-piggledy, without any recognizable arrangement, like a hebephrenic word-salad. The healthy range would be somewhere in between.

This is a good example of a quality that can be directly observed in action, not requiring to be projected on to fantasy figures. The same quality can readily be seen in other productions, such as free painting or handwriting. Another quality that enters into most of such tests, is the organization of individual responses. It is noteworthy that most of the scoring categories of the Rorschach test can be applied to a set of T.A.T. stories. They can be rated for the use of whole or detail, for the spontaneity or inhibition shown in the invention of stories, for qualities of organization and arrangement, for obsessional use of detail, compulsive avoidances and omissions, and in other ways similar to a Rorschach.

There has been so much parochialism in modern psychology that each group has cultivated its own test with its own conceptual tools. If Rorschach concepts were applied to the use of T.A.T. materials, and vice versa, the validity of scoring categories should be greatly improved. The Rorschach test uses a situation in which the subject is likely to reveal himself because the situation is novel, and he has prepared no defences, no system of conventions that he can use as a mask. Another approach is to use some activity that has been repeated so often that it is no longer deliberately controlled. Any act that is performed easily and repeatedly comes to develop features of style; and these can be used to interpret the individuality of the person that uses them. That the choice of language is expressive of character was a discovery of the Elizabethan dramatists, principally of Shakespeare.

'Go thy ways, old Jack; die when thou wilt. If manhood, good manhood, be not forgot upon the face of the earth, then

I am shotten herring. There live not three good men unhanged
in England, and one of them is fat and grows old: God help
the while! a bad world, I say. I would I were a weaver; I could
sing psalms or anything.'

> 'Let's talk of graves, of worms, and epitaphs;
> Make dust our paper, and with rainy eyes
> Write sorrow on the bosom of the earth,
> Let's choose executors and talk of wills
> And yet not so—for what can we bequeath
> Save our deposed bodies to the ground. . . .'

Both of these passages are taken from historical plays of
Shakespeare, primarily intended to be records of busy and
violent action, crises of national decision. Yet in both the action
pauses while Shakespeare exploits his new-found delight—the
intoxicating discovery that words express not merely facts and
ideas, but also the character of the person who uses them. In
the passages we have quoted the facts and ideas are negligible,
the style of the speaker is everything. It is the constant use
of this device in English drama after Shakespeare that marks
it off from the French, where the device is not used. English
people cannot understand Corneille because in his plays everyone speaks the same language. Although the use of linguistic
style has been one of the chief media for the interpretation of
character in three centuries of English literature, very little use
of this material has been made by professional psychologists.
It is only recently, and then in a limited way, that attempts
have been made to grapple scientifically with the complexities
of style analysis (Masserman and Balkan, Dingle, Yule).
    Other possibilities have been considered. Elizabethans
noticed the use of clothes as a medium of character interpretation (Flugel, Laver).
    Voice is an important source of intuitive judgments of
personality, and the mainstay of the actor's art. The vanishing
word has not proved easily accessible to scientific analysis;

nevertheless a beginning has been made with Pear's[19] investigations.

Handwriting is another tantalizing problem. All children are taught in much the same way, yet everyone emerges in adult life with a unique style of handwriting; it is as stable a quality as his voice, and much more accessible to study. Any amount of material is easily available, and its individuality is sufficiently distinct to stand as evidence in a court of law. It seems an ideal opportunity for the study of personality, and has attracted many investigators. In Germany graphology attracted dabblers in high-flown mysticism, and with the rise of objective psychology in America the whole subject got rather rough treatment. The publication of Allport and Vernon's *Studies in Expressive Movement*[20] marked a revival of interest in the subject among British and American scientific psychologists, and the use of matching methods has shown more validity than the analytical approach that was used earlier.

Principles of interpretation used in graphology are similar to those of Rorschach protocols. Qualities of handwriting are taken to be representative of general tendencies of character and behaviour. For example, regular handwriting is said to indicate a predominance of will, and irregular handwriting a predominance of impulse. Klages,[21] the leading theorist of graphology, built much of his system on the contrast between 'releases' and 'bonds'.

This corresponds in some degree to the Freudian id and ego, and to Rorschach's contrast between colour and form. Indications of a predominance of impulse are: large writing, fast writing, ascending lines, light pressure, an increasing left margin. The opposites of these indicate a predominance of 'bond', or self-control. It will be noticed that these graphologists use general impressions from a considerable bulk of writing. The experimentalists, on the other hand, have mainly used precise measures of a single letter, such as the thickness of bars on the t's.

It is not our business to review here the extensive experimental literature concerned with the validation of graphological theories. An excellent summary of this work is given by Bell. The general impression one gets is that there is some truth in graphology, but not enough to be of much practical use. The fact that its success is so limited seems to be due, not to a failure in the expressiveness of productions, but to the fact that expressive signs do not have a universal meaning. The symbolism of handwriting is not carried in the culture. In part it depends on the universal principles of spatial thinking, which we have already discussed; but for the rest it depends on private meanings arising in the course of individual experience, which cannot be understood except through a personal life history. Jones wrote his y's in this way because he was imitating Smith, whom he admired at Oxford, and also to be as different as possible from Brown, who used to write him most offensive letters. General rules are often confused and overlaid by qualities that have a purely individual meaning, and it is for this reason that the validity of graphological symbolism is not higher. Once more general psychology has to be supplemented by a study of individual lives, if we are to attain results anything more satisfactory than 'more or less', 'by and large', and 'on the whole'. Graphology has grown up in the hope of discovering a universal symbolism in which we could afford to ignore individual meanings. Yet the individual has constantly reasserted himself. The stubborn facts of individuality have restricted the extent to which general laws are applicable to psychology.

TABLE VI: Some Projective Techniques

Name of Test Author, Date	Materials	Instructions	Interpretation
Word Association. C. G. Jung, 1905, amplified by Kent and Rosanoff (1910) Kohs, and Rapaport (1946), etc.	List of 100 words. Stop-watch for timing responses.	Words are read out to subject one at a time, and he responds with the first word that occurs to him. Jung's list contained 100 words. After a short interval stimulus words are repeated and subject is asked to recall previous response.	Responses are classified in several ways. The most useful way lists 'complex indicators', or signs of association disturbance. These include: no response, naming objects in the room, definition of stimulus-word, repetition of stimulus word; clang-associations, perseveration, multi-word reactions, absurd or obscure responses, delay in response, false recall.
Sentence completion. A. F. Payne, 1928. See also Rohde and Hildreth (1947).	The first few words of a sentence are provided.	Subject is required to complete the sentence.	Various systems have been used; one system classified responses into healthy, unhealthy and neutral, and gave a total score for maladjustment.
Rorschach, 1921, amplified by Beck, Klopfer, Rapaport, etc.	Ten ink-blots, of which five are coloured.	Blot is shown to subject who is asked: 'What could this be?'	Individual responses are classified in terms of area chosen, determinant, form quality, content, and social meaning. Interpretations in terms of quality of thinking, tendencies towards inhibition or emotion, introversion - extraversion, etc.

Test	Material	Procedure	Interpretation
World Game. M. Lowenfeld. Similar devices used by Bühler, Kamp and Erikson.	A sand tray and standard set of miniature toys—humans, animals, houses, trees, etc.	Child is asked to make a 'world'; Erikson asked his adult subjects to make a 'dramatic scene'.	No established rules. One classification mentions realistic worlds, mixture of realism and fantasy; purely fantastic; incoherent worlds; metaphors; stories and myths; dramatic worlds. The most important interpretations are in terms of private symbolism.
Mosaic Test. M. Lowenfeld.	A large number of pieces of various colours and shapes (square, diamond, triangular).	Subject is asked to make a pattern.	No established rules; patterns are classified into normal, defective, neurotic and psychotic.
Controlled Projection. J. C. Raven (1944).	Paper and crayons; outline pictures 'Road' and 'Box' and several pictures of a person drawing.	Subject is asked to draw a picture, and simultaneously to tell a story. The progress of the story is stimulated by questions. With the Road the subject is asked to draw and also describe where the road goes; with the Box, what is inside the box; with the person drawing, what is he interested in, etc.	Interpretations are based on an expectation that projection will occur. No detailed rules are given.

TABLE VI: Some Projective Techniques—*continued*

Name of Test Author, Date	Materials	Instructions	Interpretation
Szondi Test, 1947.	Six sets of eight portrait photographs. Each set contains one example of each of the following syndromes: homosexuality, sadist, epilepsy, hysteria, catatonia, paranoia, depression, mania.	From each set, the subject has to pick two he likes and two he dislikes.	Interpreted according to Szondi's scheme of Drives (see Table III). Responses are classified (*a*) according to the number of pictures chosen from one clinical group; a group frequently chosen indicates submerged drives; a group that is avoided indicates manifest drives. (*b*) according to acceptance or rejection. Accepted faces indicate a drive that is accepted, though not manifest, rejected faces indicate a repressed drive.
MAPS Test. (Make a Picture Story.) E. X. Shneidman, 1948.	Twenty-two background pictures, showing such scenes as living - room, street, bedroom, raft, nursery. Sixty-seven figures, including adult males, adult females, children, legendary and fictitious characters, animals. Background pictures are 8½ in. × 11 in., figures about 5 in. high.	Subject is given a background scene, and is required to choose figures and place them on the background and then make a story about the scene. Eleven background pictures are used with each subject.	Aspects of the record used for interpretation: with respect to the use of figures, their number, repetition, placement, selection, interaction, activity, meaning, chronology, use of background, and time taken. Sixty-four signs are listed, discriminating normals from psychotics.

Test	Material	Procedure	Scoring
Thematic Apperception Test. Morgan and Murray, 1936 (an earlier set of pictures was made by Schwarz).	Thirty pictures, of which twenty are given to any one subject (some separate pictures for Boys (B), Girls (G), Men (M) and Women (F)). Pictures occur in a definite order. No. 16 is blank.	A picture is presented to subject, who is told: 'Make up an exciting story about this picture. Say what has led up to the scene, what the characters are feeling and thinking, and how the story ends. You should take about five minutes for each story.'	Murray begins by locating a hero, assuming that the storyteller has identified with this character, and then rating for the expression of needs, according to his scheme. Other methods by Tomkins, Henry, etc. Stein follows Murray's methods.
Four Picture Test. van Lennep. First used 1930; published 1948.	Four coloured pictures.	Subject is required to combine them into a single story.	Similar to that of T.A.T., with emphasis on organization.
Picture Frustration Test. Rosenzweig, 1945, children's version, 1948.	Twenty-four drawings of frustrating situations.	To fill in 'balloons' with the first reply that recurs to the subject.	Responses are classified as extra-punitive, intra-punitive and im-punitive; and as obstacle-dominant, ego defensive and need-persistent.
Unnamed Projective Test. Temple and Amen, 1944.	Fourteen pictures with blank faces; alternative heads for insertion.	Child has to decide whether a happy or a sad face should be inserted.	Scored for anxiety, measured by percentage of unhappy completions; areas of anxiety located.

REFERENCES

1. RORSCHACH, H.   *Psychodiagnostics*   Bern, Huber, 1942.
                       (original German Edi-
                       tion, 1921).

2. STERN, W.   *Cloud Pictures: A new*   Character and Personal-
                      method for testing   ity, 1938, 6, 132–146.
                      imagination.

3 and 15.
   MURRAY, H. A.   *The Thematic Apper-*   Cambridge Mass., Har-
                      ception Test.   vard Univ. Press, 1943.

4. SCHWARTZ   *Social Situations Pic-*   Chicago, C. H. Stoelting
                      tures Test.   Co., 1931.

5. KOFFKA, K.   *Principles of Gestalt*   London, Kegan Paul,
                      Psychology.   1935.

6. SZONDI, F. L.   *Experimentelle Trieb-*   Bern, Huber, 1947.
                      diagnostik.

7. HOMBURGER, E.   *Configurations in Play:*   Psych. and Quart, 6,
                      Clinical Notes.   139–214, 1937.

8. PRESSEY   *Pressey Cross-out X-*   Chicago, C. H. Stoelting
                      O Test.   Co., 1921.

9. BECK, S. J.   *Rorschach's Test.*   2 Vols. New York, Grune
                                                  and Stratton.

10. KLOPFER, B. AND   *The Rorschach Tech-*   Yonkers - on - Hudson,
    KELLY, D. M.   *nique.*   World Book Company,
                                                  1942.

11. RAPAPORT, D., GILL, *Diagnostic Psycho-*   Chicago: Year Book
    M. AND SCHAFER, R.   *logical Testing* (The   Publishers, 1944–46.
                         Menninger   Clinic
                         Monograph   Series
                         No. 4.)

12. ROSANOFF, A. J.   *Manual of Psychiatry.*   New York, Wiley, 1938.
                      Revised edition.

13. FRANK, L. K.   *Projective Methods.*   Springfield Illinois :
                                                  Charles   C.   Thomas,
                                                  1948.

14. LOWENFELD, M.   *Notes on the Nature*   London, Inst. Child
                      and Use of the Mosaic   Psychol. No date.
                      Test.

16. TOMKINS, S. S.   *Thematic Appercep-*   New York, Grune and
                      tion Test.   Stratton, 1947.

17. HENRY, W. E.   *The Thematic Apper-*   Genetic Psychology
                      ception Technique in   Monographs, 35, 1947.
                      the Study of Culture-
                      Personality Relations.

    LOWENFELD, M.   *The World Pictures of*   Brit. J. Med. Psychol.,
                      Children. A method   1939, 18, 65–100.
                      of recording and
                      studying them.

19. PEAR, T. H.   *Voice and Personality.*   London, Chapman and
                                                  Hall, 1931.

20. ALLPORT, G. W. AND *Studies in Expressive*   New York, Macmillan,
    VERNON, P. E.   *Movement.*   1933.

21. KLAGES, L.   *Handschrift und Char-*   15th Edition, Leipzig,
                      akter.   1932.

CHAPTER X

MEN IN GROUPS

TO the outsider it may seem odd that psychologists should approach the problem of personality in such devious ways. There are people all round about, millions of them. Even if they are no longer issued with immortal souls, they presumably all have individuality of some kind. There is also no shortage of the crucial events of human life. Birth, copulation and death are common as sneezing. Yet in the midst of all this passion and despair, we find psychologists peering at the crossing of t's, or curiously pondering the shape of ink-blots. Why not approach the problem more directly? Cannot we look with open eyes at people's lives, and try to draw some wisdom from what we see there?

Partly our trouble is the restless fluidity of raw facts. People will not stay still in stained-glass attitudes to be studied. Keats looked at a Grecian urn, where people stayed motionless for two thousand years, to find an image of human life. The direct experience of process may lead to good literature, but not easily to science. Partly also our trouble is due to the excessive timidity of psychologists. Many psychologists are academics who chose their career because it seemed to involve nothing more disturbing than the harmless pedantries of the laboratory, the peaceful revolutions of the calculating machine. To be faced with real people having real emotions was more than they had bargained for. It is said that in some parts of the United States morticians employ minions to listen in to the short-wave police radio, so that whenever a fatal accident is reported, they can hurry to the spot and sell a funeral. If psychologists had shown more enterprise of this kind, the subject might have progressed faster.

Many psychologists have felt safer when personal relations were restricted to the formalities of a test situation, and were not allowed to become tiresomely human. The problem is really an awkward one, and does not arise to the same extent in other sciences. The real self is defended and concealed by a variety of masks, and in casual contacts with people we meet little else. We cannot expect to learn a great deal about people from observing them in trivial situations, because it is too easy for them to keep up a mask. We expect to see the 'real' person best in situations of crisis. This helps to explain the permanent attractiveness of street accidents and murders. (This is also one reason why people are charmed by small children. Their emotions are near the surface, their responses less complicated by masks and defences.) We are not, however, at liberty to evoke emotions whenever we want to observe them. The physiologist, who wields power of life and death over his animal subjects, has an advantage. The psychologist can take only minor liberties with human subjects. He may venture to make them feel foolish or frustrated in small ways, but he cannot threaten them with imprisonment or starvation, nor can he reward them with a bride or a motor-car. The controlled situations on which the physiologist so largely relies are mostly out of our reach.

Various expedients have been tried. Landis and Blatz, making physiological studies of emotion, induced students in the interests of Science to undergo rather severe traumas like undergoing electric shock, and beheading a living rat. Luria,[1] in the early days after the Russian revolution, had opportunities to apply psychological tests to murderers awaiting trial, and students just before a final examination. Sick people, particularly those suffering from depression or anxiety in a moderate degree will often co-operate with a psychiatrist in the hope of obtaining some relief. This privileged access of the doctor to secret material has been one reason for the predominant influence of medicine on recent psychology. The doctor has only a little more oppor-

tunity than other men for the direct observation of important
moments of experience, but he may hear extensive verbal
confessions in the consulting room.

Some have turned to animal experiments to supplement
the little that we may do to humans. However, the circumstances of animal neuroses show only rather a remote resemblance to our own. Interesting though these experiments
are, they can hardly take the central place in psychology
that animal experiments do in physiology. Men and animals
resemble one another much more closely in physiology
than they do in psychology. The development of human
symbolic processes creates a gulf between men and rats.
Some psychologists have put to a scientific and therapeutic
use that curious blend of real life with fantasy that occurs
in improvised dramatic situations. Some too have used the
bait of privileged status to induce men to undergo severe trials.

Several large-scale projects in the selection of leaders were
carried out during the last war. The W.O.S.B. procedures (War
Office Selection Boards) in the British Army, and the O.S.S.
(Office of Strategic Services) in the United States employed
daring and adventurous methods of personnel selection. These
military selection procedures were improvised at short notice
in response to demands that psychologists had not formerly
known how to meet. In the course of developing these methods
they learnt how to observe and give a meaning to a great deal
of social behaviour that had formerly slipped through the
mesh. Before 1940 the established tests for personnel selection
were mainly concerned with the measurement of abilities.
They might require processes of intellectual abstraction,
perceptual tasks like tracing a maze, or manipulative tasks like
filling a peg-board; and skills like adding figures or assembling
an instrument. These tests of ability formed the core of the
selection procedure, and might be supplemented by an interests
questionnaire, a psycho-neurotic inventory and a biographical
form.

The direct observation of social process formed no part

of selection procedures. The interaction of people is not easily standardized or quantified, and therefore, in terms of the laboratory psychologist, does not belong to science. Regretfully or thankfully, according to temperament, scientific psychologists had consigned the whole process of social relations to the limbo of the unobservable. The W.O.S.B. psychologists, building on Gestalt conceptions, escaped from the paralysing nominalism in which behaviourist psychology had immobilized itself. Since they were willing to treat social groups as realities, they were able to observe all sorts of qualities that emerged from interaction. The main task of the W.O.S.B. selectors was to choose leaders; and for choosing these, tests of intellectual abilities were almost useless. Just as we can best assess intelligence by setting intellectual tasks, so we can best assess leadership by creating situations in which someone has to take the lead. This means that we have to improvise social situations in which these qualities have an opportunity to emerge. The leaderless Group Test, or (as Harris[2] calls it) the Stress Group Test, was due originally to Bion and Rickman,[3] and several others subsequently contributed to its development. One knows how the old-style selection interview used to work. Several candidates, unknown to one another and to the examining board, sat uncomfortably in a waiting room, eyeing one another silently and suspiciously until called in. The candidate entered the room alone, and found himself being stared at by half a dozen senior persons. He was not actually alive, but the moth could be seen flapping a little while the pin was being pushed into the cork. The Board saw the candidate in such a peculiar and artificial social relation that not very much could be inferred about his ordinary behaviour.

In the W.O.S.B. procedures, candidates were assembled for three days to live as a social group, along with the Personnel Selection Officers who observed and tested them. The usual military barriers of rank were eliminated, and candidates were known by numbers only. The programme contained many standardized tests of ability and interest, and certain special procedures that are our concern here. Men were divided into groups—usually eight in each group. A group was then collectively given a task—for instance, improvising a bridge across a stream. No one was appointed to take command, yet the task was one in which co-ordinated work was essential. The work could not be done by anyone in isolation, nor by all of the eight working parallel. In order to achieve it they had to become a group.

If we phrase the task as a test of leadership we may give a false impression, for if all the candidates set out with a determination to become leaders, nothing whatever would be achieved. Harris prefers to describe the quality they were assessing as 'Group-Cohesiveness'. A cohesive person is the one who tends to raise the level of the group's functioning, to make it more effective as a group. One can notice various aspects of this total quality—encouragement, tact, firmness, stability under frustration. One can also distinguish various patterns of character that fail to produce this cohesive effect. Three well-marked variants are those who develop anxiety when placed in positions of responsibility, and who need someone to lean on; those who become aggressive and domineering in positions of power; and those who work best on their own, and do not co-operate easily. (These coincide with Horney's neurotic trends of submission, power and withdrawal.) Some take the lead at the beginning, but cannot maintain it, either because their suggestions are not effective enough, or because they are not impressively presented. When their suggestions are rejected, some drop into the background, and become mere ropeholders; others sulk or loaf; others again may keep trying to recapture their lost prestige, by 'spivoid' tactics—toadying, exploiting others, and exhibition. The observer need not limit himself to rating individuals for the effectiveness of their leadership. He can also get a good deal of insight into dynamic processes.

Officer candidates in the personnel selection situation were strongly motivated by the bait of a commission that was dangled before them, and needed no further stimulus to put up the best show they could. Job-status is such an important part of our society that this can readily evoke strong motives and determined efforts, and even the willing endurance of traumatic stresses. A bold use of their opportunities enabled investigators to evoke serious and lifelike emotions. Such 'stress situations' formed an important part of the O.S.S. selection procedures at Fairfax, Virginia.

The Office of Strategic Services employed a number of men in dangerous and highly skilled jobs, such as spies and saboteurs behind the enemy lines. It was of the first importance that such personnel should be of high quality, and that hidden flaws of character should not ruin an enterprise. It was thus important to put on pressure that would break through the ordinary social defences, and serve as a rigorous test of stability. Several different stress situations were used by Murray and his associates. A rather perilous obstacle race weeded out those deficient in physical courage. In another test, candidates were required to take on, at short notice, the role of a man who has been caught, without credentials, examining a secret military file in a Washington office. He is given a few minutes to prepare a cover story, and is then subjected to a ruthless cross-examination, which always ended with the announcement 'It is our decision that you have failed this test'. Since the candidate had been placed at a hopeless disadvantage from the start, it was not difficult to convince him that he had failed. A severe stress could be built up from the humiliation of failure in another test that started much less dramatically. The task was presented as one of construction—a fairly simple job of hut-building, in which the candidate had to direct two workmen. Secretly, however, the workmen had been instructed to obstruct and humiliate the candidate in every possible way, ensuring the complete failure of the construction task. When this happened under the eyes of the instructor, it could amount to a severe trauma, quite as severe as the previous one. Lewin's[4] studies of the level of aspiration had earlier shown that success and failure in any task easily become symbolic of success and failure in general, so that important emotions are readily tied to intrinsically trivial situations. While the experimenters did not hesitate to pile on the agony during the actual test, they were careful to see that the effect did not last. Traumatic experiences were 'detensed' or 'sealed off' immediately afterwards.

Other techniques were also used, reminiscent of Moreno's[5] 'psychodrama' or 'sociodrama', The British workers spoke of a 'Human Problems' session'. Two members of the course would be asked to act an improvised scene: for example, a corporal has been too matey with the men under his command, and his officer has decided to see him about it; the corporal is told to say that he doesn't see why he should have to break off his friendships just because he has become a corporal. In every scene one played the officer part and one the other rank. Each was given a general indication of his role, but was not told how the other would react. It was an 'open' situation, in which the development of the scene depended on the interaction of the two men. It could not be predetermined or fully controlled by either of them. In the next scene the roles of officer and other rank are reversed. Another typical 'human problem' that was acted out before the group was one in which a man who was expecting promotion has to be told that he is not going to get it after all. The officer has to make the situation clear without generating resentment, and at the same time without encouraging self-pity or a belief in his own grievance. The disappointed man has to show that he really wanted promotion, and that he considered that he deserved it, but at the same time will not sulk, and is prepared to go on trying, and to be confident about the future. There is room for a lot of variation in this little scene, and for the unconscious representation of personal attitudes.

The O.S.S. group used similar tasks (called 'improvisations'), though in a slightly more informal way. Situations were chosen to impose a definite stress on each man, to put him in an uncongenial role, in which he would have to overcome some weakness in himself. A man who was intolerant of criticism might be set to play the role of an author whose book had been adversely reviewed; a man who was suspected of lacking firmness might be given the task of refusing some reasonable request. Often candidates would realize that conduct which seemed natural and proper to them in the situation would create a bad impression on the audience. A common response was momentary blocking and speechlessness. The sudden insight of seeing himself as others saw him left him momentarily defenceless. At other times a man could be found sliding away from the situation that had been posed for him, into another that was more congenial. A soft, kindly man put into the role of reprimanding a deserter might begin to make excuses for the prisoner. If a man were given a role that went too close to the bone, aroused too much anxiety in him to be tolerable, he might try to disguise this by being funny, or by ham acting. To play his part in a theatrical, exaggerated manner might serve to disguise from the audience the real embarrassment that he felt. The man who was really upset at being criticized pretends to shoot his critic.

An essential part of these projects was the audience. This consisted not merely of the testing staff, but also of the other candidates, and all were encouraged to discuss and criticize afterwards. The audience served to raise the tension and to give it more naturalness and spontaneity. Once more we note the contrast with orthodox testing procedures. Candidates were not isolated from one another, nor was each studied separately as a 'pure case'. The problems set were not vigorously standardized, and no attempt was made to ensure that exactly the same problem was given to everyone. It would rather be true to say that every problem was unique. Even if a candidate has heard all about a task beforehand from others who have been through it, he cannot do much to prepare for it, because he cannot know who will be the others with whom he has to co-operate. Stereotyped performances worked out in advance (as one spots questions for an examination) would be useless, because the prepared answers would not fit into a fluid developing situation.

The W.O.S.B. and O.S.S. groups devised ways of bringing important social emotions directly under observation, of enabling the psychologist to watch the play of feeling and the stress of action, instead of inferring them remotely from symbolic acts, or trying to assess them from ratings. There can be no doubt that methods like these will play an increasingly important part in the future of psychology. Having once seen the possibilities of directly observing significant events of human life, emotions in action, the psychologist will not be willing to withdraw to his attic again. However, although everyone might agree that real and important qualities were being exhibited, it was another thing to devise satisfactory ways of describing them.

The W.O.S.B. psychologists did not concern themselves much with the analytic interpretation of parts or aspects of personality, so far as personal selection was concerned. Their main rating was a judgment of the total personality in terms of its effectiveness for the task in hand. They did, however, also analyse this effectiveness into three aspects—a man's ability at the group task, his cohesiveness, or tendency to bind the group together into a working unit, and his stability. One man might be outstanding for the high quality of his direction and execution of the task; another, though not particularly skilful in technical aspects of the work, might have the effect of getting people to work better and more effectively together; a third might emerge chiefly in moments of frustration or defeat, as the one on whom others most readily relied, the one from whom they took the lead. The contrasting qualities were the ineffective, the disruptive and the unstable.

The O.S.S. workers adopted a somewhat more analytical approach. They rated their men on ten variables—Energy and Initiative, Leadership, Effective Intelligence, Emotional Stability, Motivation for Assignment, Propaganda Skills, Observing and Reporting, and Security. It will be noticed that there was no attempt to describe people in terms of psychologically pure qualities, nor to ensure that the variables would be independent of one another. In fact they were all positively correlated with one another, and nobody bothered. The choice of some variables arose out of the jobs that the men had to do. The heading Motivation for Assignment came in because men were being individually selected for particular roles, and a man who was otherwise excellent might have been picked for a job for which he had no inclination. Several of the variables selected themselves, because they were aspects that could conveniently be isolated in terms of the test procedures they were using. Propaganda skills were directly assessed by a work sample in which men had to draft a leaflet to be dropped in enemy territory. Judgments were made in terms of immediate needs, and not of psychological theory. The team working on this project started with several different systems of theoretical ideas, and had no time for a long preliminary debate aimed at resolving disputes. It is remarkable how much effective collaboration they were able to achieve with a minimum of theory.

The Human Problems Session was a development of the Psychodrama invented earlier by J. L. Moreno. His work, spread over some forty years, has been a remarkable blend of technical invention and philosophic breadth. As early as 1911 in Vienna he was developing the *Stegreiftheater* or Spontaneity theatre. Moreno's theatre was a place where children had a chance to act, but they acted, not plays whose words were written by someone else and fixed beforehand, but plays in which only a general situation was laid down, and details were improvised by the actors as they went along. Many anxieties and inferiorities come to the surface and are positively resolved in the course of being expressed dramatically. Moreno was a pioneer of group methods at a time when most of the active thinking about psychotherapy was individualistic.

Psycho-analysis was at first concerned only with the individual patient, and later with the relation of patient and doctor. When Freud[6] turned to consider the phenomena of group behaviour he did so mainly in terms of similarities between individual and group; the leader could be considered as a kind of father; the murder of Moses was a prototype of each son's wishes for revenge on his father, etc. Freud did not devote much attention to the special problems of group work, and it was a long time before psychoanalysts developed the technique of group study. It was Schilder[7] who first applied theoretical ideas of psycho-analysis to the technique of group works, and even to-day this is considered a side-line.

The main business of analysis is still a group of two— the patient on the couch and the analyst in the chair. Although Freud's work dealt with the stormiest of human passions, his own attitude was that of a detached, pessimistic observer. The aim of his therapy was the destruction of illusions, the building of a realistic self-image. He had no great hope of making men happier or of seeing a future brotherhood of man, but he thought that he could make men wiser than they had been. A man of this temper is not the one to undertake inspirational work with groups. The fascination of Freud's discoveries was so great, and attracted the best minds in medical psychology to such an extent that it seems to have been a long time before Moreno's ideas got a hearing in the learned world.

Many people may have underrated the intellectual quality of his ideas because of his flamboyant expansive manner. Moreno really believes in brotherly love, and the possibilities of human community. For forty years he has taught that the cure of neurosis lies in the recovery of spontaneity, release from the tyranny of bureaucracy and of the machine, and a restoration of more direct human relations. Many of the ideas later stressed by Fromm and Sullivan can be found earlier in Moreno. In recent years varieties of group psychotherapy have become widely popular, and many of them have been directly inspired by his work. While some physicians have thought of group psycho-therapy mainly as a labour-saving device, enabling a busy doctor to treat several patients at the same time, the group activity is to Moreno the central meaning and purpose of the whole treatment. To him isolation is not merely a symptom of mental illness, but a major part of the disease process. And the most important technique for breaking down this isolation is the psychodrama. An example of the way in which psychodrama has been used to break down isolation is in relation to Service patients about to leave a mental hospital. Patients whose acute phase of psychosis is over may nevertheless not feel strong enough to leave hospital and face the world on their own. They may feel that their peculiar defect will be obvious to everybody as soon as they emerge. A vague fear of the questions that people will ask may be enough to keep a patient cowering behind the bars of a mental hospital. By the psychodramatic method this fear is met directly. The patient is put on the stage to rehearse impromptu the source of his anxiety. The patient has come home, and gone out to the Post Office to post a letter; someone says to him, 'Aren't you John Smith. I thought you were in the Army. How is it you're not in uniform?' This is the question he has been dreading, and to build up his ability to answer it may be an important part of his recovery. Again, the application for a job may be rehearsed, including searching questions about his past record.

A cure is not something that the doctor does to the patient. In group therapy the cure comes from the group, and from membership of the group. Although the transference relationship occurs in a group as elsewhere, its meaning is commonly rather different. Maxwell Jones uses psychodrama as one means of breaking down isolation. In the Industrial Neuroses Unit the men he deals with are not psychotics but chronic failures, men who have drifted for years from one job to another. Often they considered themselves defeated, and did not want to renew contact with their families. In the weekly psychodrama at the Belmont Hospital (at Sutton in Surrey), the achieving of insight is a secondary aim, which is often possible only to a very modest degree. The primary aim of the psychodrama is the stimulation of positive group activity. One of the patients volunteers to act the story of his own life. A week is spent in rehearsing, and the successive scenes are carefully prepared, though the exact words are not usually pre-determined. Several people are brought in to take parts, and encouraged to improvise and produce ideas. At the end of the play (which lasts perhaps twenty minutes) the audience, which includes everyone in the hospital proceeds to discuss the moral. A lot of advice may be offered, some of which may be aggressively toned. Even if there is a rather low level of insight, an important object is achieved if patients are drawn into a co-operative activity aimed at recovery and success.

Apart from the psychodrama, the interaction of members of a group can be studied in various other ways. Moreno's sociometric method was an ingenious device for studying the living structure of a group—a device that was both an instrument of research and a programme of action. All the children in a primary school class were asked to choose from among their classmates who they would like to have stay in the same classroom and sit near them. Answers were put on to a chart showing diagrammatically the social relations of the group. Boys were represented by small triangles, girls by small circles. A red arrow from A towards B represented a liking of A for B, while if the attraction were mutual it was represented by a line joining them. Repulsions were represented by black lines. Such a sociometric chart gave a great deal of information about the structure of the group. If the group were split into two cliques, this would readily be visible. Isolates and leaders reveal themselves at a glance. The charts can be used for studying the development of race and sex attitudes. By counting the percentage of intersex preferences at various ages, a clear picture of the latency period is obtained. Small children choose either sex indifferently; but from the fourth grade (eight or nine years) to the eighth (thirteen years) boys nearly always choose boys, and girls choose girls. From thirteen years onwards choice of the opposite sex becomes common again. In a similar way the charts can be used to express attitudes about colour or race. As used by

Moreno at the New York State Training School for Girls, the charts could also be used to assess the morale of the institution. It is a place to which girls have been committed by the State; they are lodged in sixteen cottages, each containing about thirty-five girls under a house-mother. In the sociometric test the girls are asked to make five choices. Where the morale of a cottage was strong, a large proportion of the choices would be made inside the cottage, and fewer outside it. Still further details could be added when the opportunity was also given to express repulsions. The features we have mentioned by no means exhaust the possibilities of the sociometric device, but they are enough to indicate its value. Its validity depends largely on the fact that the preferences expressed by the girls must as far as possible be put into effect. If they know that their choices are taken seriously by the administration, they will be more seriously made.

Sociometry is a consequence of taking groups seriously as real existents, which most psychologists have until recent years been unwilling to do. They have believed that isolated human beings are the only realities, and that groups were some kind of a metaphor, useful, no doubt, for limited purposes, but dangerous when carried too far. Lewin and Moreno have both made important contributions to psychology by a direct study of groups.

In recent years projects of group psychotherapy have been growing up all over the place, and we are beginning to realize something of its true importance. Those whose work lay with criminals rather than with neurotics have always placed group work in the centre of the picture. Social workers have usually tended to think of crime as more than anything a disease of the social group, which must be dealt with in terms of the group. In the same way educationists and clergymen have thought of their tasks as one that would normally be done in groups. Much of what is nowadays called group psychotherapy is a re-phrasing in medical terms of activities that were formerly carried on under other auspices. The brilliant achievements of medical science in the last 100 years, and the high standards of training set by the medical schools, have given great prestige in the eyes of the public to the medical profession. What is called Mental Hygiene in America, or the somewhat similar body of ideas and attitudes called Social Medicine in Britain, are ways in which concepts originally belonging to medicine have invaded other fields.

There is a marked tendency to-day to use terms from medicine to describe all sorts of other things. We speak of a neurosis (something wrong with the nerves) when we mean that a person is queer or unhappy, even though there may be nothing ascertainably wrong with his nervous system. We speak of clinical psychology when we mean merely that we are studying an individual, not that he is sick in bed. We speak of therapy instead of comfort and of diagnosis instead of understanding. This notion of the peculiarly close relation of psychology with medicine has arisen because so much of what is best in modern psychology has been created by doctors. And the individualistic tradition of medicine has retarded the growth of group methods of dealing with psychoneurosis. To-day, however, sometimes under medical auspices and sometimes elsewhere, many group projects have arisen for dealing with various forms of unhappiness and crime, and this is clearly going to develop a great deal in the coming years.

The pre-eminence of medical men in the development of psychology was due to their tradition of moral detachment. The Hippocratic code set the patient's health as a complete, limited goal, and encouraged the doctor to confine his attention to this. This, combined with the secrecy of the confessional, gave the doctor his special value as a mental healer. The priest and the teacher did not show the same readiness to reserve judgment. In the present generation, however, there has grown up in the practice of social welfare agencies a similar custom of tolerance and utilitarian thinking. Many other people now have the attitudes and sets that enable them to do good psychotherapy. As Moreno has pointed out, the practice of group

o

therapy means a new relation between patient and physician. The authoritative father-figure who prescribes a regimen to the sick man is not required here. His status must be diffused through the group. In many ways a medical training is an unsuitable background to one whose work is the psychology of groups.

Nevertheless many concepts drawn from modern medical psychology are finding valuable application in group work. Scott Williamson's work at the Pioneer Health Centre in Peckham was a powerful synthesis of social and biological ideas. W. R. Bion's sessions for group psychotherapy showed the possibility of applying a strictly Freudian technique to the group. Bion confined himself to analysing transference within the group. Just as an ordinary analyst in modern practice may devote the greater part of his analysis to the relation of analyst and patient and the symbolism implicit in it, so Bion discussed relations between the members and the group, of whom he was one. It might seem that there would be nothing much to talk about, yet he managed to make the existence of the group a fruitful and illuminating theme of discussion for the group. Almost any statement that a person makes has a first meaning as an assertion of fact, a second meaning as an expression of an attitude to persons addressed, and a third meaning vaguely implicating a number of other persons not immediately present. Analysis consists in uncovering these second and third meanings. The observation 'nice day' made across the pavement on the way to office may mean: 'I have nothing to say at the moment that would in any way help to bind us together, but I do not want that to be misinterpreted as an attitude of withdrawal.'

Slavson[8] draws a general distinction between Activity Group Therapy and Interview Group Therapy. The purpose of the first is to provide the opportunity for a spontaneous discharge of drives, diminution of tension and reduction of anxiety through physical and emotional activity in a group setting; unimpeded acting out is permitted within the boundaries of personal safety. In Interview Group Therapy conversations are similar to those in individual psychotherapy, but influenced by the fact that several people are comparing experiences. Here insight is a major objective. Bion's groups were of this type; so was the method described by John Levy[9] as Relation Therapy. While Interview Group Therapy is a sophisticated and professional process, Activity Group Therapy is merely a conscious and purposeful use of something that is as old as human nature itself. Various groups outside the medical profession are making some deliberate use of its possibilities. Examples are the Oxford Groups, and Alcoholics Anonymous.

To the experimental psychologist the problem has been to find an effective way of assessing and measuring the influence of the group on the individual. After a long series of pioneering experiments with rather trivial results, an effective approach to the problem was made by Elton Mayo[10] and his associates in the famous Hawthorne Experiment. Mayo departed from the usual engineering approach when he decided to build up the statistical population of his tests by recording a very large number of performances by a few people, instead of a few performances by a great many people. In his experiments the performances of half a dozen workers are recorded over a period of several years. The production records, interpreted by T. N. Whitehead,[11] provide a vivid image of the social structure of the group. When two girls, sitting together at a factory bench, were on good terms, their production rose and fell in unison. When they quarrelled, the correlation dropped to nothing. By this method, delicate measures of the effect of a social relation became possible.

In another field, the work of Sherif[12] and others on Social norms has provided another approach to the dynamics of social groups. Sherif has used mainly perceptual tasks for his experiments. He has been able to show the influence of social reference frames in what might appear to be a quite impersonal task, such as judging the length of a line. In these and other ways, techniques are being developed for bringing the effect of membership of social groups within the scope of the psychologist.

REFERENCES

1. LURIA, A. R. — *The Nature of Human Conflicts.* — New York, Liveright, 1932.

2. HARRIS, H. — *The Group Approach to Leadership Testing.* — London, Routledge and Kegan Paul, 1949.

3. BION, W. R., AND RICKMAN, J. (1943). — *Intra - Group Tensions: Their study a task of the Group.* — Lancet, ii, 678.

4. LEWIN, K. — *Dynamic Theory of Personality.* — New York, McGraw-Hill, 1935.

5. MORENO, J. L. — *Who shall survive? A new approach to the problem of human inter-relations.* — Washington D.C. Nervous and Mental Disease Publishing Co., 1934.

Group Psychotherapy: a symposium. — New York, Beacon House, 1945. (Reprint of Sociometry 8, 1943, Nos. 3 and 4).

6. FREUD, S. — *Group Psychology and the Analysis of the Ego.* — London, Int. Ps-a P., 1922.

7. SCHILDER, P. — *Moses and Monotheism.* — New York, Knopf, 1939.

Psychotherapy. — New York, W. W. Norton, 1938.

8. SLAVSON, S. R. — *Practice of Group Therapy.* — International Universities Press, N.Y., 1947.

9. LEVY, JOHN — *Relationship Therapy as Applied to Play Groups.* — Am. J. Orthopsych. 8, 1938.

10. MAYO, ELTON — *The Human Problems of an Industrial Civilization.* — New York, Macmillan, 1933.

The Social Problems of an Industrial Civilization. — Cambridge, Mass., Harvard Univ. Press, 1945.

11. WHITEHEAD, T. N. — *The Industrial Worker. A Statistical Study of Human Relations.* — Cambridge, Mass., Harvard Univ. Press, 1938.

12. SHERIF, M. — *An Outline of Social Psychology.* — New York, Harper, 1948

CHAPTER XI

THE LOGIC OF VALIDATION

THE validation of a procedure means the confirmation of its results by some kind of external evidence. The great variety of unproven speculations and interesting conjectures in our field makes the confirming or disapproving of them the main task of scientific psychology. Ever since Freud's time, the psychology of personality has been full of brilliant ideas, most of which are very difficult to prove or disprove. Psychology has also been full of tests where it was not known with any certainty what they tested, and mental faculties whose existence was affirmed only by the meditations of a philosopher. It is thus not surprising that many psychologists regarded their main business as the development of techniques of validation. In the nineteen-twenties in America they thought of their work rather as one of invalidation. The scientific psychologist was the professional debunker, the man who proved that there was nothing in it. American psychologists turned their backs on introspection, intuition, and other pleasant vices, and determined to be scientists and nothing else. For a while there was a good deal of anxiety to prove that unscientific sources of knowledge were really illusory. Experiments were published in psychological journals proving that interviews were no good, handwriting was no good, palmistry was no good, phrenology was no good, psycho-analysis was no good. In the view of scientific psycho-logists, all these could be swept together in one red burial.

British academic psychologists never rejected introspection, but were distrustful of intuition. Typologists and psycho-analysts were bold in speculation and indifferent to the niceties of experimental method; their impudent probing into the secrets of private life filled many psychologists with alarm, and led them to restrict their researches to colourless and minor topics.

Often they succeeded in convincing themselves that their investigations were in some undetermined way laying the foundation of a future objective science of psychology. By refusing to have anything to do with real people they made certain that their experiments could at any rate do no harm. Some concerned themselves with the elaboration of apparatus. Others devoted their lives to the harmless necessary rat. Others again to the marmoreal beauties of a correlation matrix. Those who have been distressed by the great schism within psychology, and seek to bridge it, occupy themselves mainly with elaborating techniques of validation.

Several varieties of validation are used in current investigations. One kind consists in finding out whether a test sorts people out in the same way that life-experience does. In occupational psychology we often want to know whether some test that we have constructed will adequately predict success in a job. We construct a test which we hope will distinguish good taxi-drivers from bad ones. A few years later, after these men have been taxi-drivers for some time, we find out whether those who did well in the test have turned out to be the best drivers. The degree to which this is so is the measure of validity that the test possesses. For each type of occupation we have to search for the criterion that will serve us best. For taxi-drivers we might use the number and cost of accidents incurred over a period. Although some accidents may really be 'accidental', we may suppose that, with large numbers, there will be a clear relation between the total proficiency of drivers and the number of accidents. If then our test is a valid test of driving ability it will show rather a high correlation with the number of accidents. For a criterion of proficiency as an insurance salesman we could use the value of insurance sold in a year. If on the average those who did well in the test subsequently sell more insurance than those who did badly in the test, then the test can be considered a valid measure of proficiency in selling insurance. For a test of factory workers the validating criterion is often the amount of production. Other criteria of proficiency that have been used are: amount of spoilt work, frequency of absence from work, rate of labour turnover.

The logical conditions that need to be fulfilled for adequate validation are these: (i) the criterion selected should be of central importance to the occupation concerned and a true measure of proficiency; (ii) it should be accurately measurable; (iii) a representative sample of those originally tested should be available for re-examination. In practice, of course, these conditions are seldom perfectly fulfilled. If the test that we are seeking to validate has been used as a method of selection, then those who have failed the test, and have consequently been rejected, will not be available for follow-up. If, as a result of our test, the man has not become a taxi-driver, then we cannot say how badly he would have driven. The test will thus be validated by its ability to distinguish between those who are fairly good at the task, and those who are very good. This is much harder than to discriminate between those who are outright good and bad.

Another snag that commonly arises is that we have no valid measure of proficiency in the occupation. How shall we assess the merit of a soldier's service? Should it be by the wounds or decorations he has received, or the enemies he has killed, the punishments or promotions he has received, the battles he has fought in, or his ability to keep alive? None of these criteria would have much to recommend them in the eyes of a serving soldier. Usually we have no choice but to depend on some kind of merit rating, of the kind that we discussed in Chapter III. Ratings are themselves so subjective and so fallible that we may often feel that the blind are measuring the blind. Nevertheless there may often be nothing better available, and we must refine techniques of rating as much as possible.

Sometimes, although we cannot follow our subjects up to the final stage of validation, we may be able to follow them a certain distance. If our selection test is given at the beginning of a period of training, we may be able to use as a measure of success the results of an examination held at the end of the training period. A test of aspiring pilots may successfully predict who will get their wings, even though we have no record of their subsequent performance. Validation by examination results is a timid and inadequate criterion, but we may have no other available.

We can sometimes get a rather strong indirect confirmation of a selection test by showing that it successfully differentiates two groups whose characteristics are known to be different. For example, if we have constructed an interest scale for nurses, we may validate it by showing that nurses score much more highly on it than do the general population. Not all nurses are interested in nursing, but they are more likely to be, than people who do some other job. The same kind of validation has sometimes been used for attitude scales, where it was shown that members of a pacifist organization got much higher negative scores than the average of the population, in filling in a scale of attitudes to war. The scale is validated by the fact that, at any rate in extreme instances, answers to questions agree with the rest of his conduct. Terman[1] and his associates used the same method of constructing a masculinity-femininity (M-F) scale. A great many questions were asked of men and women, and wherever the answers of the two groups were sufficiently different, they could be given differential M-F scores. Such a test virtually validates itself, as do Strong's([2]) Vocational Interest Scores. This happens because the qualities that the test seeks to measure are not abstractions derived from psychological theory, but straightforward descriptions of what people do. We know that a certain answer is masculine, because in fact more men than women give it. In Cattell's[3] terms, they are surface traits, not source traits. Similarly, the MAPS test has a kind of validation in its power to discriminate normal and schizophrenic responses. The original scoring was established in the same way as the M-F test. If, however, we are trying to establish the existence of a source trait or factor, the problem of validity is rather different. Here the external evidence (that people having this trait make a certain kind of impact on the world) is of secondary importance. The existence of source traits depends, first of all, on the acceptance of a certain unique method of analysis of inter-correlations, and secondly on the emergence of the same set of source traits on several different occasions (varying both tests and subjects). The validity of a factor analysis comes from internal rather than external evidence.

A third meaning of validation occurs when it is used about projective tests. Projective tests are not, for the most part, designed to measure a single trait, and are not scored automatically. It is not so much the test itself as its interpretation that has to be validated. A Rorschach or a T.A.T. has no determinate meaning until it has been interpreted. While the principles of the validation of occupational tests and social attitude scales are well known, the validation of projective tests is less clearly understood, and its importance less appreciated. A T.A.T. worker may find that the picture he has built of his subject is so beautifully coherent, and the parts support one another so well, that he feels no need of external validation; and in any case a good many of the conclusions consist of qualitative statements, whose truth is not easily submitted to an objective test. The T.A.T. worker looks for much of his validation in the agreement between what he discovers in his subject's fantasies, and the known events of his life. If he sees in the stories marked fears of illness, and finds out independently that a member of the same household has just died of tuberculosis, he will feel reassured that the stories are really telling him something important about the subject.

The main confirmation of interpretations consists in the recognition of a congruence between fantasy and behaviour. It may produce a very strong subjective conviction, without fulfilling the requirements of formal proof. This is the kind of situation in which clinical and scientific psychologists find nothing but mutual irritation and loss of confidence. Because a T.A.T. (or even a Rorschach) is not reduced to a neat score, in the way that a proficiency test can be, it can usually not be submitted to the kind of validatory procedure that the occupational psychologist is accustomed to. Instead of the one quality (that of success in employment) that has to be assessed in occupational tests, the projective tester is faced with estimates of a great variety of qualities, some of which are not behaviourally defined. The validation of a projective test is usually somewhat indirect, and procedures are not very well established. Let us look at a few devices that have been used.

Rapaport, Gill and Schafer[4] carried through a large-scale project for validating certain tests as instruments of psychiatric diagnosis. Their method was to select experimental groups, consisting of various clinical categories of psychotics (depressives, paranoid schizophrenes, etc.) and a control group of fifty traffic police, who were taken to be 'normal'. The validity of various signs of psychosis was then tested. For instance, on the word association test, the various complex indicators were pooled together, and the frequency in normal subjects was compared with the frequency in the various psychotic groups. On the Rorschach, each scoring item was considered separately. Two statistical tests of significance were used. Where the material was such that scores could be expressed as averages, Student's t-test was used to determine the significance of the difference between normal and psychotic; where scores were frequencies rather than averages, differences were tested by means of chi-square. In this limited diagnostic way the validity of various scoring items could be established or refuted. But there is obviously a great deal more to be done in order to get the full value out of projective tests.

The current psychiatric classes are a very incomplete description of personality, and are so blurred that one cannot feel sure of their future. There is really no established pathology of schizophrenia, and any important discovery in that field might cut right across existing classifications. The present psychiatric classification is in a transitional state between one based on symptoms (phenotype) and one based on causes (genotype). It is not un-common on a child's card in a guidance clinic to find written: Diagnosis: hysteria, or anxiety neurosis, as if this is an explanation of what is wrong with the child. For validation studies of items in a projective test, it is more satisfactory to use some rather well-marked behavioural or somatic sign. Examples of such clearly defined groups are thieves, army deserters, alcoholics, would-be suicides, stutterers, enuretics, asthmatics. Admittedly these classes are not based on unitary traits, and cannot be expected to have a single meaning in every case studied; but at any rate we can be fairly sure when we have an example of what we are talking about; and this is not always true of psychiatric types.

If there were any other well-established psychological types, they would be a useful basis for validation studies, but type theories are at present too flimsy to serve this purpose.

A common-sense way of validating interpretations of a projective test would be to ask someone who knew the subject well to say whether the interpretations fitted the subject. This kind of validation has often been tried. An interesting example is a study in the Rorschach Research Exchange, where a case of history is compared with a blind interpretation of the Rorschach record. Another one that has impressed many readers is the large measure of agreement between du Bois'[5] descriptions of Alorese behaviour, and Oberholzer's interpretations of their Rorschach records. The method is attractively simple, and is similar to what we do in ordinary life. It is, however, not easy to evaluate. The gypsy palmist often makes a similar impression of successful interpretation, and the significance of her result remains open to argument. What was the chance of guessing right? How right was the answer? Nobody can say, so the value of the interpretation remains indeterminate. An enter-taining demonstration of the fallacy involved in this kind of validation is given by Forer.[6] He gave an Interests Question-naire to his class, and pretended, on the basis of their answers, to give a description of each one's character. He then asked the subjects to indicate on a five-point scale how well the test agreed with their estimate of themselves. Most of the students professed themselves impressed by the interpretations given. Only afterwards did they discover that the same interpretations were given to everybody. They included such items as these: 'Your sexual adjustment has presented problems for you.' 'Disciplined and self-controlled outside, you tend to be worrisome, and insecure inside.' 'Security is one of your major goals in life.' The apparent validation of the character sketch was thus shown to be entirely bogus.

On the whole, validation by a general impression of the amount of agreement is an unsatisfactory method. We want to measure the amount of agreement, to compare it with what could have been obtained by chance, and to calculate the probable error of the difference. There is no possibility of doing this in the circumstances that we usually have to deal with. And this has lead many psychologists with a scientific bent to consider that intuition is of no real value to us. We seem to have a great deal of intuitive knowledge, to see brilliantly into the other man's inside. But such knowledge (so it is argued) is deeply untrustworthy, and flatters to deceive. Since we can never determine its validity we should do best to turn our backs on the attraction of unscience, and to build psychology on what we can measure.

The scientific psychologist has worked towards the elimination of the observer. In the natural sciences, the personal observer using his own judgment has usually meant bias and lapses of attention, with consequent error; and an impersonal recording instrument can in most respects do better. A thermometer in the mouth is a better way of finding a person's temperature than feeling his forehead. When psychology came to join the natural sciences, it was widely assumed that it would also follow the general practice in eliminating the personal observer as far as possible. There are many circumstances in which this is desirable. Objectively scored intelligence tests have their uses, and there are many circumstances where a recording instrument can replace an observer. But there are also many circumstances in which the personal observer is the only possible instrument. This applies mainly to the observation of meanings. If we understand a person we observe the meaning of his acts. Out of the chaos of meaningless detail (the twitch of a muscle, the drying up of a gland, or momentary rise of blood pressure) we select for observation those details that can be given a meaning in terms of the whole person. It is this that marks the special province of psychology. We should never say: this is a psychological event, or a biological event, or a sociological event. Events are neutral, and may be studied in any department. The self-same muscle twitch could be studied in terms of physics or chemistry or psychology or sociology, or in various other ways. What makes something physical or psychological or sociological is not the event itself, but the point of view from which it is described. The distinctive point of view of physics concerns such qualities as mass, electrical charge, and temperature. The distinctive point of view of biology concerns the efficacy of the system for maintaining life. The distinctive point of view of psychology concerns the meaning of the act for the person. Its interpretation is in terms of people's motives and values, and in general of the life-space. The distinctive point of view of sociology is in terms of institutions and of individuals in so far as they exemplify impersonal processes, such as the law of increasing returns.

In terms of logical theory, it would probably be possible to translate the subject-matter of any science into another science —to translate sociology into psychology, psychology into physiology, physiology into physics and chemistry. We can make our bow to the ideal of unified science without allowing it to disturb our daily work. But in practice such translations are intolerably clumsy, and cannot be effectively carried out. Each science finds a level of complexity at which it can operate most effectively; and while excursions may be made into neighbouring territory, some rough boundaries can be observed. The psychological level is that of meaningful acts. Some of these meanings are universal, and belong to a situation by virtue of the mere humanity of the observer. The properties of perceptual unit formation studied by Wertheimer are a proper part of general psychology. Orion's belt is a unity for every man who sees it.

Other organizations are individualized, and cannot be effectively studied except through an interpretation of private symbolism. It is here that an impersonal or instrumental method of recording the environment breaks down. The same stimulus may have different meanings for different people, and the discovery of these meanings is an essential task of the psychology of personality. To understand the meaning of a person's act is momentarily to identify with him, to see the world in his terms. This has in the past been spoken of as intuitive knowledge, because it could not ordinarily be analysed and explained in detail. It has fallen into discredit among psychologists because it was felt that our knowledge should be scientifically based. So psychologists have tried to get along without intuitive knowledge, and have pretended to one another that it is useless and misleading. A generation of academic psychologists, confining themselves to external and measurable qualities of behaviour, repressed their subjective understanding of people until they effectively ceased to have any. The scientific psychologist has been right in asking 'how do you know', but he has asked it at the wrong moment. He interrupts the process of empathy, and destroys it by asking for reasons while the process is going on. Validation should rather be indirect, and should not be used to cramp imaginative identification. The observer who by a self-denying ordinance restricts himself to external and measurable aspects of action has deprived himself of psychology's most powerful instrument. The observer is, as Murray has justly remarked, psychology's forgotten man. Every effort has been made to eliminate him in favour of some machine, or routine of scoring. Subjective knowledge is felt to be incurably infected with vagueness and indeterminacy, and to be outside the proper business of science. As we saw earlier with Forer's experiment, it may indeed give the appearance without the reality of knowledge. Much of the knowledge obtained by empathetic understanding cannot be verified peacemeal and in detail. Nevertheless, this knowledge is far too valuable to be thrown overboard, and it is often possible to apply indirect methods of verification.

The main devices of indirect verification are the method of matching and the method of specific prediction. We shall begin with the method of matching, which has been more extensively used. The matching method was apparently invented by Alfred Binet, in the course of an attempt to verify the claim of a graphologist to judge character. The graphologist might say that a person's handwriting showed ambition and nervousness. But if no exact meaning could be given to these terms, they did not help in proving whether the graphologist knew his job or not. We could, however, test the reality of the graphologist's skill by redesigning the experiment as an objective one. Suppose we obtain, from someone who knows them, descriptions of five people concerned in the experiment. A is a man of fifty years, married with three children, fond of golf and afraid of cats. B is a girl of eleven, freckled and hopes to get in the hockey team . . . and so on. The 'expert' is then given specimens of all their hand-writing, and asked to match these with the descriptions. Which handwriting came from A, which from B, etc? If he succeeds, he has given some evidence of possessing real knowledge. Although the descriptions are subjective and impressionistic, the task set for the 'expert' is quite definite, and the degree of success that he obtains can be exactly known. Furthermore, the successes obtained can be compared with the probability of chance success, and the significance of the successes can be calculated. For instance, suppose we have five character sketches to be matched with five specimens of handwriting, with a definite assurance from the experimenter that each of the five characters is represented by one specimen of handwriting. We can then set up a null hypothesis, and consider the probabilities of varying degrees of success, if the matching was done blindly.

If in a series of trials the 'expert' obtained successes significantly better than chance, then we can be sure that he has some genuine skill. Instead of matching specimens of handwriting with character sketches, we might match two expressive productions with one another, for example, a free painting with a Rorschach record. Presumably, successful matching would require some understanding of both kinds of interpretation. A matching experiment has to be sensibly designed if it is to produce meaningful results. If both productions are complex, it is hard to say how the matching was done, and successful matches may be obtained, not by a knowledge of character, but by the use of some quite trivial signs. An example of an unsatisfactory matching test is one that we carried out some years ago, when we asked several judges to match descriptions of a play interview with case histories. We found it necessary to remove many indications that would have given the case away too easily. For instance, one child had been referred for a tic, and this reappeared during the play interview, but had to be omitted from the record for matching purposes. Again, it was often found that identifications were based, not on important traits of character, but on external qualities like the possession of a blazer.

Matching is most satisfactory when it is based on some rather simple expressive act like word association or handwriting. The difficulty of matching depends not merely on the relation between the two items that have to be matched, but also on the other items in the series. The difficulty of the task increases rapidly with the length of the series. The judge may find it impossible to keep the various possibilities in mind together, and his task may become impossibly confusing. The difficulty of the task also depends on the variability of the series. Where the people in the series are markedly different from one another the task of matching is easier than when they are more similar. (The same difficulty arises in using a correlation coefficient, where a larger standard deviation tends to produce higher correlations.) A successful outcome to a matching task is partly a matter of the expressiveness of the material, and partly of the judge's skill. If a judge fails, we cannot conclude that the material is useless; it may be merely that the judge is unskilful. Results cannot be better than the material permits (except in a short run by chance) but they may often be worse. While a successful matching may give a general indication that a projective method is valid, it is not easy to say just what has been proved. The dependence of separate judgments on the series in which they occur is a defect that impairs the value of the method. (In one form or another, this is of course a common phenomenon, and impossible to eliminate entirely in psychological experiments; cf. Sherif's studies of reference groups.)

A device that seems to escape some of the defects of matching is the method of specific prediction. A judge is asked to show his knowledge of a person by predicting how that person will behave in some situation where only a limited set of alternatives is available. The prediction is then compared with the actual outcome, and the degree of success is used as a measure of the judge's knowledge of the person. For example, a judge is asked to guess how his subject will fill in an attitude scale. He is asked to say which statements on a Thurstone type scale the subject will agree with. The more closely the judge's predictions agree with the subject's answers, the better the judge knows his man. It should be noted that the judge's task is to say, not what the man's real attitude is, but how he will fill in the scale. It is not a vague and indeterminate attitude that we are trying to predict, but a precise act of filling in answers to questions, an act that has been given a rigid form by the rules of the test. In a Thurstone-type attitude scale there will be perhaps twenty statements, to each of which the subject has to express agreement or disagreement. The judge has to guess what answers the subject has made, and his proportion of successes can be precisely determined by the experimenter.

In some circumstances we can measure not merely the

P

amount of success obtained, but also the amount of success that would on the average be expected by chance. We may use as the act to be predicted the filling in of a self-rating scale, and we may assume that all answers have the same initial probability. By this we mean, not that all answers are in fact equally frequent, but merely that we have no reason to expect one answer rather than another, except by knowing something about the rater. The more we know about him, the more accurately we can predict how he will respond to the form.

While the general idea of specific prediction is now becoming familiar to psychologists, very little has so far been done to develop the method. We do not know what kinds of acts are most suitable to use for prediction. In one investigation by Notcutt and Silva[7] an extract of eighteen items from Murray's Personality Questionnaire was given to fifty pairs of husbands and wives. All were asked to first answer for themselves, and then to predict how their consorts would have filled in the questions. The accuracy of the wife's knowledge about her husband can thus be precisely measured, by the discrepancy between the husband's self-rating and the wife's prediction of it. Similarly we assessed the husband's knowledge of their wives, and compared the first with the second, to obtain a measure of 'feminine intuition'. There are several other possibilities for specific prediction. We might ask our judges to say which of various toys a child will choose to play with, in what order he will recall a number of objects that have been shown to him, how well he will succeed on a learning task, etc. Any act that expresses a personal style can be used as the basis of a prediction test, provided that the error of prediction is precisely measurable. The desired precision can be obtained in either of two ways: we can either limit the act to a small set of choices, or we can make it one that is suitable for measurement (e.g. the marking of a graphic rating scale, or the level of inspiration).

The prediction of expressive acts can be used as an indirect

way of validating projective tests. At the end of reading a set
of T.A.T. stories we often feel that we understand a person;
we can validate this feeling by predicting how he will answer
specific questions. If the subject's answers to these questions
have been obtained beforehand, we can accurately test the
reality of this claim to understand the person. This is a method
that has not yet been developed, but has great possibilities.
When some standard prediction test has been developed, it
will be possible to measure the amount of insight that a psychologist possesses, like a cricketer's batting average. If a
projective test is regularly used along with a standard self-
rating scale, the prediction of self-ratings can be used as a
measure of the psychologist's insight into the subject. This
objective measure of insight will serve as a check on the
judge's interpretation of the T.A.T. protocol. If an interpreter
cannot predict accurately how the subject will behave, then we
cannot have much confidence in his understanding of the
person. Indirect though it is, this method can provide a searching and completely objective test of the validity of insight.
We saw that in the matching test, success with a particular
item depends in some degree on the other items in the series.
But in the kind of specific prediction that we have been discussing, each item can be considered by itself. The answer to
one item in the rating scale need not be influenced by the other
items. This makes it a better instrument, since the answers
are more open to analysis.

By using tests of specific prediction we can hope to combine
some of the advantages of the subjective and objective methods
in psychology. So far, the subjective psychologists have had
most of the interesting ideas, but have been distressingly
unable to prove them. The objective psychologists have made
delicate instruments of analysis, but have applied them to
trivial problems. The scientific psychologist has rejected
insight, and demanded objective evidence at inconvenient
moments. Insight into private symbolism is a real and important kind of knowledge, which psychology cannot afford to

neglect. Private symbolism is responsible for a considerable part of the variations in human nature, which account for the lack of psychological laws. If we consider the structure of private symbolic systems to be outside the legitimate scope of science, we are condemning scientific psychology to another twenty years of missing the point. With the subtleties of factor analysis at one's disposal, it may be possible to arrive at some valid generalizations in psychology, but they will be diffuse tendencies blurred by innumerable exceptions, and possessing little predictive power. The acceptance of insight as a proper means to psychological knowledge need not mean opening the gates to a flood of subjective speculation. The use of indirect methods of validation can enable experimental psychologists to keep a check on bogus insights and windy impressiveness. It can also enable them with a good conscience to make use of the powerful insights that have been achieved by psycho-analytic thought. The prosperous future of psychology depends on a proper blending of insight and validation.

REFERENCES

1. TERMAN, L. M.   *Sex and Personality.* New York, McGraw-Hill, 1936.

2. STRONG, E. K.   *Vocational Interests of Men and Women.* Stanford Univ. Press, 1943.

3. CATTELL, R. B.   *Description and Measurement of Personality.* Yonkers - on - Hudson, World Book Co., 1946.

4. SCHAFER, R.   *Clinical Application of Psychological Tests.* New York. International Universities Press, 1948.

5. DU BOIS, C.   *The People of Alor.* Minneapolis, Univ. of Minnesota, 1944.

6. FORER, BERTRAM, R.   *The Fallacy of Personal Validation: A classroom demonstration of gullibility.* J. Abnorm. Soc. Psychol. 1949, 44, 118–123.

7. NOTCUTT, B., AND SILVA, A. L. M.   *Knowledge of Other People.* J. Abnorm. Soc. Psychol.

CHAPTER XII

DEVELOPMENT OF THE CONCEPT OF PERSONALITY

IN the preceding chapters we have presented current ideas about personality drawn from psychological theory and practice. Most of the notions described belong to the present century. In the last chapter we shall be lengthening the time-perspective, to include pre-scientific views of the nature and determinants of personality. We shall try to follow (in a sketchy way) the concept of personality as it has changed and grown through the centuries in which it can be observed. In so doing it is natural to look first at ancient Greece, where so many of our modern views originated. The Greeks were the first to make serious attempts to formulate general ideas about human personality. They did not try to build an independent science of psychology, but under the headings of ethics, politics and rhetoric they were discussing the same questions that concern us, and in biographical writings they struggled with the same problems of personality.

For Greece, personality was not so much a theory as a value. It was a value that first became prominent during the breakdown of the old city State, when the old unreflecting identification of the citizen and his society was no longer possible. Personality appears as a value in two different ways—in the contrast of reason and the passions, and in the contrast of nature with custom. Reason was first of all a value that enables man to set himself apart from brute nature, to be above chance and fate. The Greeks did not usually think of the soul as existing independently of the body. Aristotle spoke of the soul as the form of the body, and thus inseparable from it. But he distinguished various parts of the soul, some of which were more closely tied to bodily processes than were others. There was the vegetative soul, controlling the involuntary processes of the body (corresponding to what we now call the autonomic nervous system). There was the sensitive soul, to which belonged sensation and perception, thought, feeling and desire—all the processes that would have been called 'the mind' from Locke onwards. And lastly there was the intellectual soul, including the faculties of reason and will. These were described more in terms of philosophical requirement than of introspective observation. Reason was the faculty that arrived at logically necessary truths; will was the free will, not determined by desire, but willing the good.

The Stoics operated with a similar scheme, though sometimes even more complicated. The Stoic sage was a man who had risen superior to the passions that move ordinary people. It was a celebrated stoic paradox that the good man is happy, even on the rack. He was completely autonomous, and what happened to him no longer mattered. The only evil that could befall him would be that he should fall beneath his own high standard, and he would not permit this to happen. His judgments become impersonal, and he is, indeed, little more than a walking copybook. In the process of achieving self-mastery he has ironed out every individual quality, everything that makes one man different from another. Thus, although Stoicism was a process of continuous self-discipline which encouraged introspection and self-analysis, it did not lead to the self-portrait of a recognizable individual. The philosopher had to identify the workings of interest or passion, only in order to reject them. In the writings of the great Stoic moralists (Seneca, Epectetus, Marcus Aurelius) there is much wisdom, but not much like a Pilgrim's Progress. At the end of the journey all individuality seems to have been purged away. The personal soul has become identical with the practical reason, the moral law in accordance with nature. In overcoming the desires of the flesh, the person evaporated altogether. In the true philosopher, the vegetative soul and the sensitive soul had been subordinated to the intellectual soul.

Similarly, in Plato's earlier metaphor, reason was the charioteer whose business it was to control the unruly horses, lust and ambition. There was a strong vein of asceticism in Plato, and this was reinforced by the Stoics. From this point of view, the achievement of a complete character would mean the subordination of passion to the moral law, the control of the body by the soul.

The second antithesis with which Greek thought operated was that between nature and custom ($\phi\acute{v}\sigma\iota\varsigma$ and $v\acute{o}\mu\sigma\varsigma$). This is the contrast between man as he really is, by his original nature, and man as he is made by society. The effective exploitation of this idea is the work of Socrates, Protagoras, and their contemporaries—the group of philosophers whom Popper has called 'The Great Generation'. They were the first men to make full use of the spirit of free inquiry. The business of the sophist was to call everything into question, to show that even the best established beliefs were the result of convention, not of nature. The usual inference was that what is merely conventional has no binding force, and that everything in morals which had formerly been considered certain, must now be considered doubtful. In the fifth century B.C. the self-contained city State was a dream of the past (perhaps, indeed, it never existed). Commerce, conquest and the wandering scholars meant that men were continually making cross-cultural comparisons; wondering whether this or that custom that had formerly been considered an inevitable expression of human nature, were not in reality just another arbitrary convention, ordered otherwise across the Channel. Plato's *Republic* can be considered as a despairing attempt to check the corrosive process, and to imagine a stable society in which convention would be protected from the inroads of sceptical reason. However, although Plato enjoyed the literary triumph, the ideas that continued to spread were those of Antisthenes. The Cynic philosophers were primarily individualists. They taught their followers to ignore the bonds of convention. It was a doctrine of the Simple Life, similar to that which fascinated eighteenth-century France, though without the sentimental prettiness of Malmaison. Cynics had no property, and did not marry. Their refusal to marry was due not to asceticism, but to a fear of obligations. Their name, of dog-philosophers, is supposed to be an allusion to their shameless habit of copulating in public, like dogs. This was the extreme symbol of rejecting convention. They even disapproved of compulsory athletics for schoolboys.

It is significant that the name of Diogenes, the effective founder of cynicism, is often coupled with that of Alexander. In a tightly integrated little city state, where everyone had an accepted role and status, there could be no room for the man who made autonomy an end in itself. But in the new world-Empire there was scope for individualism. And it seemed to many the most sensible course, because the responsibilities of of a citizen, as they had been known to earlier generations, could not be practised in the huge and despotic modern State. In these two respects, then, the value of personality was expressed for the Greeks in terms of self-sufficiency—the mind's mastery of the body, and the individual's freedom from convention.

With the rise of Christianity the individualist trend continued, but acquired a new meaning. The aim was no longer a proud self-sufficiency, but total submission to a God. And this God was not a timeless order of Nature, but a Person deeply interwoven with time and change. Christians got from the Jews the decisive notion that history as a whole is purposeful, that it has a beginning, middle and end. Greek thought as a whole had no clear-cut view about the meaning of history. Sometimes they played with notions of a cyclic process, and entertained themselves by imagining that all this had happened before, and would happen again. But it was not a notion around which they organized much of their thought. More often they pictured the time-process as coming from nowhere, and going nowhere. For the Christians, History was a meaningful whole: Paradise, the Fall, the coming of Christ, the second coming, and the Final Judgment, were stages of a single historical process. And every individual life acquired its meaning from the cosmic drama of salvation. Each life-history was in a way a microcosmic study of the significance of history as a whole. Biography was a way of seeing God's judgment at work, and learning to know God's ways. The Saint's life was full of ups and downs, a perpetual struggle replete with excitement, whose outcome was uncertain until the very last. There were foes within and foes without. The devil was always looking out for an opportunity to cheat and betray the Christian. And, in human terms, the life and fortune of an earnest Christian were very insecure. The saint did not proudly boast his victories over the flesh, his indifference to chance and change. He rather represented himself as deeply dependent, liable to temptation and failure, never secure of salvation. Christian doctrine gave a new interest and significance to the life-history. At the end of the vista was not the certainty of nothingness, but the tremulous hope of everlasting life, coupled with a dread of everlasting despair. St. Augustine's *Confessions* and his *City of God* were correlated works. The drama of redemption was displayed in both, on the scale of a single life, in the fall of the Roman Empire and in the whole history of man. The spiritual autobiography was essentially a Christian creation. It arose from an enriched idea of the significance of personality.

Medieval theories of the soul are continuous with those of the ancient world. St. Thomas Aquinas, adapted Aristotle's theory to suit the needs of the Church. As we have seen, Aristotle's usual view was that soul and body are two aspects of one whole, and cannot be separated. There is, however, one short momentous passage (De Anima III, 5) in which he takes a different view, saying that, while the vegetative and sensitive souls are born and die with the body, the intellectual soul has an independent existence. Theologians

seized on this passage as a way of reconciling the requirements
of Christian doctrine with the infallibility of Aristotle. Vegetative and sensitive souls were transmitted by the processes of
heredity, were influenced by environment, could be passed
on to offspring, and were subject to mortality. The intellectual
soul had an entirely different fate. It was created between
conception and birth (about the sixth month of pregnancy)
and was thenceforth immortal. By the Augustinian doctrine,
every soul acquires at its creation the sin of Adam, from which
he is absolved only by special grace. The general effect of the
doctrine of original sin seems to be that a stable order of Church
and State is required to keep man from going astray. The
social role is a support that protects man from himself, as well
as from the horror of outer emptiness. The soul needed human
institutions for its salvation. It passed a brief but crucial
period in the flesh, and on the basis of its performance there
was assigned to Heaven, Purgatory or Hell. The reality of this
continued existence was attested by the numerous miracles
of the saints. A saint might or might not perform miracles
in his life, but it was essential that he should begin to do so
soon after death. In Purgatory also, people's circumstances
went on changing, and could be influenced by events in the
world. It was in these ways that the doctrine of immortality
was constantly kept before people, as a practical reality of
which they had to take account. The Soul's Survival after
death was not a remote and improbable speculation, but a
fact of daily experience. In other respects, however, the
concept of personality in medieval society shows a reversion
to earlier models. We no longer see isolated individuals,
separated from their place in society, as we did in the empires
of Alexander, or of Rome. In medieval society, people were
tightly bound to their places, so much so that it was hard to
think of them otherwise.

For the ordinary purposes of life, the main concept was that
of Status Personality. When Chaucer describes his pilgrims,
he sees them firmly set in occupational roles. A man is a

knight, a monk, a miller or a man of law, and most of his qualities are expected to follow from that fact. In the Prologue to the *Canterbury Tales*, people are so completely described by their occupations, that it is not considered necessary to give them names. They are described by their place in the social structure, and by the qualities that grow from their being in that place. The squire is expected to be debonair, the lawyer to be secretive, the franklin to be a lover of meat and drink. In choosing to describe a group who are unrelated, and thrown together by chance, Chaucer has for the moment prized them loose from both occupational and kinship roles. But even when thus separated, they retain their status characteristics. And it is noticeable that in most of the other tales the characters are embedded in the social structure. Among most of Chaucer's contemporaries the identification of a person with his role went much further—so much so that characters were often given abstract names. The characters in a morality play may be dim abstractions like Wealth, Pride, or Good Deeds.

There is an extraordinary lack of clearly perceived individuals in medieval literature. People are seen through a haze of generality and exhortation.

The Middle Ages recognized two ways in which a person might been seen in isolation from his conventional role. One was the hermit, who might withdraw from society in search of his soul's salvation. The second way was that of lovers, in whom a mysterious attraction might cut through all the rules of society. The idea that one man and one woman belonged particularly to one another by reason of some unique affinity in their natures turns up occasionally among ancient writers as an idle speculation; but as an effective myth it spreads over Western Europe from eleventh-century Provence. It involves the idea of personality, that everyone has some individual quality that distinguishes him from everyone else, and is the meaning of his existence. Romantic love originally belonged not to marriage but to adultery. The great love stories of the Middle Ages mostly concerned married ladies who developed other interests—Paolo and Francesca, Lancelot and Guinevere, Tristan and Iseult. Married love was considered to contain no scope for romance. A married woman was expected to obey her husband and bear his children. The Knight, on the other hand, must obey his lady, and it was in that relation that love became significant. Marriage was too much bound up with the system of role and status to provide scope for personal feelings. Adultery alone was truly poetic. C. S. Lewis considers that it was Edmund Spenser who first suggested the way (in the fifth book of the *Faerie Queene*) by which marriage and love could be reconciled, at any rate for the English. This never seems to have happened to the same extent in France. There, love remained characteristically forbidden love.

The first unrestricted assertion of personality was through the romantic lover. In the Italian Renaissance of the fifteenth century the flourish of individualism achieved extremes never known before or since. In a society where careers were open to talents the *condottieri* could rise to any height of greatness by courage, leadership and ruthlessness. The economic restraints of the guild system were breaking down. Agreed restrictions on prices, production and competition were falling into disuse, and the world was open to the strong man who wanted to get on. Moral restraints as well as economic were thrown to the wind. In Renaissance drama we find a deliberate suspension of moral judgment, an admiration of strength and cunning for their own sake. During the sixteenth century the model of Machiavelli diffused over Europe. Marlowe's plays are studies in this ruthless self-assertion that fascinated the men of the time. Tamburlaine achieved the ultimate in terms of brutal power, and lay on his death-bed lamenting his inability to conquer America, which had not then been discovered. The Jew of Malta goes to similar extremes as a finance capitalist, and Faust as a crooked scientist. Faust's thirst for knowledge is so great that he will accept eternal damnation in order to win it. Renaissance dramatists built many tragedies around fear of the strength of the instincts. Instinctual drives so overpowering in their demands that they drive a man to destruction are the theme of Macbeth and of Antony and Cleopatra. Shakespeare liked to isolate a character, to remove him from the usual supports of the social environment, and then to observe the real man emerging from the social mask. Sometimes he is isolated by escaping from the usual social observation, as Proteus in the *Two Gentlemen of Verona*, or Sebastian in *The Tempest*, turn nasty when they think themselves unobserved. At other times a man is isolated by being freed from the usual restrictions, and given absolute power, like Angelo in *Measure for Measure*. The blackest wickedness emerges from the respectable puritan when freed from social control. The effect of isolation is not, however, always bad. Sometimes splendid virtues appear, as with Rosalind and Viola, or with Ferdinand in *The Tempest*. Another way in which a character is set free from the social process is by accident of birth. Richard III is a hunchback. Edmund in King Lear is a bastard. A breach in the kinship system releases a man from the rigidities of status personality, and enables him to be completely himself. The result may be good as with Faulconbridge, or bad as with Don John in *Much Ado*. The Renaissance regarded personality as an absolute form of self-realization, and a value in itself. To be fully and utterly oneself, like Antony and Cleopatra, was worth while, whatever the cost.

Thinkers of the Renaissance added little to the older theories about the causes of personality. The theory of the four humours continued to be used, though without much conviction. In Ben Jonson it had become frankly a metaphor. *Every man in his humour* alluded no longer to hypothetical body fluids, but to comic exaggerations of character. The use of the astrological idea was a little more serious. Some anticlericals among the Italian schoolmen used astrology as a counterblast to Christian theology, in the same way that the Emperor Julian had done a thousand years earlier. The Elizabethans often use metaphors from astrology to express the idea of destiny, and helplessness of man. Shakespeare may suggest that 'The stars above us govern our conditions' (*Lear*, iv, 3) or

> 'That this huge stage presenteth nought but shows
> Whereon the stars in secret influence comment.' (Sonnet
>   15),

But there are other passages in which he rejects the astrological explanation as a cowardly evasion of human responsibility.

> 'The fault, dear Brutus, is not in our stars
> But in ourselves, that we are underlings'.

On the whole Shakespeare is a good Elizabethan in regarding personality as something ultimate, not requiring explanation. He never makes the origin of character a serious theme of his drama. We are not offered a reason why Cordelia is good and Goneril is bad. The men of the Renaissance did not want explanations of personality. Their concern was with the fact rather than the cause. They delighted in their new-found moral and intellectual liberty, their freedom to enjoy 'the huge army of the world's desires'. They felt that any systematic explanation would be an encroachment on the freedom of the will that was their chief delight. The humanist Pico della Mirandola imagines God addressing Adam: 'We give you no fixed place, no features of your own, nor any gift peculiar to yourself, in order that you may have whatever place, features or gifts you may choose. On others we impose a definite nature under prescribed laws. You are bound by no limits, and may determine your nature by your own judgment. We have placed you in the middle of the world, in order that you may more easily look around at whatever is in it. We have made you neither heavenly nor earthly, neither mortal nor immortal, so that you may form your own image, as if the sculptor of yourself. You can degenerate to a brute or by your own decision rise to divine heights'. (*De Hominis Dignitate*). Such a belief in free will naturally discouraged interest in the origins of character, but it greatly stimulated interest in the process.

As the Renaissance advanced, people seem to become more acutely observant of one another, as well as being better equipped for describing what they observed. People began to study character for its own sake. Several times in Shakespeare we find that a character originally designed to play a conventional role in the plot has become too large and too interesting for his place. Pistol, in *Henry V*, is intended to be nothing more than the boastful coward, the traditional *miles gloriosus* of Latin comedy. Through most of the play he takes this part consistently enough, but in a short soliloquy near the end of the play, after the traditional exposure scene where he is shown up as the coward that he is, he tells us how his wife at home in England has died of syphilis. For the moment he ceases to be the conventional pasteboard object of contempt, and behaves like a three-dimensional human being. This happens many times over in Shakespeare—that a character narrowly bound by the requirements of a plot begins to behave in a more human, less stereotyped way. Sometimes this seriously distorts the impression made by the play as a whole. Shylock should, according to the dramatic conventions of the time, be a hateful villain, whose ruin is the crowning delight of the play. This may have been the impression made on a sixteenth-century audience, but to us to-day an undercurrent is indicated that would yield a different judgment.

There is thus an official or conventional result of the play, and an unofficial meaning in terms of the characters rather than the plot. Critics stress one of these or the other according to temperament. There are many more of these, Hamlet, Falstaff, Caliban and Barnadine are further examples. From one point of view this can be described as a conflict of plot and character; from another, as a contrast between public and private values.

From the late sixteenth century onwards, this interest in character became increasingly a pre-occupation of Western man. Characters were enjoyed for their curious and fantastic qualities, and there was sometimes a deliberate suspension of moral judgment, as with Falstaff. There was a brief fashion in England of writing 'characters' (such as we quoted in Chap. III). Other literary forms—the essay and the novel—responded to this absorbing interest. In France the writing of characters went on longer, and developed new psychological subtleties in the writings of La Bruyère and Vauvenargues. In the English novel, the interest in character came to predominate over the interest in plot.

Side by side with this delight in quaint individuals, there was a search for a systematic description of human motivation. Galileo and Descartes had seen the vision of a general order of nature, a system of universal law, and their hope had been triumphantly vindicated by the achievements of Newton. The lawfulness of mechanics encouraged men to search for a similar lawfulness in human nature. The many variants of moral theory that appeared in the eighteenth century can be reduced to two main kinds. The pleasure-pain theories lead on from Hobbes to Condillac, Bentham and the Reflexologists. Economists and political philosophers found the pleasure-pain psychology fairly adequate to their needs. They developed the theory of the economic man, who was entirely rational and selfish. He bought in the cheapest market and sold in the dearest, and always acted in his own interest. The pleasure-pain psychology worked rather well for describing the world of the rising eighteenth-century tradesman. Adam Smith says: 'It is not from the benevolence of the butcher, the brewer or the baker, that we expect our dinner, but from their regard to their own interest. We address ourselves not to their humanity but to their self-love, and never talk to them of our own necessities, but of their advantages. Nobody but a beggar chooses to depend chiefly on the benevolence of his fellow-citizens.' The concept of natural law applied to human personality can lead on to an exalted vision of the unity of man with nature. This is most splendidly expressed in the *Ethics* of Spinoza. Man's freedom lies in the recognition of necessity. Any other freedom would be superfluous and illusory. When we follow this line of thought, we are led to a possible harmony of man with nature, not very different from the Stoic idea. A realistic acceptance of the natural order was a canon of Spinoza's thought: 'He who truly loves God will not expect that God should love him in return.' Spinoza, like the Stoics, regarded the passions as a weakness to be overcome, and scientific understanding was the means to this end. Thus utilitarian hedonism and rationalism tended to coincide with a belief in necessity.

There are others to whom necessity is not a source of consolation and refreshment, but presents a bleak and terrifying aspect. In their positive forms, these stress the possibilities of human freedom and uniqueness. To them the passions are an expression of the riches of human personality.

These systems were those of intuitionism. The work of Hutcheson and Hume in Scotland, and of Vauvenargues in France, are the background of McDougall, Janet and the dynamic psychologies.

While pleasure-pain theories looked for a uniform human nature, in which people would be differentiated by effects of association, the intuitionists differentiated people by the strength and direction of their motives. The psychology of personality derives from these eighteenth-century philosophers of motivation.

These opposing theories of human nature turn up in eighteenth-century literature as contrasted pairs of characters—the calculating selfish man versus the good-natured impulsive wastrel. Tom Jones is contrasted with Blifil, and Charles with Joseph Surface, in each case to the advantage of the instinctual life. Sometimes the two theories are presented as contrasting systems of motives within a single person, like Goldsmith's Man in Black, who is theoretically hard-hearted towards the

Q

poor, but surreptitiously gives away everything he has. The general opinion was that the forces of order and selfishness were increasingly dominating the forces of impulse, the ego was subduing the id. 'The age of chivalry is gone,' wrote Burke; 'that of sophisters, economists and calculators has succeeded; and the glory of Europe is extinguished for ever.' Literary men on the whole took the side of sentiment against industrial discipline and time-keeping. The search for qualities in human nature that could not be reduced to enlightened selfishness led the romantics to explore many byways in search of glimpses that would make them less forlorn. Knights of chivalry, Gaelic barbarians, boys and girls growing up on distant islands, peasants, tramps, children, dogs, donkeys, skylarks—they explored every kind of character that was not dominated by the selfish ambition that was to them the worst evil of the modern world. The Greek antithesis of nature and convention reappears. The convention that philosophers are opposing is now the organized selfishness of the industrial society.

Considering how the individual is moulded by culture, the romantics were led on to the study of childhood, which to them was the age of innocence, before the shades of the competitive prison-house descended. In their anxiety to score points off the industrialist, Wordsworth and St. Pierre view children through a rosy haze, properly belonging to those delightful moments when they have been washed, and are prepared to behave. They emphasized the permanent influence of early experiences. Coleridge held up his little son to the moonlight, and hoped that its beauty would be permanently valuable to him. In terms of modern psychology, he would have been well advised to cut down his opium and give little Hartley a more consistent affection. Nevertheless, the basic idea was there, that the growth of personality is continuous, the child is father of the man.

Later in the nineteenth century, novelists begin to apply the idea, and for the first time in literature we get keenly observed studies of children growing into adults. Charlotte Brontë, Thackeray and George Eliot draw personalities in continuous development. Jane Eyre in her early battles gains the strength that later enables her to stand up to Rochester and Miss Ingram. Thackeray plays elaborately on the theme of maternal over-protection; but he follows it through the generations as a modern psychologist would. Characters no longer have the arbitrary God-given quality that they did in Shakespeare.

Towards the end of the century, the theme of individual development begins to come together with the theme of evolution. The individual's life-history begins to acquire metaphysical importance from its relation to the history of the race. (We saw this happen once before, in Augustine's time.) The theme of recapitulation is prominent both in Darwin and in Haeckel, and in Germany it seems to have constituted the main meaning of evolution. The antithesis of nature and convention is still important, but nature, in an evolutionary setting loses its pristine charm. Nature in Huxley has become mainly cruel, man's animal nature that must somehow be ironed out, or coaxed away, the ape and tiger that are unwilling to die.

Most of these ideas are, as we have seen, imbued with ideology, and do not cease to be so merely because they are investigated by scientific methods. For us, as for the Greeks, personality is a value as well as a theory. Several distinct values motivate the search for a systematic description of personality. There is still Spinoza's vision, undimmed after three hundred years, of bringing human nature within the scope of natural law. Recent advances in physiology have encouraged the searchers, and factor analysis has provided new tools. There are some to whom the interpretation of man in terms of natural law means a proclamation of order, and rescue from chaos. The recognition of necessity may appear as a release from personal guilt and responsibility. In Victorian times the puritan attempt to deny and subjugate man's animal nature had aroused acute anxieties, and the Freudian reductive analysis was an effective therapy. Freud told people that they are all really lustful. Adler told people that they are all really selfish. To explain away human motives as the derivatives of bodily processes is another aggression against parental wisdom. To debunk the higher motives as nothing but lower ones may give an experience of liberation, and restored innocence, cleansing from sin. There are others for whom personality means mainly the assertion of individuality, the uniqueness of men, and their right and duty of liberty. Personality is then treated as a defence against two threats—the scientific threat of being explained away as 'nothing but' something else, and the political threat of being managed out of existence in factory and bureau. The increase of physiological knowledge often appears as a threat, a reduction of the 'higher' to the 'lower', an attempt to bring freedom under the control of necessity. Tyranny is here identified, not with morality, but with discipline. Personality means autonomy and voluntary choice, not being regulated and controlled. The emphasis is on the integration of unique systems of values, and their contrast with an ego-alien discipline. Much controversy among psychologists is really an assertion of these two opposed systems of value. The natural scientists won their freedom in the seventeenth century by separating matter from mind, and separating fact from value. In the social sciences this separation is not possible to the same extent; yet in their claim to be scientists, psychologists are accustomed to profess indifference to values. Often the result is that surreptitious value-systems flourish in the undergrowth, unacknowledged and uncriticized, disguised as objective facts. This is particularly so in the study of personality, where strong personal motives enter. We need to think more and better about the relation of fact and value. The science of personality has only just begun.

There are three sets of references:
1. Chapter references which are given separately for each of the twelve chapters.

2. Essential references, which all refer to recent works suitable for the general reader.

3. General references, which include a wider range.

A revision of the indexes was outlined by Professor Mace, and carried out by my colleague Miss Verona Hunkin: she also read the typescript for correction. My wife and my mother also read the typescript, as did two anonymous readers and other patient friends.

GENERAL REFERENCES

References have been compiled with the following rules in mind: (i) books are preferred to articles in journals; (ii) works in foreign languages are referred to in English translation, wherever possible; (iii) where there are several works by one author on a topic, usually only the latest is given.

ABRAHAM, K. — *Selected Papers.* — London, Hogarth Press, 1927.

ADLER, A. — *Understanding Human Nature.* — London, Allen and Unwin, 1932.

ALEXANDER, F. — *Uber das Verhaltnis von Struktuur — zu Triebkoniflkten.* — Internationale Zeitschrift fur Psychoanalyse 20, 1934.

ALLPORT, F. H. — *Social Psychology.* — Boston, Houghton Mifflin, 1924.

ALLPORT, G. W., and VERNON, P. E. — *Studies in Expressive Movement.* — New York, Macmillan, 1933.

AMES, ADELBERT JR. — 'Binocular Vision as affected by Relations between Uniocular stimulus - Patterns in Commonplace Environments.' — *Am. J. Psychol.* LIX, pp. 333–57.

ANASTASI, A. — *Differential Psychology.* — New York, Macmillan, 1943.

ANSBACHER, H. L. — 'German Military Psychology.' — *Psychol. Bull.* 38, 1941, 370–92.

BAHNSEN, H. — *Beitrage zur Charakterologie.* — Leipzig, 1867, reprinted 1932.

BALKEN, E. R., and MASSERMAN, J. H. — 'The Language of Fantasy III.' The Language of the fantasies of patients with conversion hysteria, anxiety state, and obsessive - compulsive neurosis. — *J. Psychol.* 10, 1940, 75–86 (reprinted in Tomkins, S. S., *Contemporary Psychopathology*).

BARKER, R. G., KONNIN, J. S. and WRIGHT, H. F. (Ed.) — *Child Behaviour and Development.* — New York, McGraw-Hill, 1943.

BARNETT, H. G. — 'Personal Conflicts and Cultural Change.' — *Social Forces* 20, (1941), p. 171.

BATESON, G., and MEAD, M. — *Balinese Character: a Photographic Analysis.* — New York Academy of Sciences, 1942.

BENEDICT, R. — *The Chrysanthemum and the Sword.* — Boston, Houghton Mifflin, 1946.

BION, W. R., and RICKMAN, J. (1943). — 'Intra - Group Tensions: Their Study a Task of the Group.' — *Lancet*, ii, 678.

BION, W. R.   'Experiences in Groups.'   *Human Relations.* 1948, Vol. I, 314–20, 1949, Vol. II, 487–96, 1949, Vol. III, Vol. 2, 13–22. 1949, IV., Vol. 2, 295–304, 1950, V, Vol. 3, 3–14, 1950, VI, Vol. 3, 395–402.

BOUTONIER, J.   *l'Angoisse.*   Paris, Presses Universitaires de France, 1945.

BOWLBY, J.   *Forty - Four Juvenile Thieves.*   London, Baillière, Tindall and Cox, 1947.

BRADSHAW, F. F.   *Rating Scale: Its reliability, validity and use.*   Washington D.C. 1930, Amer. Council on Education.

BRILL, A. A.   'The Universality of Symbols.'   *Psycho-analytic Review,* 30, 1943, 1–18.

BROWN, J. F.   *Psychology and the Social Order.*   1936.

BRUNSWICK, EGON.   'Organismic Achievement and Environmental Probability.'   *Psychol. Rev.* 50, 1943, 255–71.

BUHLER, C., and KELLEY, G.   *The World Test.*   New York, Psychological Corp., 1941.

BURT, C.   *The Factors of the Mind.*   London, University of London Press, 1940.

BURT, C.   'Validating Tests for Personnel Selection.'   *Brit. J. Psychol.,* 1943, 34, 1–19.

CATTELL, R. B.   *General Psychology.*   Cambridge, Mass. Sci.–Art Publishers, 1941.

CATTELL, R. B.   *Guide to Mental Testing.*   London, Univ. of London Press (1936).

CURLE, ADAM   'Incentives to Work: An Anthropological Appraisal.'   *Human Relations* II, 1949, 41–8.

DELAGE, YVES   *La Structure du Protoplasma et les Theories sur l'Heredite' et les grands problemes de la Biologie generale.*   Paris, 1895, 2nd edit. 1903.

DEUTSCH, H.   *The Psychology of Women.*   2 vols. New York, Grune and Stratton, 1944.

DOLLARD, J.   *Criteria for the Life History.*   Newhaven, Hale Univ. Press, 1935.

DOLLARD, J.   *Caste and Class in a Southern Town.*   Newhaven, Yale Univ. Press, 1938.

DREVER, JAMES   *Instinct in Man.*   Cambridge U.P., 1921.

DUDLEY, D. R.   *A History of Cynicism, from Diogenes to the Sixth Century A.D.*   London, Methuen, 1937.

DUNBAR, H. FLANDERS   *Psychosomatic Diagnosis.*   New York, Hoeber, 1943.

ELLIS, HAVELOCK | *Studies in the Psychology of Sex.* | 4 vols. New York, Random House, 1936.

ERIKSON, E. H. | 'Studies in the Interpretation of Play. Clinical Observations of Play Disruption in Young Children.' | *Genet. Psychol. Monogr.* 22, 1940, 557–671.

FIRTH, RAYMOND | *Human Types.* | London, Nelson, 1938.

FLIESS, R. | *The Psycho-analytic Reader*, Vol. 1. | New York, International Universities Press, 1948.

FLUGEL, J. C. | *Man, Morals and Society.* | London, Duckworth, 1945.

FORDE, C. DARYLL. | *Habitat, Economy and Society.* | New York, Harcourt Brace, 1934.

FORER, BERTRAM, R. | 'The Fallacy of Personal Validation: A Classroom Demonstration of Gullibility.' | *J. Abnorm. Soc. Psychol.* 1949, 44, 118–23.

FORTES, M. (Ed.) | *Social Structure: Essays presented to A. R. Radcliffe-Brown.* | Oxford, Clarendon Press 1949.

FREEMAN, F. S. | *Individual Differences the nature and causes of variations in intelligence and special abilities.* | London, Harrap, 1934.

FRENCH, T. M., ALEXANDER, FRANZ and co-workers. | 'Psychogenic Factors in Bronchial Asthma' 2 vols. | *Psychosomatic Medicine Monograph*, Vol. 1, No. 4, Vol. 2, Nos. 1, 2. Menasha Wisconsin. George Banta Publishing Co., 1941.

FRENKEL-BRUNSWIK, ELSE | 'Dynamic and Cognitive Categorization of Qualitative Material.'

| I. 'General Problems and the Thematic Apperception Test.' | *J. Psychol.*, 1948, 25, 253–60.

| II. 'Application to Interviews with the Ethnically Prejudiced.' | *J. Psychol.*, 1948, 25, 261–77.

FREYD, M. | *Graphic Rating Scale for Teachers.* | Chicago, C. H. Stoelting, 1923.

FROMM, E. | *Man for Himself.* | London, Routledge, 1949.

GLATZER, H. T. | 'Relationship Group Therapy with a Mother of a Problem Child.' | in S. R. Slavson (ed.): *The Practice of Group Therapy.*

GORER, G., and RICKMAN, J. | *The People of Great Russia.* | London, Cresset Press, 1949. 10s. 6d.

GORER, G. 'The Concept of National Character.' *Science News*, **18**, 1950, 105–22.

GREENE, E. B. *Measurements of Human Behaviour*. New York, Odyssey Press, 1941.

GROSS, K. *Die Cerebrale Sekundarfunktion*. Leipzig, 1902.

HANFMANN, E. 'Thought Disturbances in Schizophrenia as revealed by performance in a picture completion test. *J. Abn. Soc. Psychol.*, 1939, 34, 249–64.

HARING, DOUGLAS G. *Personal Character and Cultural Milieu.* Syracuse V.P. $5.00. 1948.

HARTMANN, H., and KRIS, E. 'Genetic Approach to Psycho-analysis.' from the *Psycho-analytic Study of the Child.* Vol. I, 1945.

HARTSHORNE, H., and MAY, M. A. *Studies in the Nature of Character*, Vol. I. Studies in Deceit. New York, Macmillan, 1930.

HARTSHORNE, H., MAY, M. A., and MALLER, J. B. *Studies in the Nature of Character*, Vol. II. Studies in Service and Self-Control. New York, Macmillan, 1929.

HARTSHORNE, H., MAY, M. A., and SHUTTLEWORTH, F. K. *Studies in the Nature of Character*, Vol. III. Studies in the Organization of Character. New York, Macmillan, 1930.

HEALY, W., and BRONNER, A. F. *New Light on Delinquency and its Treatment.* Newhaven, Yale Univ. Press, 1936.

HECKER, J. F. C. *The Black Death and the Dancing Mania* (Eng. translation 1888). London, Cassell, (original edition 1865).

HEIDBREDER, E. *Minnesota Personal Traits Rating Scales Test Blank.* Chicago, C. H. Stoelting, 1931.

HELLPACH, W. *Geopsyche.* Stuttgart: Ferdinand Euke, 1950.

HERING, E. 'Ueber das Gedachtnis' als eine allgemeine Funktion der organisirten Materie. Vienna 1870. reprinted with two other lectures in *Memory:* Open Court, Chicago. 4th edit., 1913.

HERRIOTT, F. 'Some Uses of Psychodrama at St. Elizabeth's Hospital.' *Sociometry* 8, 1943, 292–95. Reprinted in J. L. Moreno: *Group Psychotherapy.*

HEYMANS, G. 'La Classification des Caracteres.' *Revue du Mois*, 1911.

HIPPOCRATES (of Cos) *Nature of Man.* Loeb translation Vol. IV translated by W. H. S. Jones, Heinemann, 1931.

HODGES, H. — *Wilhelm Dilthey: An Introduction.* — London, Kegan Paul, 1944.

HORNEY, K. — *Self-Analysis.* — London, Kegan Paul, 1942.

HORNEY, K. — *Our Inner Conflicts.* — London, Kegan Paul, 1946.

HULL, C. L. — *Principles of Behavior.* — New York, Appleton-Century, 1941.

HULL, C. L., and LUGOFF, L. S. — 'Complex Signs in Diagnostic Free Association.' — *J. Exp. Psychol.* 4, 1921, 111–36.

HULL, CLARKE L. — 'The Problem of Interviewing Variables in Molar Behavior Theory.' — *Psychol. Rev.* 50, 1943, 273–91.

HULL, C. L., and MONTGOMERY, R. P. — 'Experimental Investigation of Certain Alleged Relations between character and Handwriting.' — *Psychol. Rev.* 26, 1919, 63–74.

HUNTINGTON, E. — *Mainsprings of Civilization.* — London, Chapman and Hall, 1945.

JAENSCH, E. R. — *Studien zur Typologie Menschlicher Typen.* — Leipzig, Barth, 1930.

JANET, P. — *L'Evolution Psychologique de la Personnalite.* — Paris Editions, A. Chahine, 1929.

JAQUES, ELLIOT — 'Some principles of organization of a social therapeutic institution.' — *J. Soc.* issues, 1947, 3, No. 2, 4–10.

JENNINGS, H. H. — *Leadership and Isolation.* — New York, Longmans, 1943.

JENNINGS, H. H. — 'A Sociometric Study of Emotional and Social Expansiveness. — in Barker, Konnin and Wright: *Child Behavior and Development.*

JONES, E. — *On the Nightmare.* — 2nd impression, 1949. London, Hogarth Press. 21s.

MAXWELL JONES. — 'Acting as an aid to Therapy in a Neurosis Centre.' — *British Medical Journal,* 30th April, 1949.

MAXWELL JONES — 'The Working of an Industrial Neurosis Unit.' — *Occupational Therapy and Rehabilitation.* 26, 1947, 213–21.

JUNG, C. G. — *Diagnostische Assoziationsstudien.* Translated as: *Studies in Word Association.* — Leipzig, 1905.

KARDINER, A. — *The Individual and his Society.* — New York, Columbia Univ. Press, 1939.

KASANIN, J. S. (Ed.) — *Language and Thought in Schizophrenia.* — Berkeley, Univ. California Press, 1946.

KLAGES, L.	*Handschrift und Charakter.*	15th Edition, Leipzig, 1932.
KLAGES, L.	*The Science of Character.*	London, Allen & Unwin, 1929 (original German edition 1910).
KLEIN, M.	*Psycho - analysis of Children.*	London, Hogarth Press, 1932.
KLEIN, M.	*Contributions to Psycho-analysis.* 1921–45.	London, Hogarth Press, 1948.
KLINEBERG, O.	*Race Differences.*	New York, Harper, 1935.
KLOPPER, B., and KELLEY, D. M.	*The Rorschach Technique.*	Yonkers - on - Hudson, World Book Company, 1942.
KOHLER, W.	*Dynamics in Psychology.*	London, Faber, 1942.
LASAGA, J. I., and MARTINEZ-ARANGO, C.	'Four detailed examples of how mental conflicts of psychoneurotic and psychotic patients may be discovered by means of the T.A.T.	*J. Psychol.*, 1948, 26, 299–345.
LE SENNE, R.	*Traite de Caracterologie.*	Paris, Presses, Universitaires de France, 1946.
LEVY, DAVID M.	'Release Therapy.'	in S. S. Tomkins, *Contemporary Psychopathology.*
LEVY, D. M.	*Maternal Over protection.*	New York, Columbia University Press, 1943.
LEVY, JOHN	'Relationship Therapy as Applies to Play Groups.'	*Am. J. Orthopsych.* 8, 1938.
LEWIN, KURT	*Resolving Social Conflicts.*	New York, Harper, 1948.
LEWINSON, T. S., and ZUBIN, J.	*Handwriting Analysis.*	New York, King's Crown Press, 1942.
LIPPITT, R., and WHITE, R. K.	'The Social Climate of Children's Groups.'	in Barker Kounin and Wright, *Child Behavior and Development.*
LOEB, J.	*The Organism as a Whole from a Physicochemical Viewpoint.*	N.Y. and London, 1916.
LOEB, LEO	'Biological Basis of Individuality.'	Springfield, Ill., Thomas, 1945.
LOWENFELD, M.	*Play in Childhood.*	London, Gollancz, 1935.
LOWENFELD, M.	'The world pictures of children. A method of recording and studying them.'	*Brit. J. Med. Psychol.*, 1939, 18, 65–100.
LOWENFELD, M.	*On the Psychotherapy of Children:* Report of a Conference held at the Institute of Child Psychology.	London, August, 1948. (Privately Printed).

LUNDBERG, GEORGE A.	*Social Research: A Study in Methods of Gathering Data.*	2nd edition. New York. Longmans, 1942.
LURIA, A. R.	*The Nature of Human Conflicts.*	New York, Liveright, 1932.
MCDOUGALL, W.	*Introduction to Social Psychology.*	London, Methuen, 1908.
MCDOUGALL, W.	*An Outline of Psychology.*	London, Methuen, 1923.
MCDOUGALL, W.	*The Energies of Men, a Study of the Fundamentals of Dynamic Psychology.*	London, Methuen, 1932.
MACE, C. A.	*Incentives:* Some Experimental Studies (Industrial Health Research Board, Report No. 72.)	London, H.M. Stationery Office, 1935.
MACKINNON, D. W., and HENLE, M.	*Experimental Studies in Psychodynamics:* A laboratory Manual.	Cambridge, Mass., Harvard U.P., 1948.
MAIER, N. R. F.	*Frustration (A study of of Behavior without a Goal).*	McGraw, 1949, \$3.50.
MALINOWSKI, B.	*Sex and Repression in Savage Society.*	London, Kegan Paul, 1927.
MALINOWSKI, B.	*Dynamics of Culture Change.*	London, Oxford Univ. Press, 1945.
MARUM, D.	'Character Assessment from Handwriting.'	*J. Ment. Sci.,* 91 (1945), 22–42.
MASLOW, A. H.	'A preface to motivation theory.'	*Psychosomatic Medicine,* 1943, 5, 85–92.
MASLOW, A. H.	'A Theory of Human Motivation.'	*Psychol. Review* (50), 1943, (370–96).
MAYO, ELTON	*The Human Problems of an Industrial Civilization.*	New York, Macmillan, 1933.
MEAD, M.	*Growing up in New Guinea.*	New York, Morrow, 1930.
MEAD, M.	*Coming of Age in Samoa.*	London, Cape, 1929.
MEAD, M.	*Male and Female: A study of the Sexes in a Changing World.*	London, Gollancz, 1950.
METTLER, F. A. (Ed.)	*Selective Partial Ablation of the Frontal Cortex.*	New York, Hoeber, 1949.
MILLER, N. E., and DOLLARD, J.	*Social Learning and Imitation.*	London, Kegan Paul, 1945.
MIRA, E.	'Myokinetic Psychodiagnosis: a new technique of exploring the conative trends of personality.'	*Proceedings of the Royal Society of Medicine* (1939), 33, 173–94.

Misch, G. — *A History of Auto-biography in Antiquity.* 2 vols. — Routledge and Kegan Paul, 1950 (original German edition, Leipzig, 1907).

Moreno, J. L. — *Group Psychotherapy: a symposium.* — New York, Beacon House 1945. (reprint of *Sociomety*, 8, 1943, Nos. 3 and 4.)

Moreno, J. L. — *Who Shall Survive? A New Approach to the Problems of Human Interrelations.* — Washington, D.C., Nervous and Mental Disease Publishing Co., 1934.

Napoli, P. J. — 'Finger Painting and Personality Diagnosis.' — *Genet. Psychol. Monog.*, 1946, 34, 129–231.

Niebuhr, Reinhold — *Faith and History. A Comparison of Christian and Modern Views of History.* — New York. Charles Scribner's Sons, 1949.

Notcutt, Bernard — 'Perseveration and Fluency.' — *Brit. J. Psychol.*, 1943, 33, 200–8.

Notcutt, B., and Silva, A. — 'Knowledge of Other People.' — *J. Abnorm. Soc. Psychol.*

Parsons, Talcott — *The Structure of Social Action.* — Glencoe, Illinois, Free Press, 1949 (first published 1937).

Paterson, D. G. — *Physique and Intellect.* — New York, Appleton-Century, 1930.

Pavlov, I. P. — *Conditioned Reflexes and Psychiatry.* — New York, International Publishers, 1941.

Payne, A. F. — *Sentence Completions.* — New York, New York Guidance Clinic, 1928.

Pinard, J. W. — 'Tests of Perseveration.' — *Brit. J. Psychol.*, 1932, 23.

Pear, T. H. — *Voice and Personality.* — London, Chapman and Hall, 1931.

Pechey, B., and Brunton-Warner, U. — 'The Play Interview as a Means of Diagnosis in the Treatment of Maladjusted Children.' — *Pretoria, Journal of Social Research*, 1950, 1, 43–51.

Preyer, W. — *Specielle Physiologie des Embryo.* — Leipzig, 1885.

Radcliffe-Brown, A. R. — 'On Social Structure.' — *Journal of the Royal Anthropological Institute*, 70, 1940.

Raven, J. C. — *Controlled Projection.* — London, H. K. Lewis, 1944.

Rees, J. R. — *The Shaping of Psychiatry by War.* — New York, W. W. Norton, 1945.

Reich, W. — *Character Analysis.* — New York, Orgone Institute Press, 1945.

Roback, A. A. — *Psychology of Character, 2nd edition.* — London, Kegan Paul, 1928.

ROBACK, A. A.   *Bibliography of Character and Personality.*   Cambridge Mass., Sci-Art Publishers, 1927.

RODGER, A.   'The Work of the Admiralty Psychologists.'   *Occup. Psychol.,* 19, 132–39.

ROETHLISBERGER, F. J., and DICKSON, W. J.   *The Management and the Worker.*   Cambridge, Mass. Harvard U.P., 1939.

ROGERS, C.   *Test of Personal Adjustment.*   New York, General Board of Y.M.C.A., 1931.

ROGERS, C. R.   *The Clinical Treatment of the Problem Child.*   Cambridge, Mass, Riverside Press, 1939.

ROHDE, A. R., and HILDRETH, G.   *Sentence Completions Test.*   New York, Psychological Corporation, 1947.

ROSANOFF, A. J.   *Manual of Psychiatry.* Revised edition.   New York, Wiley, 1938.

ROSENZWEIG, S., FLEMING, E. E., and CLARKE, H. J.   'Revised Scoring Manual for the Rosenzweig Picture Frustration Study.'   *J. Psychol.,* 1947, 24, 165–208.

ROSENZWEIG, S., FLEMING, E. E., and ROSENZWEIG, L.   'The Children's Form of the Rosenzweig Picture Frustration Study.'   *Journal of Psychology,* 1948, 26, 141–91.

ROTTER, J. B., and WILLERMAN, B.   The Incomplete Sentences Test.'   *J. Consult Psychol,* II, 1947, 43–8.

ROUX   *Archiv fur Entwicklungsmechanik* 1895.

RUSSELL, E. S.   *The Interpretation of Development and Heredity.*   London, Oxford Univ. Press, 1930.

SACHS, HANNS   *The Creative Unconscious (Studies in the Psychoanalysis of Art).*   Cambridge, Mass: Sci-Art Publishers, 1942.

SANFORD, R. NEVITT   'Personality Patterns in School Children.'   in Barker, Kounin and Wright, *Child Behavior and Development.*

SCHAFER, R.   *Clinical Application of Psychological Tests.*   New York: International Universities Press, 1948.

SCHILDER, P.   *Psychotherapy.*   New York: W. W. Norton, 1938.

SCOTT, W. D., and CLOTHIER, R. C.   *Personnel Management.*   New York, McGraw-Hill, 1923.

SEMON, R.   *Die Mneme.*   Leipzig, 1904.

SHAND, A. F.   *The Foundations of Character.*   London, Macmillan, 1914.

SHAW, R. F.   *Finger Painting.*   Boston, Little Brown, 1938.

SHERIF, M.   *An Outline of Social Psychology.*   New York, Harper, 1948.

SHNEIDMAN, E. S.   'Schizophrenia and the MAPS test. A study of certain formal psycho - social aspects of fantasy production in schizophrenia as revealed by performance on the Make - a - Picture-Story (MAPS) Test.   *Genetic Psychology Monographs*, 38, 1948.

SLAVSON, S. R.   'Differential Dynamics of Activity and Interview Group Therapy.'   *Amer. J. Orthopsychiatry*, 17, 1947.

SMITH, W. WHATELY   *The Measurement of Emotion.*   London, Kegan Paul, 1922.

SPEARMAN, C.   *The Abilities of Man, Their Nature and Measurement.*   London, Macmillan, 1932.

SPRANGER, E.   *Types of Men.*   Halle, Max Niemeyer, 1928.

STAGNER, R.   *The Psychology of Personality.*   New York, McGraw-Hill, 1937.

STEIN, M. I.   *The Thematic Apperception Test: an Introductory Manual for its Clinical Use with Adult Males.*   Cambridge, Mass. Addison-Wesley, 1948.

STEKEL, W.   *Compulsion and Doubt* 2 vols.

STEPHENSON, W.   'An Introduction to so-called motor perseveration tests.'   *Brit. J. Educ. Psychol.*, 1934, 4.

STERN, W.   *Allgemeine Psychologie auf Personalistische Grundlage.*   2nd ed. Haag Martinus Nijhoff, 1950.

STERN, W.   'Cloud Pictures: A new method for testing imagination.'   *Character and Personality*, 1938, 6, 132–46.

STONE, C. P., and TAYLOR, D. W.   *Annual Review of Psychology*, Vol. I, 1950.   Annual Review Inc. Stanford, Calif. $6.00 (London, H. K. Lewis).

STOTT, D. H.   *Delinquency and Human Nature.*   Dumfermline, Fife, Carnegie, United Kingdom Trust, 1950.

STRONG, E. K.   *Vocational Interests of Men and Women.*   Stanford Univ. Press, 1943.

SULLIVAN, H. S.   *Conception of Modern Psychiatry.*   Washington, William Allanson White Psychiatric Foundation. 2nd ed. 1947.

SYMONDS, P. M.   *Diagnosing Personality and Conduct.*   New York, Appleton-Century, 1931.

SYMONDS, P. M. *Dynamics of Human Adjustment.* New York, Appleton-Century, 1946.

SZONDI, F. L. *Experimentelle Trieb-diagnostik.* Bern, Hans Huber, 1947.

TEMPLE, R., and AMEN, E. W. 'A study of anxiety reactions in young children by means of a projective technique.' *Genet. Psychol. Monog.* 1944, 30, 59–114.

TERMAN, L. M. *Sex and Personality.* New York, McGraw-Hill, 1936.

THOMSON, G. H. *The Factorial Analysis of Human Ability.* Univ. of London Press, 1939.

THURSTON, I. L. *The Vectors of the Mind.* Chicago. Univ. of Chicago Press. Revised Edition, 1944.

TOLMAN, E. C. 'Motivation, Learning and Adjustment.' *Proceedings of the American Philosophical Society,* 84 (1941), 543–63.

TOMKINS, S. S. (ed.) *Contemporary Psychopathology: a source book.* Cambridge, Mass. Harvard U.P., 1943.

TOYNBEE, A. J. *Greek Historical Thought, from Homer to the Age of Heraclius.* London, Dent, 1924.

TOYNBEE, A. J. *A Study of History.* 6 vols. Oxford U.P., 1934, 39.

VAN LENNEP, D. J. *Four Picture Test.* Haag, Martinus Nijhoff, 1948.

VERNON, P. E. 'The Matching Method applied to investigations of Personality.' *Psychol. Bull.,* 1936, 33, 149–77.

VERNON, P. E. 'Assessment of Psychological Qualities by Verbal Methods.' Industrial Health Research, Report No. 83, London, H.M. Stationery Office, 1938.

VERNON, P. E. *The Structure of Human Abilities.* London, Methuen, 1950.

VERNON, P. E., and PARRY, J. B. *Personnel Selection in the British Forces.* Univ. London Press, 1949.

VIGOTSKY, L. S. 'Thought and Speech.' *Psychiatry* 2, 1939, 29–54.

WEBB, E. 'Character and Intelligence.' *Brit. J. Psychol. Monogr. Suppl.,* 1915, 1, No. 3.

WEBER, M. *Methodology of the Social Sciences.* Glencoe, Illinois, Free Press, 1949.

WEISS, E., and SPURG ENGLISH, O. *Psychomatic Medicine.* Philadelphia, Saunders, 1943.

WEXBERG, ERWIN *Individual Psychology.* London, Allen and Unwin, 1930.

WHITE, R. W. *The Abnormal Personality.* New York, Ronald Press Co., 1948.

WHITEHEAD, T. N. — *The Industrial Worker: A statistical study of Human Relations.* — Cambridge, Mass. Harvard Univ. Press, 1938.

WILSON, GODFREY, and WILSON, MONICA — *The Analysis of Social Change.* — Cambridge, University Press, 1945.

WOLFLE, D. — 'Factor Analysis to 1940.' — *Psychometric Monographs* No. 3, 1940, Univ. Chicago Press.

WOLFSON, R. — *A Study in Handwriting Analysis: an experiment with the Lewinson and Zubin scales.* — New York, King's Crown Press, 1948.

WOODWORTH, R. S. — *Experimental Psychology.* — London, Methuen, 1938.

ZILBOORG, G., and HENRY, G. W. — *History of Medical Psychology.* — New York, wur Norton, 1941.

ZIRKLE, CONWAY — 'Natural Selection before the origin of species.' — *Proceedings of the American Philosophical Society,* 84, 1941, 71–123.

R

ESSENTIAL REFERENCES

References have been compiled with the following rules in mind (i) books are preferred to articles in journals; (ii) works in foreign languages are referred to in English translation, wherever possible; (iii) where there are several works by one author on a topic, usually only the latest is given.

ALEXANDER, F., and FRENCH, T.	*Psycho-analytic Therapy.*	New York: Ronald Press, 1946.
ALLPORT, G. W.	*Personality. A psychological interpretation.*	London, Constable, 1937.
ANGYAL, A.	*Foundations for a Science of Personality.*	New York, Commonwealth Fund, 1941.
BARTLEY, S. H., and CHUTE, E.	*Fatigue and Impairment in Man.*	New York, McGraw-Hill, 1947.
BECK, S. J.	*Rorschach's Test.*	2 vols. New York, Grune and Stratton, 1944–5.
BELL, J. E.	*Projective Techniques: a dynamic approach to the study of the Personality.*	New York: Longmans Green, 1948.
BENEDICT, R.	*Patterns and Culture.*	Boston, Houghton Mifflin, 1934.
BURT, C.	'The Assessment of Personality.'	*Brit. J. Educ. Psychol.* XV, 1945, 107–21.
CATTELL, R. B.	*Description and Measurement of Personality.*	Yonkers - on - Hudson, World Book Co., 1946.
EYSENCK, H. J.	*Dimensions of Personality.*	London, Kegan Paul, 1947.
FENICHEL, O.	*The Psycho-analytic Theory of Neurosis.*	London, Kegan Paul, 1946.
FRANK, L. K.	*Projective Methods.*	Springfield, Illinois: Charles C. Thomas, 1948.
FREUD, ANNA	*The Ego and the Mechanisms of Defence.*	London, Hogarth Press, 1937.
FREUD, S.	*Collected Papers,* 5 Vols. (a full bibliography can be found in Fenichel).	London, Hogarth Press, Various Dates.
FROMM, E.	*The Fear of Freedom* (the American edition was *Escape from Freedom*).	London, Kegan Paul, 1941.
GORER, G.	*The American People.*	New York, Norton, 1948.
HARRIS, H.	*The Group Approach to Leadership Testing.*	London, Routledge and Kegan Paul, 1949.
HEALY, W.	*Personality in Formation and Action.*	London, Chapman and Hall, 1938.

HEALY, W., BRONNER, A., and BOWERS, A. M.	Structure and Meaning of Psycho-analysis.	New York, Knopf, 1930.
HENRY, W. E.	'The Thematic Apperception Technique in the Study of Culture - Personality Relations.'	Genetic Psychology Monographs, 35, 1947.
HORNEY, K.	The Neurotic Personality of Our Time.	London, Kegan Paul, 1936.
HORNEY, K.	New Ways in Psychoanalysis.	London, Kegan Paul, 1940.
HUNT, J. M. (ed.)	Personality and the Behavior Disorders. 2 vols.	New York: Ronald Press Co., 1944.
ISAACS, SUSAN	Social Development in Young Children.	London, Routledge, 1933.
JONES, E.	Papers on Psychoanalysis.	4th Ed., 1938. London, Baillière, Tindall.
KARDINER, A.	The Psychological Frontiers of Society.	New York, Columbia Univ. Press, 1945.
LEWIN, K.	Dynamic Theory of Personality.	New York, McGraw-Hill, 1935.
LEWIN, K.	Principles of Topological Psychology.	New York, McGraw-Hill, 1936.
LINTON, R.	Cultural Background of Personality.	London, Kegan Paul, 1945.
MASSERMAN, J. H.	Behavior and Neurosis: an experimental psycho - analytic approach to psychobiologic principles.	Chicago, Univ. Chicago Press, 1946.
MAYO, ELTON	The Social Problems of an Industrial Civilization.	Cambridge, Mass, Harvard Univ. Press, 1945.
MEAD, M.	Sex and Temperament in Three Primitive Societies.	New York, Morrow, 1935.
MENNINGER, K. A.	Man Against Himself.	New York, Harrap, 1938.
MURPHY, G.	Personality: A Biosocial Approach to Origins and Structure.	New York, Harper, 1947.
MURRAY, H. A.	Explorations in Personality.	New York, Oxford Univ. Press, 1938.
MURRAY, H. A., and KLUCKHORN, C.	Personality in Nature, Society and Culture.	London, Cape, 1949.
O.S.S. ASSESSMENT STAFF	Assessment of Men: Selection of Personnel for the Office of Strategic Services.	New York, Rhinehart, 1948.
RAPAPORT, D.	Diagnostic Psychological Testing. 2 Vols. (The Menninger Clinic Monograph Series No. 4.)	Chicago: Year Book Publishers, 1944-46.

RORSCHACH, H.   *Psychodiagnostics.*   Bern, Huber, 1942.
                        (original German edi-
                        tion, 1921).

SARGENT, S. S., and   *Culture and Person-*   New York, Viking Fund,
SMITH, M. W. (Ed.)   *ality: Proceedings of*   1949.
                        an Inter-disciplinary
                        Conference, Nov.,
                        1947.

SLAVSON, S. R.   *Practice of Group*   International Universi-
                        Therapy.   ties Press, N.Y., 1947.

TOMKINS, S. S.   *Thematic Appercep-*   New York: Grune and
                        tion Test.   Stratton, 1947.

ZUBIN, J.   *Manual of Projective*   Madison,   Wisconsin,
                        and Cognate Tech-   College Typing Co.,
                        niques.   1948 (mimeographed).

NAME INDEX

SUBJECT INDEX